Basic Computing
for the
Older Generation

Windows 8 & RT Edition

Jim Gatenby

BERNARD BABANI (publishing) LTD
The Grampians
Shepherds Bush Road
London W6 7NF
England

www.babanibooks.com

I0268289

Please Note

Although every care has been taken with the production of this book to ensure that all information is correct at the time of writing and that any projects, designs, modifications and/or programs, etc., contained herewith, operate in a correct and safe manner and also that any components specified are normally available in Great Britain, the Publishers and Author do not accept responsibility in any way for the failure (including fault in design) of any project, design, modification or program to work correctly or to cause damage to any equipment that it may be connected to or used in conjunction with, or in respect of any other damage or injury that may be so caused, nor do the Publishers accept responsibility in any way for the failure to obtain specified components.

Notice is also given that if equipment that is still under warranty is modified in any way or used or connected with home-built equipment then that warranty may be void.

© 2013 BERNARD BABANI (publishing) LTD

First Published – June 2013

British Library Cataloguing in Publication Data:

A catalogue record for this book is available from the British Library

ISBN 978-0-85934-742-6

Cover Design by Gregor Arthur

Printed and bound in Great Britain for Bernard Babani (publishing) Ltd

About this Book

This book is intended to help anyone who is hesitant about using computers or who missed out on this new technology earlier in life. Computing as a subject is overloaded with obscure technical jargon which is off-putting to a lot of people.

This new book aims to give readers of all ages the confidence to start using computers, by explaining the basic ideas in simple terms and overcoming any fears and prejudices. Early chapters are intended to convince older people that computers are now easy to use and both young and old have much to gain in many useful, social and creative activities.

The essential components of computers and their functions are discussed so that you can make a rational choice of a machine to meet your needs. The latest Windows 8 operating system, which is both powerful and easy to use, is described in detail, including the built-in help for people with special needs. Windows 8 and its very close relative Windows RT can be used with the new touch screen technology as well as with the more traditional mouse and keyboard. Both methods of interacting with a computer are discussed in parallel throughout the book.

This book describes many exciting new developments such as the latest high performance tablet and laptop computers, faster broadband Internet and wireless home networks. You can now make free Skype Internet telephone calls around the world and keep in touch with friends and family using social networking Web sites such as Facebook and Twitter. Windows 8 and RT contain powerful new apps (software) for entertainment including music, photos and videos and these are discussed in detail.

The final chapter explains how to use the Easy Transfer software within the Windows operating system to transfer your files from an old computer to a new one. A number of other utility programs to keep your computer, its document files and photos, etc., safe from accidental or malicious loss or damage are also described.

About the Author

Jim Gatenby trained as a Chartered Mechanical Engineer and initially worked at Rolls-Royce Ltd using computers in the analysis of jet engine performance. He obtained a Master of Philosophy degree in Mathematical Education by research at Loughborough University of Technology and taught mathematics and computing in school for many years before becoming a full-time author. His most recent teaching posts included Head of Computer Studies and Information Technology Coordinator. The author has written over thirty books in the field of educational computing, including many of the titles in the highly successful Older Generation series from Bernard Babani (publishing) Ltd.

Trademarks

Microsoft Windows, Windows XP, Windows Vista, Windows 7, Windows 8, Windows 8 Pro, Windows RT, Surface, Surface Pro, Windows Live Photo Gallery, Windows Live Mail, Internet Explorer, Bing, Word, Excel, PowerPoint, OneNote, Publisher, Paint, Fresh Paint, Skype, Windows Store, SkyDrive and Hotmail are either trademarks or registered trademarks of Microsoft Corporation. BT is a registered trademark of British Telecommunications plc. Firefox is a trademark of the Mozilla Foundation. Facebook is a registered trademark of Facebook, Inc. Twitter is a registered trademark of Twitter, Inc. All other brand and product names used in this book are recognized as trademarks or registered trademarks of their respective companies.

Acknowledgements

As usual I would like to thank my wife Jill for her continued support during the preparation of this book. Also Michael Babani for making this project possible.

This book is by the same author as the best-selling Basic Computing for the Older Generation (978-0-85934-731-0).

Contents

It's Never Been Easier

Age is No Barrier

As a former teacher of computing to students from 11 to 80 years of age and as a fully paid up member of the "Older Generation" myself, I was aware that many older people felt excluded from the new technology and lacked confidence. Many felt they would struggle to learn how to use computers "at their age", especially since young children appear to have a natural talent for the subject. This impression amongst some older people is hardly surprising since children are brought up with computers in the classroom and in their bedrooms — many of us spent our schooldays poring over logarithmic tables!

To overcome this lack of confidence, in 2002 I cited a friend, Arthur, who at the age of 71 was building and repairing computers and generally acting as the neighbourhood computing expert. Now at the time of writing this book in 2013, Arthur is nearly 82 and still busy solving computing problems for people a fraction of his age.

Computers are cheaper and easier to use than ever before and this chapter is intended to show that there is no need for older people to miss out. Chapter 2 gives a taste of the diverse ways computers can be used to enhance your everyday life. The rest of the book explains in more detail, and avoiding jargon, the skills needed to get to grips with the new technology.

In addition to helping with leisure and social activities, many of the skills covered in this book may be required when applying for a new job or starting a business.

Exploding the Myths

Despite the best efforts of publishers, libraries and adult education courses, etc., to encourage older people to start using computers, negative ideas still persist within some people. You often hear statements like "Our grandchildren are whizz kids on the computer but we haven't a clue." Some common misconceptions are as follows:

You have to be good at technical subjects like maths, physics and electronics to learn about computers.

Nonsense! Most tasks involve no more than clicking with a mouse, tapping with a finger or typing at the keyboard.

Computer software is difficult to use.

Most software uses simple ***menus*** with options or lists of choices. Alternatively you click small ***icons*** or ***tiles*** to start a task. The latest ***tablet computers*** use ***touch screens*** where you simply tap the required icon or tile with your finger.

If you make a mistake you might damage the computer.

No need to worry. In many years of computing, I've never known anyone damage a computer by typing at the keyboard or clicking with a mouse. But computers should be moved about carefully.

You need to be a young computer "geek".

If you still think like this please read about Arthur on the previous page. Older people often have the time to learn new skills and there are lots of free or inexpensive courses available.

The computer might lose my correspondence, accounts, family photographs, curriculum vitae or blockbuster novel.

It's true there have been cases of people losing a family photo collection or the entire text of a novel. So it's essential to make duplicate copies of valuable data, information and photos. If you use the simple backup techniques described later in this book, you need never lose a scrap of information. In producing over 30 books I don't remember losing a single page.

Modern Computers are Easier to Use

The Early Days — Learning to Program

The first "microcomputers" (as they were then known) came on the scene about 40 years ago. In those early days it really was a laborious task to make the machine achieve the most simple result. First you had to learn quite complex instructions or *program statements* and then type them in. For example, just to print the name **COMMODORE 64** on paper you had to type in the list of instructions shown below. (The Commodore 64 was the best-selling home computer in the 1980s.)

> **10 OPEN 4,4:CMD 4**
> **20 PRINT "COMMODORE 64"**
> **30 PRINT#4:CLOSE 4**

Computer programs have very precise rules for punctuation and syntax, etc., and are very unforgiving — even a misplaced comma or semi-colon can stop a program working. No wonder many people thought starting to use computers was too difficult!

Readymade Programs

Fortunately there were also many other people who liked writing programs and a worldwide software industry soon evolved, turning out readymade programs for every conceivable task.

New computers are now supplied with a lot of software already installed and you can also buy extra programs on CDs or DVDs and install them yourself. Nowadays most of us simply use software without writing any programs; however, every task we do on a computer uses software which has been developed by highly skilled programmers. Sometimes referred to disparagingly as "geeks", "anoraks" and "nerds", their job requires great knowledge, precision and meticulous application. Without the work of programmers the world would be a very different place — there would be no Internet, e-mail, social networking, digital photography, word processing, etc., etc., etc.

Interacting with a Computer

Windows 8 and RT are designed for both mouse and touch operation. The latter requires a special touch-sensitive screen.

The Mouse

In the early days readymade programs stored on the computer were a big step forward. Programs now had menus or lists of options for different tasks such as saving documents on disc or printing on paper. Initially you moved the **pointer** or **cursor** around the screen using the four arrow keys on the  keyboard. When the cursor is moved over menus or icons it appears as an arrowhead, as shown on the right. At other times the cursor may appear as four small arrowheads or a hand.

When the cursor is over a menu item or icon which you wish to launch you click the left button on the mouse. Clicking the right button on the mouse opens a menu on the screen which is relevant to the current cursor position.

The operating system used to control approximately 90% of the computers in the world is known as Microsoft Windows and is discussed in detail throughout this book. A simple menu from 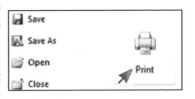 Microsoft Windows is shown on the right.

After typing a document, say, you would move the cursor over the **Save** icon shown above and click the left mouse button. **Double-clicking** the left button is used to launch programs, such as Google, from an **icon** on the Windows Desktop as shown on the right. Similarly you can open a Web site such as Amazon.co.uk by double-clicking an icon on the Windows Desktop.

The Touchscreen

Tablet computers, smartphones and other computers fitted with a touch sensitive screen can be operated with your fingers instead of a mouse. There are equivalent touch *gestures* for all of the mouse operations. These include *tapping* with a finger to select an icon or menu option. Also *swiping* the finger across the screen to launch menus, as discussed in more detail later in this book. In Windows 8 and RT, *apps* (i.e. programs or applications) are launched by tapping *tiles* on the main *Start Screen*, as shown below. The tiles are either rectangular or square and can be clicked or tapped to launch apps. Some tiles contain live information such as breaking news or weather updates.

Many of the tiles for apps shown on the Start Screen above are included when Windows 8 or RT is first installed on a computer. You can add tiles of your own when you install new software and also create tiles for your favourite Web sites.

The Start Screen is the main interface used to launch software and is discussed in more detail later in this book.

The Windows 8 Start Screen above can also be operated with a mouse and keyboard on laptop, hybrid and desktop computers.

The Keyboard

Despite the development of the mouse and touch screen to control a computer as just discussed, the keyboard remains the normal method of entering text and numbers into a computer. Laptop and desktop computers and some smartphones such as the Blackberry range use a QWERTY keyboard with separate physical keys. (QWERTY refers to the layout of the first six letter keys). Tablet computers such as the Microsoft Surface and the iPad use a touch keyboard which pops up on the screen when needed. A touch keyboard on the screen of a Surface tablet is shown below. To improve your typing skills there are typing tutor programs which can be downloaded for free from the Internet.

Separate physical keyboards can be connected to some tablet computers such as the Surface and the iPad. The Microsoft Surface tablet has a single USB port which can be connected to a full-size keyboard and mouse.

If you have difficulty operating a physical keyboard, but can use a mouse, Microsoft Windows 8 and RT include an On-Screen Keyboard. This allows you to "type" using a mouse by clicking letters and numbers on the keyboard that appears on the screen.

What is a Window?

The term **window** in computing refers to a rectangular area of the screen in which programs and information are displayed. When you start up a program such as a word processor or a photo-editing program, each is displayed in its own window. You can have several windows open on the screen at the same time.

On the left below, the picture of the swans is running in its own window in the Microsoft Paint program. On the right below, two pages from this book are shown in the Microsoft Publisher program, running in its own window.

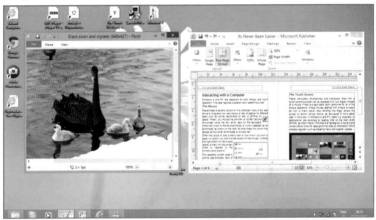

A window can be enlarged or made smaller; **minimising** changes a window to appear just as a small icon on the **Taskbar** along the bottom of the screen, as shown above.

The blue background shown above is known as the **Windows Desktop**. The small graphical images scattered about the Desktop are **icons** representing, for example, programs, Web pages or folders. Double-click an icon to open a program, Web page or folder in its own window on the screen.

Although Windows 8 and RT uses the Start Screen shown on page 5 to launch the latest apps, the Desktop is still used in Windows 8 and RT when you run traditional Windows programs.

The Microsoft Windows Operating System

Microsoft Windows is a suite of software or programs, collectively known as an *operating system* and used to manage the overall running of a computer. This is distinct from *application software* (or *apps* for short). Apps are programs used to accomplish specific tasks such as browsing the World Wide Web, writing a report, or selling unwanted items on eBay, for example.

Microsoft has dominated the market for personal computer operating systems since the 1980s, first with a suite of software known as MS-DOS (Microsoft Disk Operating System). This required commands to be typed in at the keyboard.

In 1985 Microsoft's own **Graphical User Interface**, known as **Microsoft Windows**, was launched. The Windows operating system is currently installed on approximately 90% of the world's personal computers.

Windows 8 is the latest Microsoft Windows operating system and there are several versions, as follows:

Windows 8. This is the basic OEM (Original Equipment Manufacturers) version pre-installed on brand new computers.

Windows 8 Pro. This is the consumer edition of Windows 8 which you can buy on a CD/DVD or download from the Internet. It is used to upgrade a computer running an existing version of Microsoft Windows such as Windows XP, Vista or Windows 7.

Windows RT. This is a special version of Windows 8 designed to run only on tablet computers which use the *ARM processor*. Windows RT cannot be bought or installed separately. Windows RT is supplied with some Microsoft Office 2013 software. These are special versions of Word, Excel, PowerPoint and One Note.

The above versions of Windows 8 all have the same Start Screen as shown on page 5, operate in the same way and include the traditional Windows Desktop. They can all be operated with either a mouse and keyboard or using touch gestures (if the computer has a touch-sensitive screen.)

Computers Can Change Your Life

Introduction

Some of the major developments in recent years which have affected the daily lives of many people are as follows:

- Powerful new laptop and tablet computers and also smartphones give easy access to computing facilities and the Internet wherever you happen to be.

- Much faster broadband Internet services make it quicker and easier to find information and download music and videos from the Internet to your computer.

- Microsoft Windows has been improved over the years, making computers more powerful and easier to use.

- Web sites like Facebook and Twitter enable the worldwide exchange of news, information and photos.

- The Skype Internet telephone service, providing free video calls between family and friends around the world.

- Software which replays previously aired TV and radio.

- Inexpensive wireless *routers* enabling several computers to form a home network to share resources.

- Most large companies such as Tesco and Amazon let you shop online from home. The eBay Web site helps you to sell your surplus items in an online auction.

- Many large organisations now allow form filling and financial transactions to be carried out online.

- Cheap digital cameras and personal computers enable anyone to produce high-quality photographs easily.

Keeping in Touch

Electronic mail or e-mail has been around for some years, with the ability to send messages, including photographs, to friends and relatives anywhere in the world. The development of **cloud computing**, using special **server** computers on the Internet for data storage, now makes it easier for you to share any sort of information, including photographs, with people you trust wherever they are. The arrival of **social networking** Web sites such as **Facebook** and **Twitter** allows people to exchange instant news, messages, personal information and photographs.

Facebook allows you to search for and make contact with people you knew at school or in a previous employment, or who share similar interests. Then you can choose (or perhaps decline) to become Facebook "friends" to share news and information, etc.

Twitter is a social networking Web site enabling you to send and read text messages or "tweets" up to 140 characters long, in order to share your latest news with friends and relatives.

Free Worldwide Video Calls

Skype is a free computer program which allows you to make voice and video calls across the Internet. Calls with Skype between computers anywhere in the world are free of charge. To download and sign up to Skype go to **www.skype.com** and left-click **Join us** at the top right of the screen. Then follow the on screen instructions. If you have friends or relatives abroad, Skype can save you a great deal of money.

Making a Call

To make a call, select your contact's name from the list on the left-hand side of the Skype window. Then click **Video call** or **Call** as shown below.

Receiving a Call

When you receive a call you can answer with or without video or decline the call, as shown below.

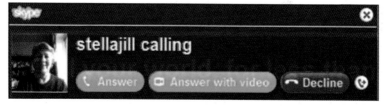

Modern tablets and laptops have a built-in microphone and a *webcam* allowing you and your contacts to see each other. If necessary these accessories can also be bought separately for a few pounds; they simply plug into a laptop or desktop computer and work straightaway. As well as free calls between computers, you can also use Skype to make cheap calls to mobile phones and landlines, if you have a Skype account with a credit balance.

Electronic Greeting Cards

Your computer can take care of all the greeting cards you send to friends and relatives, if they have a computer. For example, Jacquie Lawson Cards enable you to send electronic cards for every occasion — birthdays, Christmas, anniversary, etc. These *e-cards*, as they are known, consist of high-quality, animated graphics with a musical accompaniment, to which you can add your own message using a pre-designed, stylish template. You receive e-mail reminders when another e-card is due, for example when a friend's birthday is approaching.

You can sign up and start sending cards at the Web site:

www.jacquielawson.com

Searching for Information on Any Subject

You can find out about virtually any subject under the sun by typing a few relevant words into a search program such as **Google**. (Searching with Google is discussed in detail later in this book). I am always amazed that, no matter how bizarre a subject, there is invariably a huge amount of information available on the Internet. For example, my wife was recently concerned about swellings on the legs of our bantam chickens.

A search with Google produced a Web site with photographs which identified a condition known as "scaly mite". A further Google search for methods of treatment is shown below.

 scaly mites treatment

This quickly found numerous companies advertising sprays, etc., to treat the condition, one of which proved entirely successful.

Similarly you can find lots of up-to-date information about all the illnesses which afflict the human race. This information is provided by the NHS and other medical institutions.

Many DIY tasks are explained in detail on Web sites. For example, if you need to sharpen a chainsaw or plant and stake an apple tree, you'll find lots of helpful Web pages, pictures and videos made by experts.

You can check the train or flight details for a proposed holiday, see videos of accommodation and view live **webcams** set up in holiday resorts. Then find out about the climate throughout the year, before booking online in the comfort of your own home.

Numerous Web sites provide powerful facilities for tracing your family history (as discussed later in this book) — a task previously requiring the services of a professional genealogist. Then you can place an order online for copies of birth, marriage and death certificates to be posted to you.

General Knowledge

As mentioned earlier, search programs such as Google enable you to find information on virtually any subject — Geography, History, the Arts or Science, Sport and Medicine, DIY, etc. Many of the answers are provided by Web sites such as the free online encyclopaedia **Wikipedia**. As the content is provided by volunteers, Wikipedia sometimes requests that an article is improved or needs further work to be done by the contributors. Nevertheless, Wikipedia is an extremely valuable source of information on a very wide range of subjects.

For example, you can find out about the lexicographer Samuel Johnson, by entering his name into Google. Typical search results are shown in the extract below.

Samuel Johnson - Wikipedia, the free encyclopedia
en.wikipedia.org/wiki/Samuel_Johnson
Samuel Johnson (18 September 1709 [O.S. 7 September] – 13 December 1784), often referred to as Dr. Johnson, was an English author who made lasting ...
Life of Samuel Johnson - A Dictionary of the English Language - James Boswell

BBC - History - **Samuel Johnson**
www.bbc.co.uk/history/historic_figures/johnson_samuel.shtml
Read a biography about the life of **Samuel Johnson** who's best-known for his 'Dictionary of the English Language'.

Tap or click each of the headings shown underlined in blue above to read the full Web pages.

Games

The Windows operating system includes a lot of games which you might enjoy, perhaps using a tablet or laptop in your favourite armchair. Some of these are card games such as Solitaire and FreeCell which can be played alone; others, such as the strategy game Internet Backgammon, can be played online with other people.

FreeCell

Getting Creative

Modern computers are now very easy to use and there are lots of affordable *software* or *apps* around to enable you to accomplish virtually anything previously done by traditional methods.

Word Processing

The word processor allows you to write anything, from a short letter to a lengthy report or a book. The word processor is very forgiving, allowing you to draft and re-draft and correct mistakes to produce the perfect blockbuster you always wanted to write.

The world's leading word processor, Microsoft Word, also includes many of the features of a dedicated desktop publishing program, as discussed below.

Desktop Publishing (DTP)

Desktop Publishing software provides many additional tools to add graphic design and formatting features to a document, such as different *fonts* or styles of lettering. Large libraries of graphic images known as *clip art* are available in various categories to illustrate documents and you can also insert photographs into pages. DTP software usually includes a plentiful supply of ready-made designs for documents. These *templates* provide a professional looking format which you can customise by inserting your own text. Commonly used templates include newsletters, advertising flyers and business and greeting cards.

This book was produced using the Microsoft Publisher DTP program.

Drawing and Painting

Microsoft Windows 8 and Windows RT include their own easy-to-use drawing and painting program known as *Paint*. This allows you to draw freehand with a mouse, or stylus or pencil tool. Shapes can be moved around, changed in size and filled with various colours. A palette provides a choice of colours for both lines and for infilling shapes.

The Paint program can also be used to edit drawings and photographs. A picture can be resized or rotated in Paint and you can crop it to remove the parts you don't want.

Fresh Paint is one of the new apps for Windows 8 and Windows RT which can be downloaded free from the *Windows Store*. This can be used with a mouse but is especially suited to touch screen and pen or stylus operation. Fresh Paint provides a full range of artists' tools, even simulating oil painting. You can use Fresh Paint to create new pictures and also modify photographs.

Digital Photography

Nowadays anyone with a digital camera and home computer can take photographs and make high-quality prints using simple "point and click" techniques. Digital cameras have an automatic mode which takes care of complicated settings such as exposure, focusing and shutter speed, etc. A small screen on the back of a digital camera allows you to preview images straightaway and delete any you don't want.

Microsoft provides the Photo Gallery software shown above, which can be downloaded free from the Internet. Photos can be edited in the Photo Gallery, for example, to remove defects such as the "red eye" phenomenon caused by flash photography. The Photo Gallery is available for Windows 8 and Windows 8 Pro but not Windows RT. However, you can download photographic apps from the Windows Store, often for free. As discussed later in this book, Windows 8 and RT include the Photos app, which allows you to import and manage your photos.

After editing, the photographs may be printed on an inkjet or laser printer or sent to friends and family around the world using e-mail or by posting to a Web site such as Facebook or Flickr.

Music and Video

Your tablet, laptop or desktop computer can be used to play music and videos. Tablets and laptops are usually equipped with sound facilities and you can add speakers to a desktop computer for a few pounds. Music and videos can be downloaded from the Internet using the Music and Videos apps discussed in Chapter 16. The *Windows 8 Store* is also a source of downloads for music and video. They can then be saved on your computer's hard disc drive or *SSD* (*Solid State Drive*) and played whenever you want. A sample video is shown below playing in the Windows Media Player, which can be downloaded from the Microsoft Web site to Windows 8 and Windows 8 Pro, but not to Windows RT.

Please note:

The Photo Gallery and the Windows Media Player are not available as downloads for Windows RT. However, the Windows Store provides a wide choice of alternative apps suitable for Windows RT. Many of these can be downloaded for free or purchased for just a few pounds.

Catch Up on TV and Radio

BBC iPlayer is a free service allowing you to use your computer to replay TV and radio programmes which have recently been broadcast. iPlayer can also be used to watch live television.

www.bbc.co.uk/iplayer/

ITV Player, shown below, is a similar Web-based service which allows television programs to be viewed on your computer up to 30 days after first being shown on ITV. Launch ITV Player from:

www.itv.com/itvplayer/

Watch Live TV on Your Computer

You can buy a TV Tuner which plugs into a laptop or desktop computer (or tablet if it has a USB port). This turns your computer into a television, able to receive a full range of live programmes. These can be saved on your hard disc drive, SSD for viewing later. Tuner packages start around £20 and include an aerial and remote control handset. Watching live TV on a computer requires your home to be covered by a TV licence.

Online News and Weather

Many local and national newspapers are available to be viewed on your computer via the Internet. National newspapers like The Times charge a small monthly fee for the online version but this is considerably cheaper than buying the newspaper every day. The online versions of many other newspapers are free. Online newspapers may be updated with the latest "breaking news", available to you as it happens, unlike the traditional paper which is usually printed the night before you read it.

Crosswords like those in The Times can be tackled online or printed out on paper. Online solutions are available the next day.

Several Internet services such as MSN, Google and Bing provide the latest news headlines, accessible at any time. Online weather forecasts from the BBC and others are immediately available for your local area or for holiday destinations at home or abroad.

www.bbc.co.uk/weather/

Watching the Pennies

It's probably more important nowadays to keep a grip on your spending than at any time in recent years. Microsoft Excel is known as a spreadsheet program, designed for handling tables of figures. It is used by large organisations around the world to produce accounts, statistics and graphs; it can equally be used to enter details of your own personal spending so that you can keep tight control of your financial affairs. The following sample spreadsheet and pie chart, based on entirely fictional data, can easily be produced using Excel on your computer without doing any arithmetic yourself, as described in detail later in this book.

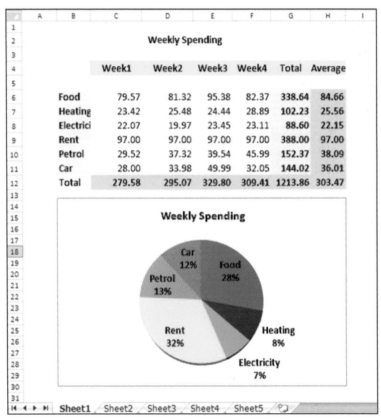

Saving Time and Money

There are many everyday tasks that can now be done *online* i.e. using a computer connected to the Internet, instead of having to travel and stand in a queue or wait days for the traditional post. Many mundane tasks can now be done more quickly from the comfort of your favourite armchair, using a tablet or laptop, at any time of the day or night. Here are just a few examples:

- Order your weekly supermarket shopping for delivery at a convenient time — saving you several hours a week.
- Raise cash by auctioning your surplus chattels on eBay.
- Complete your Income Tax Self Assessment Return.
- Tax your car by entering just a single reference number.
- Manage your bank account, check statements, set up or cancel standing orders, transfer money.
- Manage an investment portfolio — if you have one.
- Order a repeat prescription from your doctor.
- Obtain price comparisons, buy virtually anything, usually cheaper and easier than in the High Street.
- Buy or rent a house or flat, after watching an online video of the property.
- Use an online Web site to view the details and numerous photographs of second-hand cars.
- View descriptions and technical specifications of prospective purchases, e.g. electronic equipment.
- Research holidays, book flights and accommodation.
- Check in for a flight online and print a boarding pass.
- Renew your passport.
- Apply for a job, send your Curriculum Vitae by e-mail.
- Obtain a state pension forecast.
- Order copies of birth, marriage and death certificates.

Types of Computer

Introduction

While working in industry in the early 1960s I remember the first computers being introduced. These were *mainframe* machines made up of numerous cabinets and occupying several rooms. Data and programs were stored on massive reels of tape over a foot in diameter. The typical mainframe computer serviced the needs of an entire company, including financial, payroll and technical departments. In the mid 1960s, *minicomputers* were introduced. These were small enough for individual departments to have their own machine. Some of the manufacturers of these early computers such as IBM and Hewlett-Packard are still big names in computing today, although the industry has undergone enormous changes in the intervening years.

Nowadays the laptop and handheld tablet computers in the home may have more computing power than the monster machines in business in the 1960s. In recent years the personal computer has steadily evolved, getting progressively more powerful while at the same time becoming physically smaller.

Nowadays the most popular types of computer are:

- The Touchscreen Tablet
- The Laptop Computer
- The Desktop Computer

As discussed on the following pages, these three types of computer all have their own advantages in different situations. There are also variations on the above configurations with *hybrid* computers, *ultrabooks* and *all-in-one* computers as discussed later in this chapter.

The Tablet Computer

At the time of writing tablets are changing the face of computing. Although only the size of a small exercise book, they are fully functional, powerful computers. Apart from their tiny size, the other new feature is that they can be operated by touch, i.e. the computer is controlled by the use of finger *gestures* such as tapping or swiping. This is possible because the various functions of the computer are represented by *touch-sensitive* icons and tiles on the screen. The first and most popular tablet was the Apple iPad. This was soon followed by models from many other manufacturers. One of the latest tablets is the Microsoft Surface shown below.

Tablets such as the Microsoft Surface shown above and the iPad have a screen size of about 10 inches, measured diagonally. New *mini tablets* are also becoming available with a screen size of about 7 inches.

Microsoft has dominated the computer software industry for many years with most personal computers running a version of the Microsoft Windows operating system. Also the Microsoft Office suite, which includes programs like Word and Excel, is the leading office productivity software. The introduction of Windows 8 and Windows RT and also the Surface RT and Surface Pro tablets have made it possible to employ the same user interface on the entire range of computing platforms i.e. tablets, laptops, desktop computers and even smartphones.

The basic Surface RT tablet is supplied with special versions of Microsoft Word and Excel already installed. However, the Surface RT tablet cannot run the vast back catalogue of traditional Microsoft Windows software. Instead it runs specially written *apps* installed from new or downloaded from the Windows Store. Thousands of apps are available and most are free or cost just a few pounds.

The Microsoft Surface Pro tablet is compatible with the full range of traditional Windows software. As discussed later in this book, the Surface Pro, unlike the Surface RT tablet, uses the same type of Intel or AMD processor as millions of existing laptop and desktop computers found in many homes and businesses, etc.

The Microsoft Surface RT tablet and the Surface Pro tablet run different versions of the Windows 8 operating system. However, the Windows RT operating system used on the Surface RT tablet looks identical and is used in the same way as Windows 8 Pro used on the Surface Pro tablet and also on laptop and desktop computers. Some smartphones also use a version of the operating system known as Windows Phone 8.

The tablet computer is capable of most computing tasks from browsing the Internet, sending and checking e-mails, word processing, spreadsheets and entertainment such as music, video and watching live and "catch-up" television.

The tablet computer is in every sense a fully-fledged computer, but its small size and light weight mean it can be used anywhere from the settee in your home to an airport, train or hotel room, etc. I use a Surface tablet every day for reading e-mails, catching up on news and weather, browsing online newspapers and checking my bank account. Although the on-screen pop-up keyboard on a tablet is adequate for entering small amounts of text, I wouldn't, for example, use a tablet for producing a book such as this one, writing long e-mails or editing a photograph.

The Hybrid Computer

Some manufacturers have recognised the need to make tablets more suitable for prolonged work by producing *hybrid computers*. These are tablet computers which can be integrated with a keyboard if necessary. The Microsoft Surface shown below has a separate keyboard which clips on magnetically and also forms a cover when the computer is not being used.

The Surface can be operated as a handheld tablet for lighter tasks or attached to the keyboard for more demanding work.

The hybrid computer design enables you to use a tablet like a laptop computer. Tablets like the Microsoft Surface have a USB port and other tablets like the Apple iPad have adapters which include a USB port. This enables various devices to be connected to the tablet. I personally find the touch screen difficult to use for some tasks such as selecting an item from a menu – a mouse is more precise in my opinion. You can connect a full size wireless keyboard and mouse to a tablet if your tablet has a USB port into which you can plug a wireless receiver. Alternatively *multi-port USB hubs* are available which convert a single USB port into  several, as shown on the right. This would, for example, allow you to connect a USB keyboard and USB mouse to the tablet. A USB port might also be used to copy photos from a digital camera or to connect a printer.

The Smartphone

The latest smartphones such as the iPad and the Blackberry range have many of the functions of a full-blown computer. These include browsing the Internet, sending and receiving e-mails, social networking with Facebook and Twitter, playing music and video and downloading apps as well as taking photographs with  the built-in digital camera. Some smartphones use Windows Phone 8, a version of the Windows operating system with a similar user interface to the versions of Windows 8 used on tablet, laptop and desktop computers.

The Laptop Computer

The laptop was originally developed to provide portable computing for people who travel in their work, such as sales representatives and members of the armed forces. The keyboard and monitor are permanently hinged together and fold into a single unit when not in use. The laptop typically has a 15-inch or 17-inch screen, measured diagonally. Laptops are also known as *Notebook* computers.

Nowadays the laptop is widely used both in the home and at work. Although early laptops were heavy and lacking in power, the latest machines are much lighter and are comparable to the desktop machine in performance.

The *Netbook* is a smaller version of the laptop, with a typical screen size of 10 inches, and usually lacks the CD/DVD drive provided on laptops.

Using a Laptop

In recent years laptops have improved by leaps and bounds and are now more than a match for desktop machines in terms of performance, screen display and price. As a result, sales of laptop machines now exceed those of desktop machines and this trend is expected to continue for the foreseeable future. While the new tablet machines are undoubtedly very popular and useful on the move, they are expected to supplement, rather than replace, the more versatile laptop machine in the next few years.

My wife Jill is not particularly interested in computers for their own sake but more as a tool for useful work, to make life easier, to save time and money and for entertainment. Jill's laptop is several years old but still going strong and used every day for diverse tasks such as checking e-mails, supermarket shopping online, booking a holiday, managing her bank account and finding out about anything from solving obscure crossword clues to the health problems of humans, cats and poultry. One particularly useful recent task was finding a spare part for a vacuum cleaner on the Internet and ordering a replacement — the whole process only taking a few minutes. This was much easier than sending for a service engineer or visiting a shop. It's very common now for the manufacturers of appliances, etc., to include instruction manuals on their Web sites.

Laptops can be prone to overheating, especially if literally used on your lap, where the flow of air may be restricted. In this situation it's worth buying a laptop cooling pad and fan, as shown on the right. The laptop sits on top of the cooling pad, which is connected by a USB  cable, as shown on the far right of the above screenshot.

We also have a Dell Inspiron laptop bought in the last two years. This has quite a good technical specification. (Criteria for comparing the specification and performance of computers are discussed in Chapter 4).

The Dell Inspiron laptop is used for work such as writing this book in the evening, in the relative comfort of the house, rather than using the desktop machine in our home office (actually a shed in the garden). I tend to use the laptop for relatively short periods of work — for longer periods of sustained effort during the day I prefer a desktop machine, as discussed shortly. For precision work I personally find it easier to use a mouse with the laptop. You can buy a plug-in wireless mouse or a mouse connected via a USB cable for under £10.

A recent newspaper article quoted a well-known physiotherapist as saying that laptops promote poor posture as you tend to look down at the screen and this can cause neck and back pain. To avoid this it was recommended that a laptop should be raised by a book or similar object so that you can see the screen without dipping your head. The report also suggested that, if a laptop is used for long periods, a separate keyboard and mouse should be used, as discussed below and in Chapter 5.

The Desktop Replacement Laptop

You might need to use the same computer both on the move and as an office machine, e.g. for word processing, Desktop Publishing (DTP) and spreadsheets (accounts and number crunching). You can quickly turn the laptop into an effective desktop replacement machine — simply buy and plug in a full size monitor, keyboard and mouse, as described on page 66. The connecting sockets or *ports* into which these various devices are connected are discussed in Chapter 5. Some computers are marketed as **Desktop Replacement** laptops. These are larger than the standard laptop with more powerful components, making them more expensive and not as portable.

Temporarily converting a laptop to a desktop equivalent with an extra keyboard and monitor will allow you to use the same machine both on the move and as a home office machine. This will, however, make for a rather cluttered desk as shown on page 66.

The modern laptop computer normally has built-in speakers, so it can be used for listening to music and watching videos and previously shown television programmes. You can also plug in headphones so that music or a video sound track doesn't interfere with other people in the room who may be watching television, etc. If the sound quality from your built-in speakers is not very good, this can be improved by plugging in some separate speakers costing a few pounds.

Modern laptops have built-in webcams and microphones, so they can be used for live video calls to other people around the world using Skype (discussed elsewhere in this book). The webcam allows your contacts to see you as you speak and you can see them if they also have a Web cam. By moving the laptop around you can also show your friends or relatives live pictures of your home, family, pets or surroundings.

The Ultrabook

This is a very slim and light version of the laptop. Traditional laptop and desktop computers have generally used a magnetic *hard disc drive* on which to store all the software and data, as shown on page 40. The hard disc drive consists of a number of revolving metal discs and is relatively heavy. The slim size of the latest *ultrabooks*, i.e lightweight laptops, (and also the tablet computer) is made possible by the use of smaller and lighter components such as the *SSD (solid state drive)*. This is not actually a revolving disc drive but a form of permanent memory which uses no moving parts, similar to the *flash memory* used in removable *USB flash drives* or *dongles*.

The Desktop Computer

The desktop computer normally has a separate keyboard, monitor and **base unit** (also known as a **tower**). The tower is a box containing most of the working parts of the computer and usually stands on the floor, while the monitor, keyboard and mouse sit on the desk or work surface, as shown below.

The flat-screen monitor, wireless mouse and keyboard shown above can be freely moved around to give the most comfortable working conditions. A large monitor is helpful when doing exacting work such as desktop publishing or computer-aided design, for example. The large monitor is also helpful if your eyesight is not what it used to be. Instead of a floor-standing tower as shown above, some desktop computers have a base unit which sits flat on the desk underneath the monitor.

The desktop computer needs quite a bit of space in your home – perhaps a special computer desk set up in a corner of your lounge, or in a spare bedroom if you have one. When setting up a home office, many people, including myself, use a shed in the garden. The desktop machine needs several power points or a power strip for the separate tower unit, monitor, printer and speakers, etc. Despite the above drawbacks, many people including myself, continue to prefer the desktop machine for some applications.

My main desktop machine is of indeterminate age. This is because, like the woodman's axe, you can replace the main parts easily and mine has had several replacement monitors, keyboards and major internal components over the years. This is cheaper than buying a complete new machine to keep up with the latest developments in software, which often require more powerful computers.

To make text easier to read, I recently added an extra large monitor (24 inches measured diagonally) shown on page 32. A new full size replacement keyboard was bought for under £10.

In the tower unit of a desktop computer, the critical electronic components needed to control facilities, such as the graphics displayed on the screen or the sound quality, are stored on small removable circuit boards called *expansion cards*. Each of these is usually held in place by a single screw. An expansion card which controls the screen graphics is shown below.

A graphic designer, writer, photographer or games player, for example, might want to improve the graphics capability of their machine. They could simply buy and fit a better graphics card. Similarly a musician could improve the sound quality by fitting a better **sound card** (also known as an **audio card**). Such improvements are simple to carry out on the desktop computer but impossible or at least very difficult with a tablet or laptop.

The desktop computer tower unit is very easy to assemble and many people, including myself, have built their own computers from kits — it's really just a case of screwing the parts together and connecting the cables. This can save a lot of money and at the same time you learn a lot about the computer — it's no longer just a complicated magic box that can perform miracles.

Unlike modern tablets and laptops, the traditional desktop computer doesn't normally have built-in devices like a webcam, speakers, card reader or microphone, although these items can each be bought separately for a few pounds. You simply plug them into one of the sockets or **ports** on the tower unit (discussed in Chapter 5). They usually work straightaway or very soon after a short, automatic installation process. Some monitors have built-in speakers and you can also buy plug-in head phones, which may incorporate a microphone. A webcam clipped to the top of a monitor on a desktop computer is shown below.

The All-in-One Computer

This is a computer design which has similarities to both the tablet and the desktop computer. The All-in-One computer, like the desktop, has a large monitor which sits on a desk or table. The computer may be operated with a mouse and a separate keyboard, although touchscreen versions are available.

Like the tablet computer, the main components are integrated within the monitor — avoiding the "bird's nest" of cables often found on desktop computers. As shown above, the All-in-One computer with a wireless keyboard and mouse provides an efficient and uncluttered work space. The keyboard and mouse can be moved around freely to optimise the working position.

The All-in-One computer, with its crucial components in a more confined space in the monitor, may be harder to expand or repair than a desktop computer with its separate tower unit. The tower unit is a spacious box allowing easy access to the components.

Features of the Tablet Computer

Pros

- Small and light, easy to carry — can be used anywhere.
- Built-in camera, webcam, microphone, speakers.
- Doesn't need a power point except for battery charging.
- The tablet uses very few cables.
- Low power consumption gives long battery life.
- The touchscreen gives fast and easy operation.
- A huge number of *apps* are available cheaply or free, covering news, weather, games, music, video, etc., etc.
- The tablet is very quiet compared with older laptop and desktop computers.

Cons

- The tablet may be difficult to repair or upgrade.
- The small screen size, on-screen keyboard and touch gestures may not be suitable for prolonged typing tasks or those requiring great accuracy.
- The tablet has a high value, is currently very popular and being very small is an easy target for thieves.
- The tablet doesn't have many *ports* to allow flash drives, external CD/DVD drives, etc,, to be connected.

However, the tablet can be expanded to increase productivity by the addition of a physical keyboard. This approach is used in *hybrid* computers from companies such as Samsung and Dell. The Microsoft Surface and Surface Pro tablets also have a magnetic clip-on keyboard so they can be used like a laptop computer. USB hubs, adapters and *docking stations* can be bought separately to allow peripheral devices to be connected.

Features of the Laptop Computer

Pros

- While not as light and portable as the tablet, the laptop can be used on the move or in any room in your home.

- The laptop has a bigger screen than the tablet and a real keyboard, making it more suitable for serious work.

- The laptop has several *ports*, i.e. sockets, allowing you to connect devices such as cameras, SD cards, a large second monitor, mouse and printer.

- A laptop (like a tablet) can run on either mains or battery power. So you can keep using it during a power cut.

- A laptop only needs one power point for occasional use.

- Unlike the desktop machine, a laptop can easily be stored when not in use. A modern laptop has built-in speakers, microphone and webcam and few cables.

Cons

- Laptops are not as easy to repair or upgrade as the desktop machine, though easier than the tablet.

- The fixed position of the keyboard relative to the monitor makes it difficult to optimise your working position.

The laptop and tablet have much in common. For many activities we find the two types of computer are equally suitable. These include browsing the Internet, listening to music, watching videos and keeping up with news and weather, etc., etc.

Like the tablet computer, the laptop can be used on the move (though somewhat bulkier) and for those activities which can be generally classified as entertainment. In addition, the laptop can serve as a competent workhorse for more weighty tasks for which a tablet may not be suitable. The latest *ultrabooks* and *hybrids* bridge the gap between tablets and traditional laptops.

Features of the Desktop Computer

Pros

- Desktop machines generally have larger, separate screens and keyboards, making them easier and less tiring to use for demanding work over long periods.

- Components are larger, more robust and more easily replaced in the desktop machine, making repairs and upgrades simpler and cheaper.

Cons

- The desktop machine takes up more space than a laptop and needs to be permanently set up in a fixed location.

- The desktop machine can't be used on the move on trains and in airports and hotels, for example.

- The desktop machine needs several power points for the monitor, tower unit and speakers, etc.

- Peripheral accessories such as speakers, microphones, webcams and card readers are not usually built into desktop computers and need to be bought separately.

- The fully equipped desktop computer uses a lot of cables which can be unsightly, if not unsafe.

You might choose a desktop machine if you were setting up an office with a permanent, fixed computer. You might also choose the desktop if you want the ability to upgrade it easily with special components such as better graphics or sound cards, extra memory or a faster processor for demanding applications.

If I could only have one computer, the laptop or its lightweight relative the ultrabook would be my first choice. These combine the portability of the tablet with the greater productivity of the desktop computer.

Essential Know-how

Introduction

Chapter 3 argued the pros and cons of various types of computer. Tablets are an exciting innovation for people on the move and for news and entertainment wherever you happen to be. The desktop machine is a serious workhorse, normally situated in a permanent position, ergonomically suited for long periods of demanding work. It is also very simple to repair or update with the latest components. The laptop is a useful compromise between the desktop machine and the tablet. Modern laptops and ultrabooks are very light and portable, while still being capable of serious office-type work.

The vast majority of laptop and desktop computers in the world (and some tablet computers and smartphones) are managed and controlled by the Microsoft Windows operating system. The latest versions, Windows 8 and Windows RT are referred to throughout this book.

This chapter describes the essential components common to all computers and attempts to demystify the jargon surrounding them. If you understand the basic principles underlying the operation of all personal computers, you will be able to:

- Choose a computer with a specification which meets your own present and future needs.

- Avoid being blinded with science by people trying to sell computers, equipment or software.

- Use your computer more effectively and understand the need for sound backup and security procedures.

What is a Computer?

One definition of a computer is a machine which can carry out a *program* or sequence of stored instructions in a special language. These tell the computer what to do, such as printing a word, making a sound or drawing a line, etc.

Where are Programs Permanently Stored?

So that programs are always available to be *executed* or "run", they are permanently stored or recorded on a magnetic disc. This is usually the *hard disc drive*, as shown below, which revolves at high speed inside the case of the computer.

Some computers, especially tablets and ultrabooks, now use an *SSD* (*Solid State Drive*) instead of a hard disc drive. The SSD has no moving parts. When you buy a new computer, some programs will already have been installed, i.e. saved on the hard disc drive or SSD. You can buy additional programs on a CD or DVD and copy them to your hard disc drive or SSD. Nowadays many programs can also be *downloaded* from the Internet over the telephone lines and saved on your hard disc drive or SSD. Tablet computers do not normally have a CD/DVD drive so downloading software from the Internet may be the only option.

Apart from programs, the hard disc can also hold **data files**, i.e. the information you are working with such as names and addresses, photos, videos, music or the text of a document.

What is the Memory?

In order to run or execute a program, it is copied or "loaded" into a temporary storage area known as the *memory*. The memory consists of one or more **modules** each containing a number of chips mounted on a small circuit board, as shown below.

The memory only holds the program(s) you are temporarily running at a given point in time, unlike the hard disc drive or SSD which contains your entire collection of programs. The memory also holds the data files such as documents you may be working on using the current program.

When the computer is switched off the contents of the memory are completely wiped. This sort of memory is said to be *volatile* and is known as *RAM* or *Random Access Memory*.

How are Programs Run or Executed?

In order to carry out the instructions in a program they are fetched from the memory and executed in the *processor*, also known as the *microprocessor*, *CPU* or *Central Processing Unit*, as shown on the right. The processor is a single chip, often called the "brains" of the computer since it carries out calculations and logical operations.

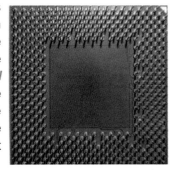

After an instruction has been executed, the result of the operation is transferred back to the memory and may be displayed on the screen.

Saving a Document

If you are working on a document such as a report, for example, the data consists of the letters you type in using the keyboard. This data will be held in the memory or RAM until you overwrite it with new data or switch the machine off. In either case the document will be lost. So to keep a permanent copy of a document you must carry out a *save* operation to record it permanently on your hard disc drive, SSD or other storage medium such as a *flash drive* or CD/DVD.

Volatile versus "Permanent" Memory

Programs and data stored in the memory, i.e. RAM, are lost when the computer is switched off. The memory is said to be *volatile*.

The hard disc drive, SSD, flash drive and rewriteable CD or DVD are a type of permanent or *non-volatile* storage. Programs and data stored on these media are not lost when the computer is switched off. The word permanent is used loosely here, because you can, if you wish, remove programs and data from a hard disc drive, SSD, flash drive or rewriteable CD or DVD (designated CD -RW and DVD-RW). All of these rewriteable media can be repeatedly used for saving data, which can, if necessary, be deleted or overwritten. Discs designated CD-R and DVD-R can only be written to once and cannot be overwritten with new data.

Flash Memory

This is a type of non-volatile or permanent memory which can be used to save data. It can also be wiped and re-used like the hard disc drive. Flash memory is used in SSDs, flash drives (also known as memory sticks) and *SD (Secure Digital) cards*. SD cards in various sizes are used in cameras, mobile phones and computers, especially tablets.

Computer Performance Criteria

The previous pages described some of the main components involved in the computing process, namely:

- The hard disc drive (or SSD in tablets and some laptops) used for permanently storing programs and data.
- The memory or RAM which temporarily holds the instructions and data for the programs currently running.
- The processor or CPU used for carrying out instructions such as calculations and other logical operations.

The above components are critical to the performance of a computer and are often the main criteria used to compare and sell computers. Obviously the larger the hard disc drive or SSD, the more programs and data can be stored before you need to start deleting *files*. If a computer has insufficient memory or RAM for the program or data being executed, the computer will run very slowly. Similarly a slow processor may be unable to handle complex calculations or fast-moving graphics in a game.

The following is part of a typical specification used to advertise a computer:

ACE Laptop Computer

- **Intel Core Duo 2.6GHz**
- **4GB Memory**
- **320GB Hard Drive**

£399 including VAT

The above jargon is explained on the next few pages.

Jargon Explained

Intel Core Duo 2.6GHz

This note on the previous page refers to the processor or CPU as discussed earlier. *Intel* is the name of the manufacturer and *Core Duo* is the type of processor. *2.6GHz* is a measure of the speed of the processor to carry out instructions such as arithmetic, for example. The processor incorporates a *clock* which generates electronic pulses or cycles. This determines the speed at which the computer can carry out instructions.

1GHz is a measure of frequency and means 1,000,000,000 cycles per second.

I use a 1.60GHz computer for general tasks such as typesetting books like this one, creating spreadsheets (financial calculations) and surfing the Internet. The performance of a 1.60GHz processor is quite adequate for this type of work. However, for certain applications, such as complex graphics, multimedia work and the latest games, a more powerful processor may be required. Processor speeds ranging from 2 to 3GHz or more are common on new computers at the time of writing.

Microsoft recommend a processor speed of 1GHz or faster to run the Windows 8 and Windows RT operating systems.

4GB Memory

When notes like **4GB Memory** appear in advertisements it refers to the size of the memory or RAM measured in Gigabytes (GB), as explained on the next page. Memory or RAM is introduced on page 41 and is used to temporarily store the instructions and data for the programs currently being run or executed.

At the current time, new computers costing around £300-£400 have a typical memory of 3 or 4GB while more expensive machines have 6 or 8GB. We run the Windows 8 operating system successfully on machines with 2GB of RAM and Microsoft recommends at least 1GB or 2GB, depending on the specification of the processor. (Please see page 48).

Adding Extra Memory

If a computer doesn't have enough memory, a program will run slowly. Increasing the size of the memory is one of the simplest and cheapest ways to increase the performance of a laptop or desktop computer. In a laptop or desktop computer it is quite easy to insert extra memory modules. Tablet computers like the Surface, being much smaller and possibly less robust, are less easy to repair or expand than desktop or laptop computers.

Bits and Bytes — Units of Memory Size

Inside the computer, data and instructions are converted to the *binary code*, where everything is represented electronically by strings of 0s and 1s. So, for example, the letter A might be coded as 1000001. The 0s and 1s are known as *binary digits* or *bits* for short. Every letter of the alphabet, number, punctuation mark, keyboard character or program instruction can be represented by groups of bits. These are usually arranged in groups of 8 bits each known as a *byte*. As computers have become more powerful over the years, memory or RAM sizes have been quoted first in *kilobytes*, then in *megabytes* and nowadays in *gigabytes,* as defined below.

Byte	A group of 8 binary digits (0s and 1s) or bits. A byte may be used to represent a digit 0-9, a letter, punctuation mark or keyboard character, for example.
Kilobyte (K):	1024 bytes
Megabyte (MB):	About 1 million bytes (1,048,576 to be exact).
Gigabyte (GB):	About 1 billion bytes (1,073,741,824 to be exact).

*When buying a new computer, choose one with as much **RAM** and as fast a **processor** as you can afford.*

320GB Hard Drive

The hard disc drive, as shown on page 40, is like a filing cabinet containing all your programs and data files. The terms *hard drive*, *hard disc* and *hard disk* are all terms used to refer to the *hard disc drive*. (*Disk* is the American spelling). As mentioned elsewhere in this book, tablet computers and some ultrabook laptops use an SSD (Solid State Drive) with no moving parts, instead of a hard disc drive rotating at high speed. However, in other respects the SSD is similar to the hard disc drive and is managed in the same way.

320GB above refers to the amount of space on the hard disc drive available to store programs and data. As a rough guide, and referring to the definitions at the bottom of page 45, a book such as this one stored on the hard disc drive would take up about 50MB (megabytes) or a twentieth of a gigabyte.

As well as data files such as text and photographs, etc., the hard disc drive also contains all of the programs, including all the files which make up the Windows operating system. Microsoft recommend at least 16GB or 20GB of free hard disc space to accommodate Windows 8, depending on which version of Windows 8 you are using — *32-bit* or *64-bit*. These refer to the size of the "chunks" of data that the computer can handle and move around. A computer costing around £300-£400 would have a typical hard disc drive capacity of around 300-500GB. More expensive machines might have a hard disc drive of 1 or 2 *Terabytes*. (1 Terabyte (TB) = 1,000GB). Tablet computers typically have an SSD of 32-64 GB capacity, while Ultrabooks (the latest, very slim laptops) might have an SSD of 128GB.

Adding Storage Capacity

You can increase the non-volatile (permanent) storage capacity of any computer using SD cards and flash drives or, on a laptop or desktop computer, by fitting a larger capacity hard disc drive. The SkyDrive "cloud" app in Windows 8 and RT allows you up to 7GB of free Internet storage for your files.

Checking the Specification of a Computer

Hard Disc Drive : (Laptop or Desktop Computer)

From the Start Screen click the **Desktop** tile and then click the **File Explorer** icon on the Desktop Taskbar as shown on the right. Click **Computer** to display the hard drive and any other devices connected to your computer such as CD/DVD drives and removable flash drives, etc. Hover the cursor over the hard disc drive icon or click **View** and **Details** to see the capacities as shown on the right.

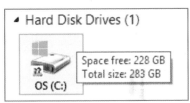

Solid State Drive (SSD): (Tablet Computer)

Tap the **File Explorer** icon on the Desktop Taskbar shown on the right and then tap **Computer** as before. If necessary tap **View** and **Tiles**. The **Computer** window for a Surface RT tablet is shown below. The SSD is designated as hard disc drive **Windows (C:)**. The Surface RT has either a 32GB or 64GB SSD capacity while the Surface Pro has 64GB and 128GB SSD options.

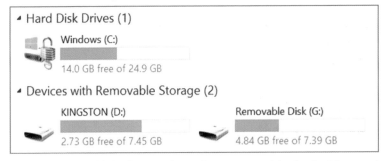

The **Kingston (D:)** shown above is a removable flash drive and **Removable Disk (G:)** is an SDHC camera card inserted in a USB card reader. These devices were connected to the single USB port on the Surface RT tablet using a *USB multi-port hub*.

Memory and Processor Speed

Tap or click the **File Explorer** icon as shown on the previous page. Then tap or click **Computer** on the left-hand side of the Explorer window and then tap or click **Computer** on the menu bar at the very top of the screen. Now tap or click **System properties** from the ribbon at the top of the screen to display the information shown in the screen extract below. This example is for a Dell laptop computer running Windows 8 Pro.

System	
Rating:	**3.4** Windows Experience Index
Processor:	Pentium(R) Dual-Core CPU T4500 @ 2.30GHz 2.30 GHz
Installed memory (RAM):	4.00 GB
System type:	64-bit Operating System, x64-based processor

The Windows Experience Index of 3.4 above is the lowest rating, (in the range 1.0 to 9.9), of several performance parameters such as processor speed and disc data transfer rates.

Listed below are the specifications of the machines I use to run Windows 8 or Windows RT, together with the minimum requirements specified by Microsoft.

Computer System	Processor Speed	Memory RAM	Hard Disc Or SSD
Surface RT Tablet	**1.3GHz**	**2GB**	**32GB**
Dell Laptop	**2.3GHz**	**4GB**	**300GB**
Desktop	**2.6GHz**	**2GB**	**149GB**
Min. requirements **32-bit** **64-bit**	**1GHz** **1GHz**	**1GB** **2GB**	**16GB** **20GB**

Most new machines currently available easily exceed the minimum requirements for Windows 8 and RT as listed above.

Input and Output Facilities

Introduction

As discussed in the previous chapter, the essential components of a computer are the processor, the memory and some form of permanent storage such as the hard disc drive or solid state drive. You also need *peripheral devices* to handle the *input* and *output* of information and media, such as text, pictures music and video. Some of the main peripheral devices include the monitor or screen, the keyboard and the CD/DVD drive.

On the traditional desktop computer the connection of the peripheral devices has been by cables inserted into input and output *ports* or sockets. A fully equipped desktop computer might have a monitor, printer, mouse, keyboard, webcam, speakers, microphone and Internet adapter all connected by cables. Together with the power cables which some of these external devices require, you might have 12 or more cables at the back of the desktop computer creating quite an untidy jungle.

In tablet and laptop computers many of the common peripheral devices such as monitor, speakers, microphone and camera(s) are already built into the computer. The only essential cable with tablets and laptops is the AC adapter used to charge the battery after several hours of use. (Typically 4-12 hours).

The tablet computer does not usually have many input or output ports and this limits its range of applications. Without special adapters, the absence of a *video port* may prevent a full size monitor or a projector being connected. Laptop computers are generally better equipped with input and output ports than the tablet. Unlike the tablet, the laptop has a built-in CD/DVD drive for recording and playing music and information, etc.

Input and Output Ports

The VGA (Video Graphics Array) Port

This is the standard 15-pin port, used on desktop and laptop computers to connect a monitor. Laptop computers, as well as having their own integral monitor, normally also have a VGA port, shown on the right, to enable a second monitor to be connected.
The VGA port can also be used to connect a projector. This might be useful for giving a talk or lecture, for example.

The DVI (Digital Video Interface) Port

Some computers have a *DVI* port which gives a superior quality screen display on a suitable monitor. The monitor must have a DVI socket to accommodate the special cable from the DVI port on the computer. On desktop computers it's easy to fit a new DVI graphics card to replace a standard VGA graphics card. Some expensive laptop computers are fitted with a DVI port as standard. Shown below is a graphics card from a desktop computer containing both a blue VGA port and a white DVI port.

The graphics card in a desktop computer is simply pushed into a slot in the *motherboard* and is held in place by a single screw.

The Ethernet Port

WiFi (or wireless technology) is widely used for networking and connecting to the Internet, but some businesses such as hotels use a *wired network* using *Ethernet* technology.
Laptop and desktop computers generally have an *Ethernet port* as shown on the right. This connects the computer to a wired network via a special
Ethernet cable. An Ethernet cable may also be used to connect a computer to a *broadband router*, as discussed later.

The Audio or Sound Ports

Laptop Computer

Tablets and laptops normally have a built-in microphone and speakers. There may also be small round input and output audio ports to connect external devices such as a microphone, headphones and speakers.

Desktop Computer

The ports shown on the right are used to connect audio devices to a desktop computer. The green port is used for sound output to speakers or headphones, pink is for input from a microphone while light blue is used for audio input, such as from an external CD drive. You might want to fit a better sound *expansion card* to improve the quality of the sound produced by the sound components. Fitting a better sound card to a desktop computer is a job anyone can accomplish.

PS/2 Ports

These are still used on some desktop computers to connect the cables for a keyboard and a mouse. The green PS/2 port shown on the right is used to connect the mouse cable while the purple PS/2 port is used for the keyboard connection.

The laptop computer, with its built-in keyboard and touch pad, doesn't need PS/2 ports as shown above. Also many people now prefer to use a *wireless* mouse and keyboard, thus reducing the clutter on the desk or work surface. You can also buy keyboards and mice with cables which plug into the *USB* ports on laptop and desktop computers (and tablets if a USB port is available).

Tablets do not usually have many built-in ports, although it may be possible to add them using plug-in adapters. The Surface tablet has a built-in USB port and ***multi-port hubs*** are available to convert one USB port into several. There is also a port to connect a VGA or HDMI monitor via an adapter.

USB (Universal Serial Bus) Ports

A few years ago, most personal computers had a variety of different ports to connect specific devices. These included the *parallel* or *Centronics* port for connecting a printer and the *serial* or *COM* port for connecting a mouse or *modem*. Nowadays these ports have largely been replaced by USB ports, although they are still present on some desktop computers.

USB ports are a relatively new development but they have taken over as the standard method for connecting virtually any sort of peripheral device. The USB ports are small rectangular slots as shown on the right. The USB port is used to plug in devices such as mice, keyboards, printers, flash drives, etc. The USB ports can accommodate USB *dongles*, as show on page 54. These plug directly into the USB port. Alternatively it may be necessary to use a USB cable, as shown on the right, to connect devices, such as a printer or webcam, to the USB port.

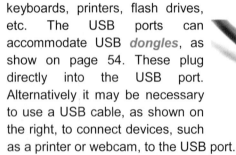

On a desktop computer there may be four USB ports at the back of the base unit and sometimes a further two at the front. Laptops usually have three or four USB ports on the side of the computer. The Microsoft Surface tablet has one USB port but this can be increased by the use of a *multi-port hub*. Some tablets like the iPad have no built-in USB ports but you can add them by connecting a special adapter or *docking station*.

USB technology has developed over recent years to give increasing speeds for data transfer between computers and peripheral devices. More expensive computers may have a mixture of USB 2.0 and USB 3.0 ports. USB 2.0 is still in widespread use while USB 3.0 is the latest high-speed standard.

The USB port has many advantages over the earlier *serial* and *parallel ports*, which were bulky and expensive:

- USB devices, such as a digital camera, can be plugged in or removed while the computer is up-and-running, a process known as *hot swapping*. You should, however, wait until the computer has finished saving data before removing a device like a flash drive, as discussed shortly.

- USB connections are simple, cheap and light and easy to plug in and remove.

- Some USB devices are known as *plug and play*, because they work as soon as they are plugged in for the first time. These plug and play devices don't need special installation software, known as *device drivers,* supplied on a CD/DVD by the manufacturers of some devices.

- The USB specification in general use over the last few years is USB 2.0, while the latest standard, USB 3.0, is becoming increasingly available in new devices such as flash drives. USB 3.0 is also known as SuperSpeed as it gives data transfer rates many times faster than USB 2.0 devices. Some new laptop computers are supplied with a mixture of some USB 2.0 ports and a USB 3.0 port for high speed devices. These include applications where large amounts of data need to be transferred between the device and the computer, such as flash drives, external hard disc drives, digital cameras, camcorders and CD/DVD and Blue Ray external drives.

- USB 3.0 devices are designed so that they can still work with computers designed for the older USB 2.0 standard. Similarly computers built to the new USB 3.0 standard can still run devices designed for the older USB 2.0 standard. Obviously to get the maximum benefit of the high speed technology, both the device and the computer ports need to be of the USB 3.0 design.

USB Dongles

As just described, USB ports can be used for connecting a diverse range of devices. Some of these devices, such as printers, are connected to a USB port on the computer using a USB cable. However, many other small USB devices plug directly into a USB port and are collectively known as *dongles*. A typical dongle may only be the size of a little finger but can contain the electronics to carry out some very complex functions. Shown below are several dongles for various purposes.

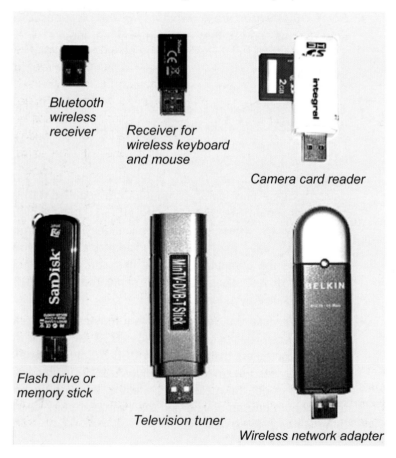

Bluetooth
wireless
receiver

Receiver for
wireless keyboard
and mouse

Camera card reader

Flash drive or
memory stick

Television tuner

Wireless network adapter

The USB Flash Drive (Memory Stick)

This is a very popular type of USB dongle. It's used for saving data files such as text, music and photographs. Flash drives are particularly useful for transferring files between computers in different places, such as work and home. The flash drive can also be used to make *backup* copies of files saved on the hard disc drive, for security.

Unlike the computer's main memory or RAM, the data on the flash drive is *non-volatile* — you don't lose it when the power to the computer is switched off or the dongle is removed. The flash drive behaves more like the computer's internal hard disc drive. Like the hard disc drive, the flash drive is a read/write device — allowing files to be saved or deleted repeatedly. This includes overwriting an earlier document by a later one with the same name. Unlike the hard disc drive, which rotates at high speed, the flash drive contains no moving parts and is a form of *solid state* memory, similar to the memory cards used in digital cameras and the main storage (instead of a hard disc drive) in tablet computers.

Some dongles can be *write-protected* by moving a small switch as shown in red on the flash drive above. In the closed position no data can be written to, or deleted from, the flash drive.

At the time of writing an 8GB USB 2.0 flash drive can be obtained for under £5.00, while a 64GB USB 3.0 drive costs around £25. (Please see page 45 for definitions of units of memory size such as GB). As discussed earlier, you will only get the increased speed of data transfer from a USB 3.0 flash drive if your computer supports the USB 3.0 standard. Methods of upgrading laptop and desktop computers from USB 2.0 to USB 3.0 are discussed on page 57.

Devices Connected via USB Ports

- A *dongle* or receiver for a wireless keyboard and mouse, giving a less cluttered desk and freedom of movement.

- A USB *broadband modem* to connect a single computer to the Internet via the telephone lines.

- A USB *wireless (WiFi) adapter* to connect a desktop computer to the Internet via a *wireless router*. (WiFi connectivity is built-in on tablets and laptops).

- A USB adapter to connect a *Bluetooth* device such as a mobile phone to a computer to transfer data wirelessly.

- A USB inkjet or laser printer used to print text, pictures or photographs, etc.

- An external hard disc drive giving additional storage and enabling the backup of the internal hard drive.

- USB flash drive, also known as a *memory stick*, used to backup data files and transfer files between computers.

- USB headphones, webcam, speakers and microphone for improved sound or to make free video calls on Skype.

- A digital camera or camera phone connected via a USB cable, enabling photos to be transferred to a computer.

- A *card reader* to transfer photographs from a memory card removed from a digital camera. Laptops often have a built-in card reader, as do some tablets.

- A *mobile broadband dongle*, used to connect a tablet or laptop to the Internet wherever a signal can be obtained using a mobile telephone network.

- A *TV Tuner dongle* enabling you to receive and record live television on a laptop or desktop computer.

- An external CD/DVD to watch videos or make backups.

- A flatbed scanner for inputting paper documents.

Adding USB Ports

USB ports are now used for so many peripheral devices that you may need to add some extra ones in addition to the 3-6 ports already provided on a new laptop or desktop computer. A tablet may need an adapter to add a single USB port, which can then be expanded.

To increase the number of ports on a tablet, laptop or desktop computer, a simple way is to buy a *multi-port USB hub* such as the one shown on the right.

With a desktop computer you can also add extra ports by fitting a USB expansion card. As discussed earlier, you simply remove a few screws and take off the computer's casing. The USB expansion card plugs into a slot in the *motherboard*, the main circuit board inside the computer's casing. The expansion card is held in place by a single screw. Shown on the right is an expansion card providing four extra USB ports.

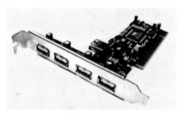

Upgrading from USB 2.0 to USB 3.0

You can add USB 3.0 ports to a desktop computer by fitting a PCI Express USB 3.0 expansion card, similar to the one shown above. Some laptops have an *ExpressCard slot* which can take a USB 3.0 ExpressCard as shown on the right.

Summary: Input and Output Facilities

The Tablet Computer

(Based on the Microsoft Surface)

USB Port

One USB port expandable to several ports. Can be used to connect a keyboard, mouse, printer, flash drive, camera, etc.

Speakers+Microphone

These items are built-in as standard but there may also be an audio port to connect external speakers or headset.

Keyboard

On-screen keyboard pops-up when needed. Also an actual keyboard which clips to the tablet and forms a cover.

Stylus or Digital Pen

For freehand drawing and painting, e.g. with Fresh Paint app.

WiFi

Built-in capability to connect to the Internet and a home network via a wireless router. Can be switched on or off.

Camera

Front and rear facing cameras built-in, for Skype, etc..

AC Adapter

For recharging the battery, clips into place magnetically.

MicroSD Card Slot

A small slot for extra storage using microSD cards and for transferring photos from a camera..

Video Output

Connect a VGA or HDMI monitor using an adapter.

CD/DVD Drive

Small size of tablet prevents the use of a built-in CD/DVD drive. External CD/DVD and hard drives may be connected to a tablet computer if a USB port is available.

The Laptop Computer

(Based on a Dell Inspiron laptop).

USB Ports

3 built-in USB ports as standard.

Ethernet Port

Built-in on most laptops. Connects to a wired network or directly to a router, using an Ethernet cable.

Speakers+Microphone

Built-in as standard. Also two audio ports allowing external microphone and speakers to be connected for superior quality.

Keyboard+Touchpad

Keyboard with built-in touchpad. The touchpad replicates the actions of a mouse with left and right buttons. The touch sensitive pad is used to control the cursor with finger gestures.

WiFi

Built-in capability to connect to the Internet and a home network via a wireless router. Can be switched on or off.

Camera

Built-in camera, for video calls with Skype, etc.

AC Adapter

For recharging the battery, plugs into the side of the laptop.

SD Card Slot

Slots for a range of SD cards of various sizes, etc., for extra storage and for transferring photos from a camera.

VGA Port

Built-in as standard. Connects a VGA monitor or projector.

CD/DVD Drive

Laptops normally have a built-in optical CD/DVD drive. External hard disc drive may be connected via a USB port.

The Desktop Computer

USB Ports

6 ports built-in as standard — 4 at the back and 2 at the front.

Speakers+Microphone

Not built-in. Several built-in audio ports provided to plug in separate external speakers, microphone or headset.

Keyboard+Mouse

Separate keyboard and mouse connected via cables to USB ports, PS2 ports or wirelessly to USB wireless receiver.

WiFi

Not built-in. USB wireless dongle or expansion card needed.

Ethernet Port

Built-in or added on an expansion network card. Connects to a wired network or directly to a router, using an Ethernet cable.

Camera

Not built-in. A separate webcam can be added via USB dongle for use with Skype or video conferencing, etc.

SD Card Slot

For transferring photos and for extra storage. Built in on some desktop machines. Otherwise a camera connected by USB cable or a USB card reader can be plugged in.

Power Supply

Requires a desk with several adjacent power points.

VGA Port

Standard on desktop computers for connecting a monitor. Extra ports for high quality DVI and HD monitors may be available.

Expansion Cards

Easily fitted to give extra USB, audio and video ports, etc.

CD/DVD Drive

The desktop computer has a built-in CD/DVD drive.

Connecting Peripheral Devices

Introduction

The Universal Serial Bus has transformed the connection of external devices. Most devices now plug easily into a USB port in the computer. You can even insert a USB device or cable while the computer is up and running — there's no need to stop work and shut everything down. Some of the most common USB devices which you are likely to connect to a USB port are:

- Flash drive, also known as a memory stick or dongle.
- Inkjet or laser printer.
- Keyboard and mouse with USB cables.
- Wireless receiver for a wireless keyboard and mouse.
- Digital camera for transferring photos onto the computer.
- SD card reader for transferring photos or extra storage. (Some computers have a built-in SD card reader).
- Some digital cameras for charging the battery.
- External hard disc drive for extra storage.
- External CD/DVD drive for backing up data, such as photos and inputting and outputting music and video, etc.

The installation of USB devices is usually very simple – it's usually just a case of plugging in and waiting a few seconds until the device is ready. This is often referred to as "plug and play". This chapter describes how to connect some of the most common USB devices.

Using a USB Flash Drive

You can insert a flash drive (or any other USB device) into any of the USB ports in your computer. If the computer has a mixture of USB 2.0 and USB 3.0 ports, you would obviously use the USB 3.0 port if high-speed data transmission was needed for transferring very large files, such as videos, etc.

When you install a flash drive into a computer for the first time, it is automatically detected. The Windows operating system then looks for and installs the necessary *device driver* software to make the device work with your computer.

After a very short time, the software installation process is complete and, all being well, the following note appears in the bottom right-hand corner of the screen.

Installing the device driver software is a one-off operation, only needed the first time you insert the flash drive into a particular computer. If you remove the flash drive and insert it in a different computer for the first time, the one-off driver installation process will need to be done on that computer.

When you insert a flash drive in a machine in which it has been previously inserted (and the driver installed) the following notification may appear in the top right-hand corner of the screen, accompanied by some short musical sounds. Now tap (or click if using a mouse) the notification to open the *Autoplay* window shown on the next page.

KINGSTON (E:)
Tap to choose what happens with removable drives.

KINGSTON (E:)

Choose what to do with removable drives.

 Speed up my system
Windows ReadyBoost

 Configure this drive for backup
File History

 Open folder to view files
File Explorer

 Take no action

Tap or click **Open folder to view files File Explorer** to see the files stored on the flash drive. The *File Explorer* (also known as the *Windows Explorer* in some versions of Windows) lists the documents, pictures, music and videos, etc., stored on a flash drive, hard disc drive, SSD or CD/DVD, as shown below.

Depending on the settings on your computer, the File Explorer may open directly after you insert the flash drive. Double-tap or double-click the icon for a file in the File Explorer to launch it in its associated program or app such as Word or Paint.

| BP601 Colour | autorun.inf | ReadyBoost.sfcache | unInstaller.exe | urDrive.exe |

If the AutoPlay Menu Doesn't Open

Swipe in from the right-hand edge of the screen or allow the cursor to hover in the top right or bottom corner of the screen. Tap or click the **Search** charm shown on the right, then select **Settings** and enter **AutoPlay** in the Search bar. When you tap or click the search icon the following window appears.

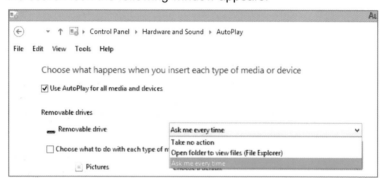

Open the drop-down menu on the right of **Removable drive** shown above and select **Ask me every time**. Tap or click the **Save** button. The notification shown at the bottom of page 62 should now appear whenever you insert a flash drive or other removable drive.

Viewing a Flash Drive in the File Explorer Window

When you insert a flash drive into a USB port it is assigned a name such as **Removable Disk (E:)** or **(F:)**. The flash drive can then be used like a hard disc drive or SSD for saving and deleting files and folders. From the Start Screen tap or click the **Desktop** tile and then tap or click the **File Explorer** icon shown on the right. The flash drive **KINGSTON (F:)** appears in the File Explorer window below the hard disc drive **Local Disk (C:)**. Tap or click the name of the flash drive to open a list of the files and folders on the drive.

Removing a Flash Drive (or another USB Device)

When using a flash drive to save a document or photo, etc., always wait until the saving process is complete before removing the flash drive — otherwise some of your data may be lost.

Windows provides an icon with a tick in a green circle which tells you when it's safe to remove hardware from a USB port. This icon appears on the Taskbar at the bottom right of the screen, as shown on the right and below.

 If the green icon doesn't appear on your Taskbar, tap or click the **Show hidden icons** icon shown here on the left and on the Taskbar above. A small window appears and this should include the green icon.

Pass the cursor over the green icon, which then displays the words **Safely Remove Hardware and Eject Media**. Now tap or click the green tick icon and then tap or click **Eject** next to the required device on the pop-up menu, in this example the flash drive **KINGSTON (F:)**, **DT 101 G2**, as shown below.

After tapping or clicking the device to be removed, such as a flash drive, the following note appears.

Using a Tablet or Laptop Like a Desktop

A laptop computer usually has some USB ports and a VGA video port, which can be used to attach a keyboard, mouse, monitor and printer, for example. These peripheral devices can also be connected to tablet computers if they have a USB port. Expanding a laptop or tablet in this way enables a single computer to be used both for computing on the move and also for demanding, extended tasks requiring the more ergonomic and productive configuration of the desktop machine.

A full-size USB keyboard and mouse can be added for about £15 or less. These plug into the USB ports on the tablet or laptop and are immediately detected and soon ready for use. Alternatively you can plug a *USB mini receiver* into a USB port on the laptop to connect a *wireless* mouse and keyboard. A 19-inch TFT slimline monitor can be bought for under £100 and this connects to the VGA port on the laptop or tablet, if available.

As shown below, the small laptop or tablet computer can now be used with all the advantages of a desktop machine.

Connecting a Printer

A printer is essential for many applications of a personal computer, such as printing holiday photographs, preparing a newsletter, producing flyers to advertise a local event, or writing a book, such as this one, for example.

There are two main types of printer used with most personal computers, the *inkjet* and the *laser*. Many of these are called MFPs (multifunction printers) as they combine in one device the roles of printer, photocopier and scanner. Scanning allows you to input or "digitize" an existing document which might consist of pages of text or pictures and photographs. Then the document can be saved on your hard disc, SSD or flash drive, or shared with someone else via e-mail or posting to a Web site.

Shown on the right is a typical multifunction inkjet printer. The lid on the top is shown in the raised position, ready for documents up to A4 size to be placed on the glass flat bed for scanning or copying.

Many printers have slots on the front which allow you to insert a memory card from a digital camera. The photos from the camera card can be input to the computer, edited on the screen, then saved on the hard disc drive or SSD before printing on paper. Highly valued photos should be backed up onto a CD or DVD for extra security.

Some inkjet printers are specifically designated as *photo printers*, but most inkjet and laser colour printers are capable of producing high quality prints. For best results, glossy *photo paper* is widely available from stationery shops, currently costing around £5 for a hundred 6x4 inch sheets, for example.

Printer Consumables

Many companies now offer quite serviceable inkjet printers at very modest prices, sometimes as low as £50. However, on top of this you must budget for replacement ink cartridges which can soon eclipse the purchase price of the printer, if you do a lot of printing. The inkjet colour printer usually has four cartridges, namely *cyan*, *magenta*, *yellow* and *black*. These are usually abbreviated to *CMYK*, where *K* is black. (In commercial printing, black is known as the *Key* colour). Prices vary greatly but you can easily pay well over £30 for a set of four cartridges, unless you shop around — on the Internet for example.

Colour and monochrome laser printers can be bought for under £100 and are faster than the inkjet, especially useful if you need to do large print runs. The cost of the toner cartridges for a laser printer ranges from about £30 — £100.

You can also buy cheaper *compatible* cartridges rather than the *original* versions from the printer manufacturer. Another option is to buy *refilled* cartridges or you can get a *refill kit* to do the job yourself. If you intend to do a lot of printing, the cost of the printing consumables is a big expense and it's worth investigating this thoroughly before buying a printer.

Installing a USB Printer

This is a task which anyone can accomplish. The basic methods are the same for most printers, but always read the user guide and instructions before unpacking and any light assembly such as the insertion of paper and cartridges, etc. There are usually only two cables — a power cable which plugs into a normal power point and a special *USB printer cable* which connects the printer to a USB port on the computer. The USB printer cable carries the data i.e. text and pictures, etc., from the computer to the printer, before printing on paper. As discussed later, you can also buy *wireless printers* which, after setting up, do not need to be permanently connected to a computer via a USB cable.

Some manufacturers of devices such as printers advise you to install the software from their CD, before connecting the device to a USB port and switching on. This software CD contains programs called *device drivers*, necessary to make the device work properly with a particular version of the Windows operating system, such as Windows 8 or Windows RT.

If there are no contrary instructions from the manufacturers, simply switch the device on and plug it into any of the USB ports with the computer switched on and connected to the Internet. Windows detects the device and immediately tries to find the necessary drivers and install them. If the correct drivers are available they are downloaded from a Microsoft Internet service called *Windows Update*.

When a Brother USB printer was connected to a USB port on my Windows 8 Pro laptop computer, the drivers were found and the installation proceeded automatically, as shown below.

Installing device driver software
Click here for status.

If you select **Click here for status** as shown above, the following window appears displaying the progress of the driver installation.

In my experience, Windows usually finds the right device drivers for recent makes of printer. If Windows Update can't find the correct drivers you are advised to use the manufacturer's CD, if available. Finally, if all else fails, log on to the manufacturer's Web site where it should be possible to download the drivers to make the device work with your version of Windows.

Once the printer drivers have been installed you will see the message **Your device is ready to use**.

Checking the New Printer

Hover the cursor over the bottom or top right-hand corner of the screen to display the Charms menu. On a touch screen swipe in from the right. Then tap or click **Settings** and **Control Panel** and **View devices and printers**. In this example, the **Brother DCP-195C** printer had just been installed as shown below.

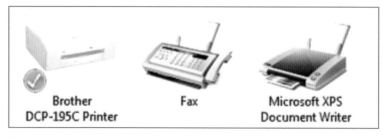

Brother   Fax   Microsoft XPS
DCP-195C Printer   Document Writer

The tick in the green circle above shows that the Brother is the *default printer*, i.e. the one which will be used automatically if you have more than one printer connected to the computer. If you right-click, (or press and hold on a touchscreen), the icon for the printer, a menu pops up with options including setting a printer as the default printer or removing the printer drivers from the computer. Double-clicking or double-tapping the icon for the printer shown above displays another set of options including viewing the list of jobs in the *print queue* and cancelling print jobs if necessary. (Mouse operations such as double-clicking and right-clicking, together with the equivalent touchscreen gestures, are discussed on pages 86 and 87).

An Overview of Windows 8

What is Windows?

Stored inside every computer there is a suite of software known as the *operating system*. This manages and controls every aspect of the computer's operation, no matter what *application* or *app* (such as a Web browser, music or photo-editing program) you are running. The operating system provides the *Start Screen* with *tiles*, *icons* and other screen objects used to launch programs. The operating system used in over 90% of the world's computers is called *Microsoft Windows*.

Recently the explosion in the use of *tablet* computers has seen a corresponding increase in the use of *touchscreens* as a method of input. The latest version of Windows, Windows 8, can be used with the new breed of touchscreen tablets, as well as desktop and laptop computers which use a mouse and keyboard. Shown below is the Windows 8 Start Screen, based on *tiles* which are tapped with a finger or clicked with a mouse to launch programs or apps. Some tiles display live information such as news, weather and sport which is regularly updated.

The Modern User Interface

The user interface refers to the way humans interact with the computer. In the last few years this has generally been with a keyboard and mouse (or a touchpad on a laptop). Before that programs and data were launched and run using just a keyboard. (Some of us are old enough to remember entering programs (now called apps) on a deck of punched cards.)

When Microsoft first announced Windows 8 with its radically different user interface, the design was initially called *Metro*. At the time of writing the new interface is called the *Modern UI*.

At the centre of the Modern UI is the Start Screen shown on page 71. There are several editions of Windows 8 but all of them use the same Start Screen, with a common core of default tiles. As you add new apps yourself they are given new tiles and you may have to scroll the Start Screen to see them all. The Start Screen is used to launch programs and this can be done in two ways:

- On a computer with a touchscreen, tap the tile for the app with your finger.

- On a laptop or desktop computer which doesn't have a touchscreen, click the tile with the left mouse button.

The Windows Desktop

Windows 8 can still run the traditional Windows Desktop, used to launch programs in earlier versions of Windows, such as Windows 7. Programs can be launched from the Taskbar across the bottom of the Desktop, as shown below.

Programs can also be launched by double-clicking or double-tapping icons on the Desktop, as shown on the next page. The Desktop can be used with a mouse or with a touchscreen.

All editions of the new Windows 8 operating system give access to a version of the Windows Desktop, as shown below.

The Desktop in Windows 8 is similar to the Desktop in Windows 7, for example, but does not have the Windows 7 Start Menu. The Desktop in Windows 8 is used to run programs which were designed for earlier versions of Windows. These programs may appear as apps on the Start Screen, alongside apps specifically designed for the Modern UI. When you tap or click the tile for a program designed for an earlier version of Windows, the program is launched in the Windows 8 Desktop.

There is a tile for the Desktop on the Start Screen, shown below (displaying flowers), which takes you straight to the Windows 8 Desktop. You can switch from the Windows 8 Desktop back to the Start Screen in several different ways, as discussed in Chapter 8. One very simple way (if you are using a suitable keyboard) is to press the Windows Logo key, as shown on the right.

Windows 8 & Windows 8 Pro

The basic edition, Windows 8, and its close relation Windows 8 Pro, can run on most laptop, desktop or tablet computers that can use Windows XP and Windows 7, for example. Windows 8 is intended to be installed by the manufacturers of new computers. Windows 8 Pro is intended for consumers wishing to upgrade a computer running an earlier version of Windows.

Windows 8 and Windows 8 Pro can be used on most laptop, desktop or tablet computers having the common PC architecture known as *x86*. This means computers using processors made by Intel or AMD, for example. These processors have been at the heart of most PC-type computers for many years. The minimum requirements for running Windows 8 are given on page 48.

Windows RT

This is a special version of Windows 8 and has been designed for tablet computers which use the *ARM* processor. The ARM is a very popular processor used in many tablets and smartphones and has a low power consumption. Windows RT cannot generally run traditional Windows software, but relies on new *apps* written specially for the ARM processor and obtainable from the *Windows Store,* as discussed elsewhere in this book.

Windows RT is not available to buy separately — it is only available preinstalled on a new tablet computer which uses the ARM processor, such as the Microsoft Surface shown on the next page.

The Microsoft Surface tablet is designed to be used in touchscreen mode. However, there is also a cover which contains an integral keyboard and touchpad. Windows RT includes special versions of Microsoft's widely used Office suite of software, i.e. Word, Excel, PowerPoint and OneNote.

The Surface can be used as a tablet, e.g. while on the move, etc. It can also be used for more demanding work by using the integral keyboard cover.

The Microsoft Surface shown above is supplied with Windows RT already installed. The Surface Pro is a more expensive version of the Surface tablet, based on the x86 processor and designed to run Windows 8 Pro.

Windows 8, Windows 8 Pro and Windows RT are all suitable for the home user. Windows 8 Pro is the same as the basic Windows 8 but contains additional features for the professional or advanced user, such as extra security.

Please Note:

- All three versions of the new Windows operating system, Windows 8, Windows 8 Pro and Windows RT, all look alike and are operated in the same way.

- The main difference is that, unlike Windows 8 and Windows 8 Pro, Windows RT cannot run traditional Windows software unless it is specially adapted.

- In the rest of this book the term Windows 8 also applies to Windows 8 Pro and Windows RT, unless otherwise stated.

Key Points: Windows RT and Windows 8

Windows RT

- To obtain Windows RT you must buy a tablet computer with an ARM processor and Windows RT preinstalled.

- Windows RT will not generally run software written for earlier versions of Windows such as Windows 7. Some Windows software such as Office 2013 has been specially converted to run on Windows RT.

- You cannot upgrade an older x86 machine to run Windows RT, or buy separate retail versions of the RT software.

Windows 8 & Windows 8 Pro

- Please see page 48 for minimum requirements.

- You can upgrade a x86 laptop, desktop or tablet computer to Windows 8 Pro from an earlier version of Windows such as Windows XP, Vista or Windows 7.

- You can buy a new x86 laptop, desktop or tablet computer with Windows 8 (but not RT) already installed. This should run software designed for earlier versions of Windows, such as Windows XP and Windows 7.

Please Note:

- Windows RT and Windows 8 can be operated either with a touchscreen or by using a mouse and keyboard.

- Touchscreen tablet computers like the Microsoft Surface may also have an optional keyboard and touchpad.

- Some tablets, such as the Surface, have either a USB port or an adapter, enabling a full-size USB keyboard and mouse to be connected for more demanding work.

- Most laptop and desktop computers do not generally support touchscreen operation unless fitted with a special touchscreen monitor.

The Start Screen in Detail

This is the most striking change between Windows 8 and earlier versions such as Windows XP and Windows 7. On starting up the familiar Desktop is replaced by the new Start Screen. Gone is the previous Start Menu, to be replaced by a matrix of square and rectangular tiles, shown in the sample below.

Tiles on the Start Screen

Some tiles behave in a similar way to Desktop icons. For example, the tile shown on the right is used to open a new version of the Microsoft Web browser, Internet Explorer 10. The program is launched by tapping with a finger or clicking with a mouse. Internet Explorer 10 is included with Windows 8 and the tile shown on  the right above appears on the Start Screen by default.

When you install additional apps, tiles for them may be automatically created on the Start Screen. The tile on the right appeared after the Adobe Reader software was installed. (Adobe Reader is used to read documents in the Portable Document Format (PDF), widely used on the Internet).

Live Tiles

Some tiles, such as **News**, **Sport**, **Weather** and **Finance**, display constantly changing headlines and live information. A sample headline on the **Finance** tile is shown on the right. After a few seconds the headlines in the **Finance** tile change, to display the FTSE index, as shown below right. Tapping or clicking the **Finance** tile leads to a full screen of news reports, as shown in the example below. To scroll through the news items, swipe across the screen or use a mouse to drag the horizontal scroll bar, as shown at the bottom of the screenshot below.

As discussed in Chapter 8, there are several ways to return to the Start Screen at any time or to launch new apps. You can have several apps running in the background at the same time and cycle through them, before switching to a different app.

Tiles for Launching Apps

The Travel App

When you tap or click the **Travel** tile, you can choose from an array of small images of the world's major cities. The **Destinations** feature shows full screen photos of attractions including 360-degree panoramic views such as the **Eiffel Tower** below.

Rio de Janeiro, Brazil

The **Travel** app also lists hotels, restaurants and tourist information, as shown in the Rome example below.

The Mail App

Many of the apps which appear as tiles on the Start Screen are discussed in more detail later in this book. The **Mail** tile leads to a new, fully featured e-mail program as shown below. E-mail is discussed in more detail in Chapter 14.

The People App

This helps you to keep in touch with friends on social networking sites such as Facebook and Twitter. Social networking is discussed in detail in Chapter 14.

The Weather App

This allows you to find out 10-day weather forecasts for any selected location, both where you live or worldwide.

The Photos App

This gives access to all of your photos stored in various locations such as the Pictures Library on your computer, on the Internet in the SkyDrive "Clouds", or on the Facebook or Flickr Web sites. The  Photos tile is live, presenting a regularly changing mini slideshow of your photos.

The Maps App

This presents a map of the world but also allows you to zoom in on a particular area such as your own location. Zooming in and out is achieved with the pinching and stretching gestures with two fingers on a touchscreen or by holding down the **Ctrl** key and using the central scroll  wheel on a mouse. Maps can be displayed in Road view, as shown below, or in Aerial view. (Touchscreen gestures and the equivalent mouse actions are discussed in the next chapter).

The SkyDrive App

SkyDrive is a storage facility on the Internet where you can place copies of your documents and photos, etc. This means they can be shared with friends, family or colleagues anywhere in the world. All they need is an Internet connection and a Web browser on any device such as a smartphone, tablet computer, laptop or

desktop machine. This form of remote storage of documents and photos, etc., away from your own computer is referred to as *cloud computing*.

Viewing All of Your Apps

All of the apps or programs installed on your computer can be displayed using the **All apps** icon shown on the right. To display the icon on a touch screen, from the Start Screen shown on page 71, swipe in from the top or bottom edge. Alternatively right click over the Start Screen to display the **All apps** icon. Tap or click the icon to reveal all of the apps. If it's necessary to scroll the screen, flick the screen with a finger or use a mouse to drag the scroll bar at the bottom of the screen.

Many of the apps are included with Windows 8 itself, while others can be downloaded from the *Windows Store* as discussed on the next page.

The *Windows Explorer* used in previous versions of Windows is still present in *Windows 8*, though it is now known as the *File Explorer*. This is used to manage all of your documents and other files in a hierarchical system of folders. As mentioned earlier, apps need to be specially written or converted for the Windows RT tablet with its ARM processor.

Also present in Windows 8 are the graphics program *Windows Paint* and the *Control Panel (*shown below), used to manage the computer's settings for various devices, discussed later.

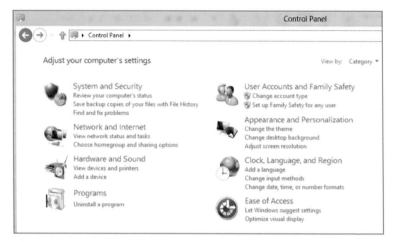

Obtaining More Apps from the Windows Store

This allows users of all versions of Windows 8 to download and install on their computers, both free and paid for apps in a wide range of subjects, such as games, music and video and photography.

Working with Windows 8

Introduction

You can use all editions of Windows 8 (including Windows RT) with a touchscreen or with a mouse and keyboard. Users of tablet computers may be able to choose between these two modes of operation, while many desktop and laptop computers can only be controlled by a mouse and keyboard. To use touch operation with a laptop or desktop computer, a special touch-sensitive screen is required.

When you switch the computer on, it quickly boots, i.e. starts up, to display the Lock Screen, shown below. Either swipe your finger diagonally across a touch screen or click anywhere on the screen using a mouse. Then enter the password for your Microsoft account. This is set up during the sign-up process when Windows 8 is first installed. (Alternative Lock Screen images or photos can be selected, as discussed in Chapter 9).

The next two pages list some common Windows 8 mouse operations and the corresponding touchscreen *gestures*.

Basic Mouse Operations

Click

Press the left mouse button to select an object on the screen at the current cursor position, such as a menu option. Opens an app from its tile on the Start Screen.

Double-click

Two left clicks in quick succession to open a folder in the Windows (or File) Explorer. Also launches an app from an icon.

Right-click

Press the right mouse button to open a shortcut or context sensitive menu. These menus list options relevant to the current cursor position.

Drag

Click over a screen object then, keeping the left button held down, drag the object to a new position, before releasing the left button. Can be used to change the position of a tile on the Start Screen or move a file or folder to a different folder in the File Explorer. Drag is also used to move horizontal or vertical scroll bars to advance forwards or backwards through a long document. Dragging an object to another disc drive, *copies* the object. Dragging an object to a new location on the same disc drive *moves* the object. Dragging with the right button held down displays a menu when the button is released. This includes options to move or copy the item.

Scroll Wheel

This wheel in the centre of a mouse is used to scroll through a long document on the screen.

Ctrl + Scroll Wheel

Hold down the Ctrl key and turn the scroll wheel. This zooms in or out of whatever is currently displayed on the screen.

Basic Touch Gestures

Tap

Tap quickly on the screen with a finger to launch an app from a tile on the Start Screen, or select an option from a menu.

Double Tap

Two quick taps to open a folder or flash drive, etc., in the File Explorer. To find out about devices such as a printer, double tap its icon in Devices and Printers in the Control Panel.

Press and Hold

Keep your finger gently pressing against an object or area of the screen for a few seconds then release to display a shortcut menu relevant to the current screen location.

Drag

Keeping your finger over a screen object such as a tile on the Start Screen or a file in File Explorer, move your finger over the screen and release to drop the object in its new location.

Swipe

This involves sliding your finger across the screen, usually from one of the four edges. Swiping has many uses for displaying running apps and menu options and these are discussed in detail shortly.

Flick

The finger is quickly moved across the screen horizontally or vertically to scroll through a long document.

Rotate two fingers to turn an object.

Pinch or move two fingers together to zoom out.

Stretch or move two fingers apart to zoom in or enlarge.

The *bezel* or border around a tablet screen is touch-sensitive. When you swipe from the left, right, top or bottom edge of the screen, always start with your finger in the bezel area.

Launching Apps Using Tiles

After you enter your password, the Start Screen appears as shown below. The background colour can be changed if you wish, as discussed in Chapter 9.

If you want to change the position of a particular app it can be dragged and dropped to a new position, as mentioned on the previous pages.

To launch a particular app, such as Internet Explorer, tap or click its tile, as shown on the right and above.

Near the top of the screenshot at the bottom of the previous page there is the **web search** bar. Here you can enter keywords to find information about topics which interest you, such as **Magna Carta**, for example. At the bottom of the Internet Explorer window on the previous page is an Address Bar, which by default displays **http://t.uk.msn.com/** as shown below.

  http://t.uk.**msn.com**/

To open another Web site, type the address in the Address Bar above, replacing **http://t.uk.msn.com/**, then press Enter/Return.

Returning to the Start Screen from an App

There are several ways to return to the Start Screen at any time. With the Surface tablet there is a Start button on the bottom bezel or edge of the screen. A Start *Charm* also appears on the Charms Bar when you swipe in from the right-hand edge, as discussed on page 93. With a mouse, hover the cursor in the top or bottom right-hand corner of the screen and move the cursor over the Start Charm.

Alternatively swipe in and back again (a few centimetres) from the left-hand side of a touchscreen screen without lifting your finger off. A thumbnail image of the Start Screen appears in the bottom left-hand corner of the screen, as shown on the right. This thumbnail also appears if you hover a mouse cursor over the bottom left-hand corner of 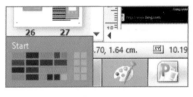 the screen. Tap or click the thumbnail to open the Start Screen full-size as shown at the top of page 88.

If you are using a physical keyboard it should have a Windows Logo key like the one shown on the right. This allows you to switch between the Start Screen and the app, i.e. program, you are currently running.

Launching an App by Typing its Name

If you are using a keyboard and can't see the tile for an App on the Start Screen, a quick way to launch an App is to begin typing its name while the Start Screen is displayed on the screen. For example, to launch the **Weather** app, as soon as you type **W** a list of the apps beginning with that letter is displayed.

However, as soon as "**We**" is entered only the **Weather** app is listed, as shown below.

Tap or click inside the small rectangle containing the word **Weather** on the left above, to launch the application.

With a touchscreen, select the Start Screen and swipe inwards from the top or bottom edge. The **All apps** icon appears, as shown on the right. Tap the **All apps** icon to view all of the apps on the computer and then tap the appropriate tile to launch the app you require.

Switching Apps

You can have lots of apps running in the background at the same time. To cycle through the apps that are currently running, swipe in from the left-hand edge, starting from the bezel. With a mouse, keep clicking in the top left-hand corner. The apps are displayed one at a time on the full screen. Stop at the app you want to use.

Swipe in a few centimetres from the left-hand edge and back again to see thumbnails of all the apps currently running, as shown down the left-hand edge below. Or hover the cursor over the top or bottom left corner then move the cursor up or down the left edge of the screen. Alternatively hold down the Windows Logo key and press the Tab key. Tap or click on a thumbnail as shown down the left-hand side below to switch to the new app.

Holding down Alt and pressing Tab displays all the running apps as thumbnails across the centre of the screen, as shown below. Stop pressing Tab and release the Alt key when you have highlighted the app you want to run on the full screen.

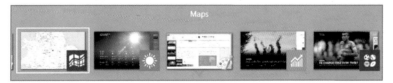

Multi-tasking: Displaying Two Apps Side-by-Side

Normally one app fills the whole screen while several others may be running in the background. However, you can have two apps running side-by-side in separate windows. Swipe an app about six centimetres in from the left edge and briefly hold until the app fills the left panel as shown below. Alternatively, with a mouse drag the top of the app downwards and to the left or the right. The app then appears in a narrow window on the left or right of the screen, with a vertical line separating the apps.

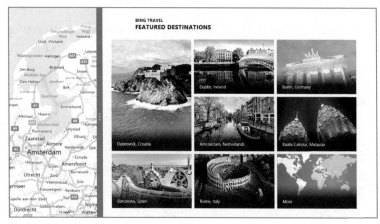

To change the app in a panel, swipe a new app in from the left-hand edge. Stop in either the left or right panel and the new app will open to fill that panel. When you open a new app from the Start Screen by clicking with a mouse, it fills the larger screen.

To close the split screen, place your finger or cursor over the dividing line then drag to the left-hand edge of the screen.

Closing an App

An app can be closed by swiping down the app from the top edge of the screen. Alternatively, with a mouse, drag the top edge of the app down the screen. The app shrinks and can be dragged and dropped completely off the bottom of the screen.

The Charms Bar

Swipe in from the right-hand edge of the screen to reveal the Charms Bar shown here below on the left. Alternatively, use a mouse to hover the cursor in either the bottom right-hand corner or the top right-hand corner of the screen. The charms are transparent at first but appear as shown below on the left after you move the cursor upwards or downwards through the charms. The touch cover keyboard on the Surface tablet has keys for each of the charms. Alternatively, hold down the Windows Logo key and press **C**.

The top charm, **Search**, can scan many categories of information stored on your computer or on the Internet. Searching for an **App** was discussed on page 90. There are many other categories to search through, such as **Settings**, **Files**, **Finance** and **Internet Explorer** as shown below.

In the example below, with **News** selected, the keyword **Inflation** was entered into the Search bar. When you tap or click the magnifying glass search icon, the screen displays a large selection of

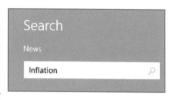

headlines and extracts from news agencies and newspapers, as shown below. Some of these stories are very new, perhaps posted in the last hour, for example. Drag or scroll to see all of the headlines and abstracts.

Tap or click a headline, etc., to read the full article.

The **Share** option on the Charms Bar on page 93 allows you to share information or photos, etc., with other people.

Start returns you to the Start Screen. If you're already on the Start Screen, the computer switches to the most recent app.

Devices on the Charms Bar lists any printers, speakers, etc., connected to the computer or on a home network. These only appear when you are using an app with something to print, such as the **Mail** app.

The Settings Charm

The **Settings** charm shown below on the right and on the Charms Bar on page 93 leads to some of the most important settings on your computer.

When you select the **Settings** charm shown on the right, the icons shown below appear at the bottom right of the screen. These give information about your Internet connection, (e.g. **BTHomeHub...**) and your sound and brightness settings, for example.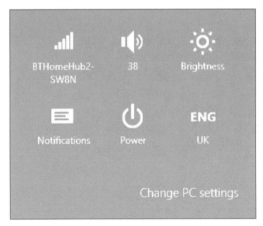

Change PC settings shown on the bottom right below leads to a list called **PC settings** as shown on the next page.

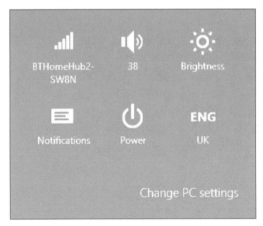

Personalize shown below provides different colour schemes and designs for your screens. **Ease of Access** near the bottom of the screenshot below allows you to make adjustments and select features designed to help with special needs.

Important settings and personalizing the computer are discussed in more detail in the next chapter.

Shutting Down the Computer

At the end of a computing session always shut down correctly. Otherwise you might damage any files that are open. Select the **Settings** charm as discussed on the previous page and tap or click the **Power** icon shown on the right above and in context below. Then tap or click **Shut down** from the small menu which pops up, as shown on the right. This closes all apps that are currently running and switches off the computer.

Sleep Mode

Selecting **Sleep** on the small **Power** menu at the bottom of the previous page puts the computer in a low power consumption mode. This saves electricity while you are not using the computer. Your work and settings are saved and to resume work later press the Power button on your computer.

Your computer will enter **Sleep** mode automatically if it is not used for a period of time. The period of time can be set in the computer's Control Panel as shown below. The Control Panel is a feature of Windows used to alter many important settings as discussed on the next two pages.

As shown above, there are separate settings for laptop and tablet computers, when operating **On battery** or **Plugged in**. Tap or click the arrow on the right of **2 minutes** shown above to display a menu of optional time periods, ranging from 1 minute to 5 hours before Sleep mode is launched. There is also a **Never** option. Select the required time and tap or click **Save changes**.

To exit Sleep mode, press the Power button and the computer will resume where you left off with the same files and apps running. The Control Panel can be used to set the Lock Screen (shown on page 85) to appear when the Power button on the computer is pressed. Tap or click anywhere on the Lock Screen, then enter your password to resume your previous activities.

The Control Panel

This important feature was included in earlier versions of the Windows operating system such as Windows 95, Windows XP and Windows 7. The Control Panel is also included in Windows 8, Windows 8 Pro and Windows RT.

The Control Panel appears on the screen in its own window, as shown below.

The Control Panel contains a large number of features to adjust the settings on the computer. These include setting the security, connecting to the Internet and other networks, setting up printers, personalizing the screen display and removing programs. The Control Panel is shown above in **Category** view. To change the view to **Large** or **Small** icons, tap or click the small arrow to the right of **Category**, shown on the right and above. Then tap or click the required view.

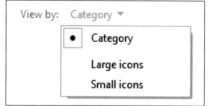

Opening the Control Panel

The alternative methods listed below describe opening the Control Panel with either touchscreen or mouse and keyboard. You may need to refer back to this page, since opening the Control Panel is discussed frequently in the rest of this book.

Method 1: Using the Settings Charm from the Desktop

Tap or click the **Desktop** tile on the Start Screen. Next swipe in from the right or hover the cursor in the top or bottom right of the screen. Then tap or click the **Settings** charm as shown on page 93 and tap or click **Control Panel** from the top of the blue panel.

Method 2: Type the First Few Letters from the Start Screen

With a keyboard attached to the computer and the Start Screen displayed, as shown on page 88, start typing "**Con...**". Tap or click the icon for the **Control Panel** which quickly appears, as shown on the right above.

Method 3: Displaying All Apps

With the Start Screen displayed, swipe in from the bottom or, with a mouse, right-click over the Start Screen, to display the **All apps** icon shown on the right. Tap or click the **All apps** icon then, from the **Apps** screen, scroll across to find the **Control Panel** icon. Tap or click the icon to open the **Control Panel**.

Method 4: The Shortcut Menu

Using a mouse, right-click over the bottom extreme left-hand corner of the screen. Then click **Control Panel** from the menu which pops up, as shown on the right.

Keyboard Shortcuts

If you use a keyboard like the one below with keys such as **Ctrl**, **Alt**, **Tab** and the Windows Logo key, shown on the right, you may find the following key presses useful as alternatives to the touchscreen or mouse, etc. The *function keys* **F1**, **F2**, etc., are located across the top of the keyboard.

Keyboard Shortcuts

Alt+F4   Close the current app.

Alt+Tab   Cycle through all open Desktop and Modern UI apps displayed horizontally across the screen.

F1   Help.

Win   Alternate between current app and the Start Screen.

Win+C   Display the Charms Bar.

Win+F   Search files.

Win+X   Display shortcuts menu.

Win+Tab   Display open Modern UI apps as thumbnails down the left of the screen.

Example:

Alt+F4 means: "While holding down the **Alt** key, press the **F4** key".

Personalizing Windows 8

Introduction

Windows 8 provides a number of ways for you to customise the computer to suit your own particular needs and preferences. These include:

- Selecting a different background design for the Lock Screen. This appears when you first start the computer or if you wake it up from sleep mode.

- Changing the colour scheme for the Start Screen. This is the main screen used to launch apps, shown on page 71.

- Creating or changing your account picture used to identify you, e.g. by including it in the e-mails you send.

- Selecting a different background design for the Windows Desktop discussed on pages 72 and 73.

- Changing the colour scheme for the windows borders and the Taskbar along the bottom of the Desktop.

- Changing the *screen resolution*. This is the number of *pixels* or picture elements in the horizontal and vertical directions. Windows 8 requires a minimum resolution of 1024x768 pixels, with more needed for some tasks.

- Using the Ease of Access Center, which provides features to help anyone with special needs, such as the magnifier to enlarge text and the on-screen keyboard for anyone struggling to use a physical keyboard.

The Lock Screen

This is the screen which appears when the computer starts up or when you wake it from sleep. Open the Charms Bar as described on page 93 and, from the **Settings** charm, shown on the right, select **Change PC settings**. Then select **Personalize** from the left-hand panel, as shown below. With **Lock screen** selected at the top of the screen you can see the current design in the right-hand panel, while along the bottom there's a choice of different Lock Screens.

Using Your Own Picture for the Lock Screen

If you don't wish to use any of the designs provided, select **Browse** to search the photos and pictures on your computer, etc. Next select with a tick the picture you wish to use and then select **Choose picture**, as shown below.

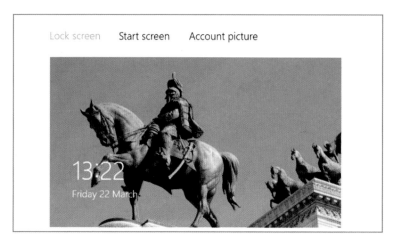

Apart from your chosen picture, as shown above, the Lock Screen also displays the current date and time.

The Start Screen

As shown at the top above, there is an option to change the colour scheme for the Start Screen. Tap or click the colours on the bottom horizontal bar or drag the arrow heads to experiment with different colour schemes. The grid of 20 small squares shown below allows you to choose an artistic pattern to superimpose on the main background colour you have chosen.

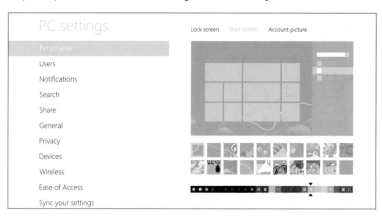

Your Account Picture

You can create or change your account picture after selecting **Account picture**, as shown below on the top right.

If you have a suitable image stored on your computer's hard disc or on a removable disc or flash drive, select **Browse**, as shown above under the picture, to search for and insert the image. Select with a tick the image you wish to use then select **Choose image**.

Alternatively if you have a tablet or laptop computer with a built-in camera or a desktop machine with a plug-in webcam, tap or click the camera icon shown on the right and above to create a new account photo.

Your account picture appears in several places, such as the Welcome screen as the computer starts up, on the right-hand side of the Start Screen, as shown on the right, and on the top of any e-mails you send using the Windows 8 Mail app.

Locking the Screen

If you tap or click your account picture on the Start Screen, a small menu pops up as shown below.

Change account picture shown above opens the PC settings window shown on the previous page. **Account picture** is already selected and the picture can be changed after selecting **Browse** as described on the previous page.

If you select **Lock** shown above, the Lock Screen is displayed. The computer can now only be used by someone who knows the password. This is entered after swiping diagonally upwards from the bottom left of a touchscreen or, with a mouse, clicking anywhere on the screen.

Sign out shown in the top screenshot returns you to the Lock Screen shown on the right above and requires a new user to sign in as shown on the right.

Changing the Windows Desktop Background

The Desktop will probably be used a lot on your computer so you may wish to give it your own personal touch. First open the Control Panel. With a touchscreen, swipe in from the bottom of the Start Screen, select the **All apps** icon which appears and then scroll across and select **Control Panel** from the large array of apps which fills the screen.

To open the Control Panel when using a keyboard and mouse, from the Start Screen, start typing "**con...**", etc. and then select **Control Panel** when

it appears on the screen, as shown above. Under **Appearance and Personalization**, select **Change desktop background**. Windows provides several designs for the Desktop background. If you select more than one, the background takes the form of a slide show.

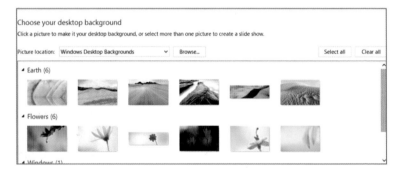

Quick Ways to Open the Control Panel Using a Mouse

Right-click in the extreme bottom left-hand corner of the screen and then select **Control Panel** from the shortcut pop-up menu as shown on page 99. Alternatively right-click over **Control Panel** in **All apps** as discussed earlier and select **Pin to Start**. This places a tile for the Control Panel on the Start Screen.

Using Your Own Photos as the Desktop Background

If you have photos of your own, these can be used as the desktop background. In the screenshot below, the **Browse** button was selected, then **Computer** was selected from the pop-up **Browse For Folder** window. (The Computer feature displays a list of all of your hard discs and removable discs). After selecting the hard disc **(C:)** the required folder was selected and opened by tapping (or clicking) **OK**.

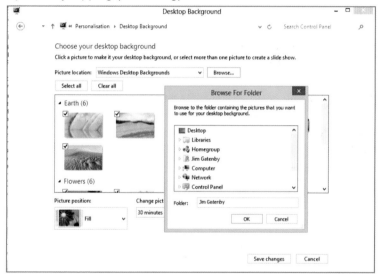

All of the required photos were selected with a tick in the top left-hand corner. After selecting **Save changes**, a slide show of the photos is placed on the Windows Desktop.

Changing the Windows Border Colours

This includes the colour of the Taskbar along the bottom of the Windows Desktop. Open the Control Panel as described on page 99. Select the green heading **Appearance and Personalisation** and then under **Personalisation** select **Change the colour of your taskbar and window borders**.

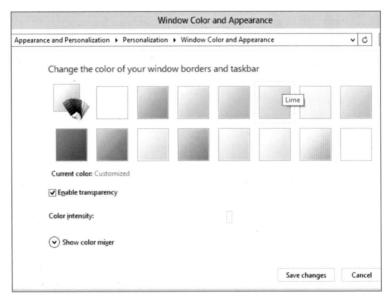

Before finally selecting a colour for your windows' borders and the Taskbar along the bottom of the Desktop, you may wish to experiment with **transparency**, **Color intensity** and the **color mixer**, as shown above. Then select **Save changes** to put the new settings into effect. In the example below, the colour **Twilight** was chosen for the border and the Taskbar, with transparency disabled and the intensity set at high.

Changing the Size of Text and Icons, etc.

If you're finding the text and other items difficult to see on the screen, there are ways of enlarging them. From the **Control Panel** select **Appearance and Personalization**, followed by **Display** and then **Make text and other items larger or smaller**.

The **Display** window opens, as shown below. To change the size of all of the objects on the screen including icons, images and text, select **Custom sizing options**. Then either select a different percentage or drag the ruler which appears. To change only the size of the text in windows, for example in the title bars or in menu options, use the drop-down menu under **Change the text size only**. As discussed shortly, the **Magnifier** allows you to enlarge a small selected area of the screen.

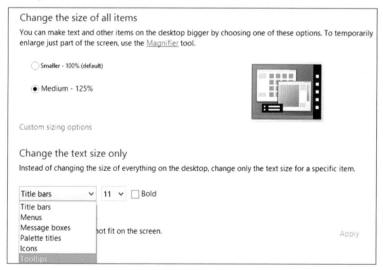

The text on a tablet or touchscreen may be enlarged or made smaller using two-fingered stretching or pinching gestures.

Changing the Screen Resolution

A *pixel* (picture element) is a single point in a screen display. The screen resolution is usually quoted in the format 1024x768, representing the number of pixels in the horizontal and vertical directions respectively. 1024x768 is stated as the minimum resolution for Windows 8 with 1366x768 recommended for some applications. At the higher resolutions, objects appear sharper and smaller. The maximum resolution available depends on the specification of the monitor and the graphics components in the computer which control the screen display.

To check the resolution on your computer, from the **Appearance and Personalization** section in the **Control Panel**, as discussed earlier, select **Display** and **Adjust screen resolution**, as shown at the top of the previous page. To change the setting, tap or click the small arrow to the right of the current **Resolution** setting and drag the slider. Then select **Apply** at the bottom right of the Screen Resolution window and either **Keep changes** or **Revert**.

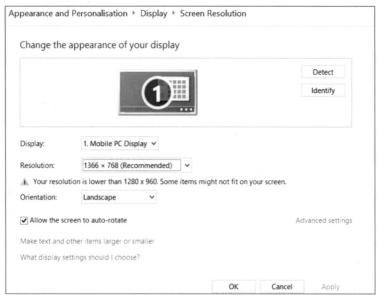

Ease of Access

This chapter describes features in Windows which are designed to help people with special needs, such as impaired eyesight, defective hearing or reduced manual dexterity.

The Magnifier

This makes the screen easier to read by enlarging the entire screen area or just selected parts.

The On-Screen Keyboard

This is intended for anyone who finds the normal physical keyboard difficult to use.

The Narrator

This reads aloud the text on the screen including the title bars and text in Windows as well as documents you're working on.

High Contrast

The screen display is converted to very clear white text on a black background.

Speech Recognition

You control the computer and input data entirely by speaking.

The above features are discussed shortly. You can launch some of the features quickly after selecting the **Settings** charm, then **Change PC settings** and **Ease of Access** as shown on pages 102 and 116 respectively. More settings for the Ease of Access features are found in the Control Panel. Open the Control Panel as described on page 99. At the bottom right of the Control Panel there are links to the **Ease of Access** features, as shown below.

Programs
Uninstall a program

Ease of Access
Let Windows suggest settings
Optimise visual display

If you select **Let Windows suggest settings**, shown at the bottom of the previous page, you are presented with a series of statements about any possible limitations you might have, such as defective eyesight, hearing or manual dexterity.

Eyesight (1 of 5)

Select all statements that apply to you:

☑ Images and text on TV are difficult to see (even when I'm wearing glasses).

☐ Lighting conditions make it difficult to see images on my monitor.

☐ I am blind.

☐ I have another type of vision impairment (even if glasses correct it).

After completing the on-screen statements, Windows recommends a series of settings based on the ticks you have placed in the check boxes, covering the whole range of common impairments. You can accept or reject these settings.

Alternatively select **Ease of Access** as shown at the bottom of page 111, then select **Ease of Access Center**, as shown below.

Ease of Access Center
Let Windows suggest settings   Optimise visual display   Replace sounds with visual cues
Change how your mouse works   Change how your keyboard works

The **Ease of Access Center** is used to start the **Magnifier**, **On-Screen Keyboard**, **Narrator** and **High Contrast** screen.

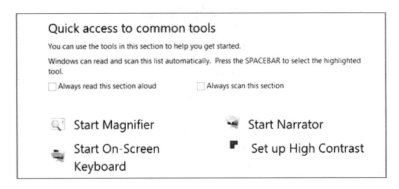

Quick access to common tools

You can use the tools in this section to help you get started.

Windows can read and scan this list automatically. Press the SPACEBAR to select the highlighted tool.

☐ Always read this section aloud   ☐ Always scan this section

Start Magnifier   Start Narrator

Start On-Screen Keyboard   Set up High Contrast

The Magnifier

Tap or click **Start Magnifier**, as shown on the previous page. The **Magnifier** window opens, initially set at 100% but this can easily be changed using the plus and minus buttons shown below.

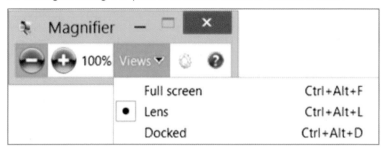

If you tap or click the arrow next to **Views**, shown above, you can choose whether to enlarge the **Full screen** or just the **Lens**. The Lens is a small rectangle which can be dragged around the screen with a finger or mouse, enlarging different areas. The example below uses 200% magnification.

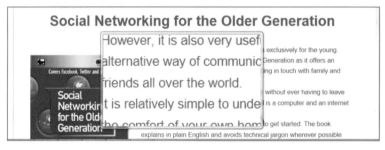

In **Docked** mode a horizontal strip across the top of the screen is enlarged. This can be scrolled to display the whole document in large text. After a short time the Magnifier window shown at the top of this page changes to a magnifying glass icon, as shown on the right. This icon can be tapped or clicked to make the Magnifier window reappear on the screen. Tap or click the cross at the top right of the Magnifier window to switch off the Magnifier.

The Narrator

Tap or click **Start Narrator**, as shown at the bottom of page 112. The computer starts to read aloud all of the text on the screen. You also hear the name of any key you press. The Narrator appears as an icon on the Taskbar as shown on the right and below.

If you tap or click the Narrator icon, the **Narrator Settings** window opens, as shown below. This includes options to alter the speed, pitch and volume of the Narrator voice or to choose a different voice altogether. The Narrator is closed by tapping or clicking the cross in the top right-hand corner of the Narrator Settings window shown below. Alternatively tap or click **Exit** at the bottom of the window.

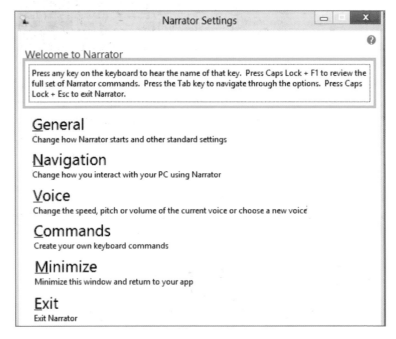

The On-Screen Keyboard

If you have trouble using a physical keyboard, the **On-Screen Keyboard**, shown in Microsoft Word below, may help. This can be operated with a mouse or joystick or another pointing device.

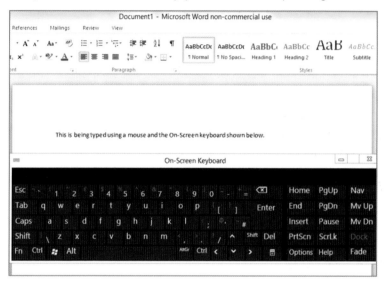

Upper-case and lower-case letters and alternate characters on a key can be obtained by first tapping or clicking either **Caps** or **Shift**. If you have a touchscreen computer such as the Microsoft Surface, you may find it easier to use the larger keys on the virtual keyboard provided as standard with the computer.

High Contrast

Select **Set up High Contrast** as shown on page 112 and then **Choose a High Contrast Theme**. Experiment by selecting and applying different Themes to find one that suits you.

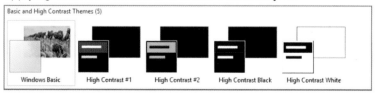

As mentioned earlier, you can quickly open the Ease of Access settings from the Settings charm, as discussed on pages 95 and 96. After selecting **Change PC settings**, select **Ease of Access** under **PC settings** shown highlighted in green below. Tap or click the small rectangles shown below to switch **High Contrast** on or off or make everything on your screen bigger. If you have a computer such as a tablet with a volume control, you can use this to switch the On-Screen Keyboard, the Magnifier or the Narrator on or off. First from the drop-down menu select either **On-Screen Keyboard**, **Magnifier** or **Narrator**. The selected feature can then be switched on or off by holding down the Windows Logo key together with the **Volume Up** control.

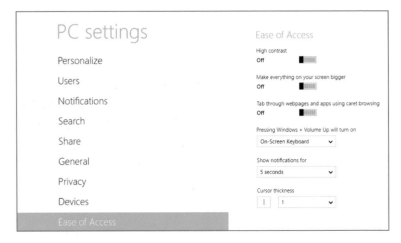

Alternative Methods

In the Windows operating system, there are usually several alternative ways of launching a particular app or feature. The Ease of Access features can be set up for a particular person using the Control Panel, as discussed earlier in this chapter. As shown above, you can also quickly launch the Ease of Access features such as the Magnifier, Narrator, etc., using the PC settings window of the Settings Charm, discussed earlier.

Another way to launch the Ease of Access features is from the Apps screen. From the Start Screen, swipe inwards from the top or bottom edge or right-click with a mouse. Then tap or click the **All apps** icon which appears, as shown above on the right. If necessary, scroll across the **All apps** screen until you see the **Ease of Access** features such as the **Magnifier**, etc., as shown on the right. Tap or click to launch the **Magnifier**, **Narrator** or **On-Screen Keyboard**, as discussed earlier in this chapter. **Windows Speech Recognition** is discussed on the next page.

Alternative Ways to Open the Control Panel

As discussed earlier, the Control Panel can be opened by tapping or clicking its name in the All apps feature. Or by typing the first few letters such as "**con**" while the Start Screen is displayed. If you are using a mouse or touchpad, moving the cursor to the bottom left-hand corner of the screen and right-clicking opens the Shortcut Menu as shown on the right. This enables you to launch many important Windows features, such as the **Control Panel**, shown highlighted on the right. Also listed on the right is the **File Explorer** which is used to manage all the documents and pictures stored on your computer. The File Explorer is also known as the Windows Explorer in earlier versions of the Windows operating system.

Programs and Features
Power Options
Event Viewer
System
Device Manager
Disk Management
Computer Management
Command Prompt
Command Prompt (Admin)

Task Manager
Control Panel
File Explorer
Search
Run

Desktop

Speech Recognition

This feature allows you to control the computer entirely by spoken commands. The necessary sound facilities are normally built into a tablet or laptop computer but on a desktop machine you may need to add speakers and a microphone. Tasks such as starting programs and opening menus, dictating text and writing and sending e-mails can be achieved without using a touchpad, mouse or keyboard. First you need to learn some spoken commands, by following the Windows Speech Tutorial; you must also "train" the computer to recognise your voice and dialect if you have one.

Tap or click **Speech Recognition** from Ease of Access in the Control Panel, as discussed earlier, and as shown below.

The main **Speech Recognition** window is shown below.

Experienced users can click **Start Speech Recognition** or beginners can select **Take Speech Tutorial** as shown above. You can also launch this feature by tapping or clicking **Windows Speech Recognition** on the All apps screen shown near the top of page 117.

As shown on the previous page, there is a **Set up microphone** option. When you first start Speech Recognition you are given advice on the use of the microphone and you are asked to read a piece of sample text. The Speech Tutorial helps you to practise all of the basic spoken commands such as **Start Listening**, **New Line**, **New Paragraph** and **Correct**. You are given practice at correcting mistakes on the screen and shown how to use voice commands to select menus. Selecting **Train your computer to better understand you**, shown on the previous page, launches extensive practice exercises in which you speak into the microphone, while the computer learns to recognise your voice.

After you've finished training yourself (and the computer) you are ready to tap or click **Start Speech Recognition** as shown on the previous page; this displays the microphone user interface shown below:

The user gives voice commands such as **Start listening** to make the computer begin interpreting the commands spoken into the microphone. The microphone button shown on the left above changes colour – blue indicating that the computer is listening to you, grey indicating not listening. The small window in the centre gives text feedback such as **Listening** or **Sleeping**. The message **What was that?** shown in the text window below indicates that a command was not understood by the computer.

If the above message appears you are advised to repeat the command or try a different command.

The Speech Recognition feature allows anyone who can't manipulate a mouse, touchpad or keyboard to use programs such as Microsoft Word, or e-mail, for example. Using only spoken commands, you can create, edit, save and print documents. I have found it quite easy to use the Speech Recognition system to dictate fairly simple documents. Although a microphone headset is recommended, I found the built-in microphones on my Surface tablet and Dell laptop worked well. If necessary, a useful plug-in microphone headset for a desktop computer can be bought for a few pounds.

However, it is important to work through the tutorials thoroughly and to spend time training the computer to recognise your voice. It also helps to speak slowly and clearly into the microphone.

Further Help

In the **Control Panel**, select **Ease of Access Center** and then **Make touch and tablets easier to use**. The following window opens, including an option for tablet users to choose an accessibility tool (such as the Magnifier, Narrator or On-Screen Keyboard) to be opened by holding down the Windows Logo button and pressing the Volume Up button on the tablet.

Learn about additional assistive technologies online at the bottom of the above screenshot is a link to the Microsoft Accessibility Web site. This gives details of products and companies involved in the design of accessibility aids, such as head-mounted input devices to overcome physical problems.

Getting Online to the Internet

Introduction

In the last few years the Internet has become an essential part of the lives of many people and some of us probably wonder how we ever managed without it. With the increasing use of laptops, tablet computers and smartphones, it's now possible to connect to the Internet whether you're at home or travelling abroad. In recent years *broadband* technology has enabled information to be delivered much faster via the telephone cables from the Internet to your computer. Some general categories of Internet activity are as follows:

- Searching for up-to-date information on any subject using a *search engine* (an *app* or program) such as Google or Bing, instead of a traditional encyclopaedia.

- Using specialist Web sites, e.g. to trace family history.

- *Communicating* electronically with people around the world using e-mail and social networks such as Facebook and Twitter to share text messages and photos. Also telephone calls with live video (Skype).

- *Shopping online* for virtually anything from one of the many online retailers. Also selling items on the eBay online auction Web site.

- *Downloading* music, videos, TV programmes and computer software from the Internet to your computer.

- Carrying out *online banking*, financial transactions and many form-filling tasks such as a Self-Assessment Tax Return and online applications like Car Tax.

Broadband

For several years the only way home users were able to connect to the Internet was using a device called a *dial-up* modem; this linked the computer to an ordinary telephone line. In recent years a much faster system known as *broadband* has become the standard; this enables you to surf the Internet more quickly and download large files such as videos and music. These tasks were too time-consuming using the earlier dial-up systems.

The latest high speed broadband service from BT, known as *BT Infinity*, uses *fibre optic* cables rather than the earlier copper wires. BT Infinity is only available in certain areas at the time of writing — you can find out if your home can get Infinity by logging on to **www.bt.com/infinity** and entering your telephone number.

Before you can connect to the Internet, the line to your home has to be *activated* by BT. You also need a special *ADSL modem* or a *router* to connect to a broadband Internet service.

If you already have access to an Internet computer, you can find out which broadband services are available in your area by logging on to **www.broadbandchecker.co.uk** and entering your postcode. An example of the results is shown below:

If you don't already have access to an Internet computer to find this information, you can probably log on in a local library or Internet cafe.

Many people use the BT Broadband service while others use companies such as Sky and TalkTalk, who deliver an Internet service over the BT phone lines. Virgin Media provide Cable Broadband to areas covered by cable television and Sky also offer TV and Broadband via satellite. Some mobile phone companies provide *mobile broadband* using a dongle which plugs into a USB port on your computer, as discussed shortly.

Internet Service Providers

Web sites such as **www.uswitch.com/broadband** allow you to enter your postcode and find the various competing offers from Internet Service Providers, as shown below.

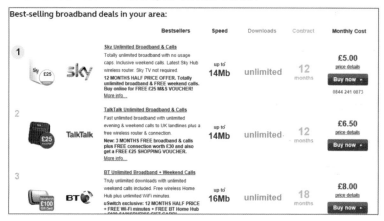

The cost of a 12-month or 18-month contract may be anything from about £4 to £20 for a month. **Speed** is the *maximum* download speed — currently 20Mb or more over fibre optic cables. The BT Infinity download speed is currently quoted as up to 76Mb. Areas without fibre optic BT cables may be lucky to achieve the British average of 7Mb. (Mb or megabits means millions of *bits* or *binary digits* per second — bits are discussed on page 45). The **Downloads** column above refers to the amount of data (pictures, video, etc.), you can download per month. A free wireless router worth about £50 is often included in a broadband package.

Broadband Requirements

The next few pages explain how to set up one or more computers to use an ADSL broadband service based on the BT telephone lines. The essential requirements are:

- An account with an Internet Service Provider such as BT, Sky or TalkTalk, etc.

- A BT telephone socket and a telephone line which has been tested by BT and activated for ADSL broadband.

- A wireless router containing an ADSL modem. Many Internet Service Providers now include a free router as part of the package.

- One or more *filters* allowing a telephone socket to be used for broadband and phone calls at the same time.

- A cable to connect the router to the filter.

- An Ethernet cable to connect the router to a computer to assist in the initial setup of the router.

- Tablet and laptop computers normally have their own built-in wireless networking capability. However, to connect a desktop computer to a wireless router you need a *wireless network adapter*. The adapter may be in the form of a PCI expansion card fitted inside the computer or it can be a *USB dongle* as shown on pages 54 and 128.

- Software and instructions for setting up the router, usually on a CD/DVD included in the start up package from the Internet Service Provider, such as BT.

- In the case of a wireless router, a *network name* and a *security key* to prevent other people from logging on to your Internet connection from outside your home. (Wireless home networks may have a range of 100-300 feet, depending on obstructions like walls and floors.)

The Wireless Router

A wireless router with a built-in ADSL modem is one of the most popular ways of connecting to the Internet, even if you only have one computer. Many Internet Service Providers include a free router in their start up kit. If you have more than one computer, the wireless router can connect them all on a wireless network, using a single telephone socket. I have found a wireless network to be extremely reliable with computers scattered about the house in different rooms and in the home office in the garden.

The initial setting up of the router may require a computer to be sitting next to the router and connected to it by an Ethernet cable. However, once the network is up-and-running the wireless router can sit on its own near to your telephone socket, with no computers physically connected to it. Our router sits in the dining room next to the telephone socket, providing Internet access and networking for a variety of tablet, laptop and desktop computers, around the house. The router requires virtually no attention except for switching off and on again several times a year. This simple operation is an effective cure for a wide range of computing problems.

The Wireless Router Startup Kit

If you subscribe to an Internet Service Provider such as BT, you may obtain a free wireless router and the various components needed to get you started, as shown below.

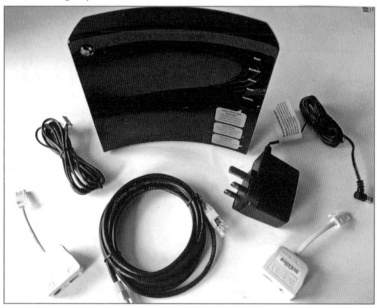

In the above photograph, the router itself is the large black box at the rear. On the right is the power supply cable and transformer. The white cables and sockets are known as *filters* or *microfilters*; these plug into the main telephone socket(s) in your home. Each filter has two sockets; one socket in the filter connects an ordinary telephone handset while the other socket accepts the broadband cable from the router. This is the black cable shown to the left of the router above. The filter enables an ordinary telephone to be used at the same time as the broadband Internet.

The black cable with yellow ends shown above is an *Ethernet* cable, which may be needed in the initial setting up of the router.

The Router Ports in Detail

Shown below are ports on the rear of a wireless router supplied by BT as part of their broadband package.

The left-hand socket in the group above is used for the cable which connects the router to the broadband telephone socket, via a filter, as mentioned on the previous page. The green socket is for a special BT Internet telephone. The four yellow Ethernet sockets have several uses, such as the initial setting up of the router using an Ethernet cable connected to a computer. The Ethernet sockets can also be used to create a wired network, using Ethernet cables and adaptors instead of wireless technology. Wired networks are often preferred in business, since they can be faster than wireless. Also, unsightly cables in the wired network may not be such an issue in business as they are in a home environment.

On the right of the router above is the socket for the power cable; finally there is a USB socket to connect a cable to a USB port on a computer (as an alternative to an Ethernet cable.)

BT Vision

One of the Ethernet sockets on the router can be used to connect an Ethernet cable from the router to a BT Vision digital television box. This allows a large number of Freeview programs to be viewed and recorded; live television can be paused and restarted. A daily program guide can be downloaded and extra programs and films are available on demand (for a fee).

Instruction Manuals

The router package should include an instruction manual and a quick-start leaflet; a more comprehensive manual may be provided on a CD/DVD which accompanies the router or alternatively on the router manufacturer's Web site.

Wireless Network Adapters

Each computer on a wireless network must be able to communicate with the wireless router. Tablet and laptop computers are normally supplied with built-in wireless networking capability. This facility may need to be switched on by a physical switch or by pressing a designated function key on a laptop.

USB Wireless Dongle

Desktop computers may need to be fitted with a separate *wireless network adapter,* in the form of a "dongle" which plugs into a USB port on the computer, as shown below.

Alternatively, a desktop computer can be fitted with a network adapter in the form of an internal PCI expansion card.

Installing a Wireless Router

Before you can start to set up a wireless network based on a wireless router, your telephone line must be tested and activated for ADSL broadband by BT. If you are using an Internet Service Provider other than BT, they may make the arrangements for you. You might have to wait a week or 10 days for the activation to be effective.

Once the telephone line is activated you can start installing the router. Ideally the router should be in a central position in your home if you are connecting several computers. If possible, avoid installing the router near to a microwave oven or cordless phones as these may interfere with the broadband.

Place a filter in the main telephone socket in your home. If you want to use an ordinary telephone in this part of your home, there is a socket for this on the filter. Now connect the special broadband cable (known as an *RJ11 cable*) from the router to the other socket in the filter. (The broadband and ordinary telephone sockets in the filter are quite different, so you can't connect the cables incorrectly.)

Now connect the power cable from a power point to the router and switch on. In the case of our BT Home Hub router, initially the diagnostic lights on the front flash yellow and then after a minute or two the power, broadband and wireless lights should be a constant blue.

Set up a computer within a few feet of the router. This computer should be fitted with a wireless network adapter as discussed earlier. Most modern tablet computers and laptops have built-in wireless networking capability although this may need to be switched on. Some desktop computers are also "wireless ready" but otherwise they need a USB or PCI wireless adapter fitted, as discussed earlier. BT provides an installation DVD which is intended to be used on every computer, although this may not always be essential to make the connection to the Internet.

Making the Connection

This section describes the steps needed to connect a computer to a WiFi network. This might be a wireless router in your home or an access point in a public place such as a hotel or restaurant, etc. Each computer must have an Internet adapter and Web browser software. If necessary the Internet connectivity in a tablet or laptop should be switched on. In the case of a home network, the router should be connected by a cable to a telephone line which has been activated for broadband by an Internet Service Provider such as BT. The router connects to the telephone socket through a *filter* which has two sockets, one for the router and one for the telephone handset. This allows the Internet and an ordinary telephone to be used at the same time.

Detecting the Router or Internet Access Point

Switch on the computer and enter your password to open the Windows 8 Start Screen. Swipe in from the right edge or click in the top or bottom right-hand corner of the screen to display the Charms Bar. Then tap or click the Settings charm shown on the right. You should see the following displayed at the bottom right of the screen.

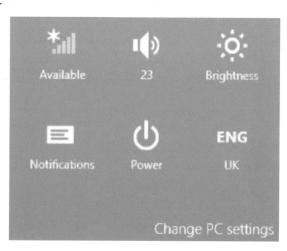

The WiFi icon shown on the right and on the top left of the previous screenshot indicates that network connections are available. In the home situation this should include your router and possibly some of your neighbours' networks if they are within the WiFi range. Depending on  your equipment, this might be up to 150 feet indoors or 300 feet outdoors. An Internet access point in a public place would be detected in a similar way. Tap or click the icon shown above to list the available networks, as shown below.

In the example above, **BTHomeHub2-SW...** is our own BT router while **EE-BrightBox** belongs to a neighbour. These routers are up-and-running and within WiFi range. **Flight mode** above must be **Off** to connect to the Internet. It is switched on and off by tapping or clicking the small rectangle shown above next to **Off**. Flight mode **On** prevents the transmission of radio signals, which could interfere with an aircraft's systems. With Flight mode **On** you can still use the computer for non-Internet activities like music saved on your computer or word processing.

Connecting to the Router

Tap or click the name of your router in your list of routers, similar to those under **WiFi** on the previous page. You are then asked for a *security key*, often a string of numbers and letters stamped or printed on the back of the router. Without the protection of the security key, anyone within WiFi range could detect and connect to your router and possibly access the information on any of the computers on your home network. For this reason you should always use a router which requires a security key.

After selecting your own router from the list and entering the security key, tap or click **Connect** to complete the Internet connection. There is also a box to tick if you wish to connect to the Internet automatically at the start of every computing session. The word **Connected** now appears against your chosen router, as shown on the right.

Now, whenever you select the **Settings** charm, the name of your router, **BTHomeHub2-SW8N** in this example, should appear as shown on the right and below.

Checking Your Internet Connection

Open the **Control Panel** as discussed on page 99. Tap or click
Network and Internet and then **Network and Sharing Center**.
This displays the dialogue box shown below, allowing you to view
many aspects of your new wireless network. You can also set up
your network so that printers, files and other resources can be
shared by all of the computers on the network, as discussed
shortly.

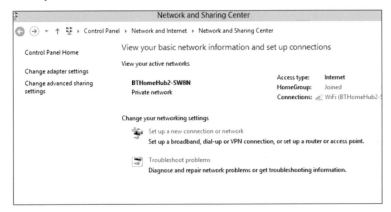

You can also check the speed of your broadband Internet
connection. At the time of writing, many services offer a
download speed of up to 10Mb while a few offer up to 70Mb or
more. The latest BT Infinity service, currently becoming more
widely available, offers nominal speeds of up to 76Mb. In practice
this speed may not be achieved due to limitations such as your
distance from the telephone exchange. You can check your
speeds by logging onto a Web site such as:

www.broadbandspeedchecker.co.uk

Now follow the instructions on the screen to test the upload and
download speeds of your broadband connection.

The results of a speed test on one of my computers are shown
on the next page.

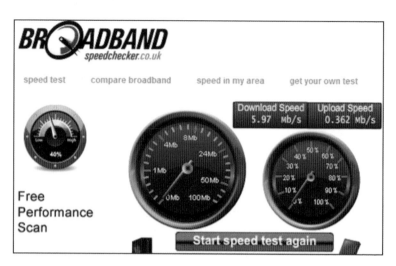

As can be seen above, my computer recorded a download speed of 5.97Mb (megabits per second) and an upload speed of 0.362Mb. I live on the same road as a telephone exchange which has been upgraded to provide BT Infinity 40Mb download speeds over fibre optic cables. The Web site **www.bt.com/infinity** lists reasons why some people may not be able to get BT Infinity, even if their telephone exchange has been upgraded. These reasons include your distance from the green roadside cabinets and perhaps the need to modify the cabinets themselves.

To check the availability of BT Infinity to your home, log on to **www.bt.com/infinity** and enter your landline telephone number.

Your broadband checker results

Broadband option	Broadband speed range	When you can get
BT Total Broadband ⑦	Between 7.5Mb and 17.5Mb (Estimated speed: 13.0Mb)	Now

Sorry, you're not currently able to get BT Infinity. This may be because your area has not been enabled yet, or your individual line does not support super-fast broadband. Register your interest and we'll let you know if this changes.

Summary: Getting Online Using a Router

The following list outlines the general method of connecting to the Internet using a BT ADSL broadband telephone line and a wireless router:

1. Check that you can receive ADSL broadband from your local telephone exchange.

2. Sign up with an Internet Service Provider.

3. Wait for BT or another company to test and activate your telephone line to receive broadband.

4. Obtain a wireless router with a built-in ADSL modem. Your Internet Service Provider may supply this.

5. Insert a microfilter into the main telephone socket in your home.

6. Insert the cable from a telephone handset into the telephone socket in the microfilter.

7. Connect the broadband cable from the router into the broadband socket in the microfilter.

8. Connect the power lead for the router and switch on. The power light on the router should be on; then the wireless and broadband lights should stop flashing.

9. Set up a "wireless enabled" computer near to the router. If necessary attach an RJ45 Ethernet cable between the router and the computer.

10. Start up the computer and connect to the Internet using a Web browser such as Internet Explorer. Enter the wireless key and/or any other information for your router or supplied by your Internet Service Provider.

11. Remove the Ethernet cable and repeat steps 9 and 10 for any other computers on the network.

12. You should now be able to connect wirelessly to the Internet from any computer on the network.

Internet Connections on the Move

Tablet and laptop computers make it easy to use the Internet when you are away from home and your wireless router.

Wireless Hotspots

Hotels, airports, etc. have *wireless hotspots* or Internet access points. When you're within range (up to 100ft indoors, say), a tablet or laptop can detect the access point. To connect to the Internet, just enter the password provided by the establishment. In some cases you enter your mobile phone number and the password is sent back to your phone in a text message. There may be a charge to use the access point. Alternatively many hotels allow you to plug an Ethernet cable (discussed on page 50) from your laptop into their wired network. Small wireless routers are available to provide a WiFi access point to a wired network via an Ethernet cable in an establishment such as a hotel.

Mobile Broadband

4G (4th Generation) is the latest telecommunications standard which applies to mobile phones and smartphones capable of broadband Internet connections. Many of the mobile phone companies enable you to connect a computer to the Internet using the 3G or 4G mobile phone network. The company provides you with a SIM card (Subscriber Identity Module) containing information to connect you to the Internet. They may also provide a *mobile broadband dongle* (shown below) which

plugs into one of the USB ports on the computer, as discussed on page 52. The dongle has a slot into which you slide the SIM card. Some computers, such as tablets, have a built-in slot for a SIM card.

As with mobile phones, there is a wide choice of pay-as-you-go and fixed-term contracts for mobile broadband. If you already have access to the Internet, try typing **mobile broadband** into a search engine such as Google or Bing to see what's on offer.

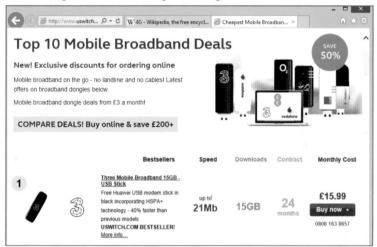

Mobile broadband pay-as-you-go services typically include 30 days preloaded credit, after which you pay to top up. Alternatively, contracts might cost £3-£20 per month and last from 1 to 18 months.

The SIM card may be inserted directly into a slot in a tablet. Alternatively, slide the SIM card into the dongle provided and plug the dongle into a USB port on the computer. USB ports are discussed on page 52. The installation process will probably be automatic but it's always advisable to follow any instructions on the screen and in the installation guide. On completion an icon for the new mobile broadband Internet connection appears on the Windows Desktop, as shown on the right. You should now be able to use your computer to connect to the Internet from wherever there is an adequate signal for your chosen phone network.

Installing a Printer on a Wireless Network

The wireless router allows several computers in your home to share an Internet connection through a single telephone socket. The wireless router also enables a *network* to be created so that computers anywhere around the home can communicate with each other and share resources such as files and printers.

For the home or small business with more than one computer, the ability to share a printer on a wireless network is very useful. This is obviously cheaper than having a separate printer connected to each computer. As discussed below, to share a printer on a network you need to switch on the **File and Printer Sharing** option and also make the printer itself *shareable*.

Turning on File and Printer Sharing

This option may already be switched on, but it's a simple task to make sure anyway. Open the **Network and Sharing Center** as described on page 133 and from the left-hand panel select **Change advanced sharing settings**.

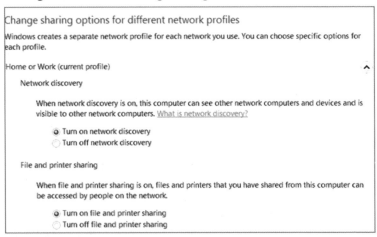

Make sure **Turn on file and printer sharing** is selected as shown above, then click the **Save changes** button at the bottom of the screen.

Making a Printer Shareable

A printer is usually attached to one of the computers on a network via a USB cable. Setting up a printer in this way was discussed in Chapter 6. The other computers on the network can then connect to this printer wirelessly.

First the printer has to be set as *shareable* so that other computers can use it. Working on the computer with the printer attached by a cable, open the Control Panel using one of the methods described on page 99. Then under **Hardware and Sound**, as shown below, tap or click **View devices and printers**.

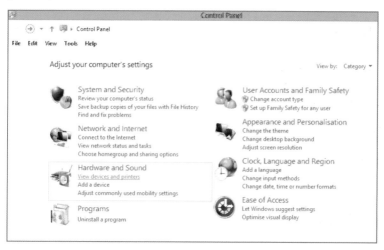

The **Devices and Printers** window for the computer with the printer attached opens, as shown on the next page, with the default printer, **Brother DCP-195C**, marked with a tick. The default printer is the one used automatically when you print a document. This printer is physically attached with a USB cable to the computer named **HPOFFICE**.

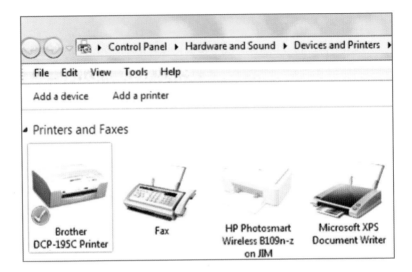

The **HP Photosmart** printer shown above is physically connected to **JIM**, another computer on the home network. Other computers on the home network can share this printer wirelessly, if it has been set as shareable and detected by the **Add Printer Wizard**, as discussed shortly.

Right-click over the printer icon similar to the **Brother DCP-195C** shown above. Next select **Printer properties** from the menu which appears. The **Printer Properties** window opens and from this select the **Sharing** tab as shown on the next page.

Now make sure the check box next to **Share this printer** is ticked. The printer is now available for other computers to detect and share. However, as stated above, other computers cannot detect this printer unless the host computer and the printer are fully up-and-running and not "sleeping". There is also an opportunity to give a different **Share name** to the printer to make it easy to identify if you have more than one printer on the network.

Detecting a New Printer on a Wireless Network

The next task is to connect the other computers to the printer, using the wireless network. Make sure the host computer with the printer physically attached is fully up-and-running and that the printer has not slipped into sleep mode. Then from each of the other computers (sometimes known as *workstations* or *network clients*) carry out the following procedure.

Open the **Devices and Printers** window as described on page 140 and tap or click **Add a printer**, as shown below.

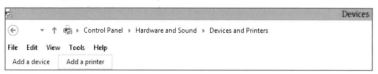

The computer starts searching for available printers on the network and, all being well, finds the required one, as shown highlighted in blue below. This is the **Brother** printer attached by a cable to the printer host computer called **HPOFFICE**, also on the wireless home network.

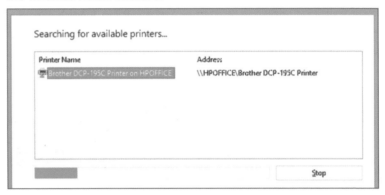

When the required printer is listed click **Next**. You should quickly see the following window, confirming that the printer has been successfully installed with the correct driver software. If Windows cannot find the correct driver software, you may need to insert the manufacturer's CD which came with the printer.

If a computer cannot wirelessly detect the shared printer, try temporarily disabling any firewall or Internet security software. You may need to alter a setting in the security software in the computer to allow wireless printing across the home network.

12

Browsing the Web

Introduction

Microsoft Windows 8 includes Internet Explorer 10, a *Web browser*. This is a program used for displaying Web pages and navigating between Web sites. A tile for Internet Explorer (shown on the right) is pinned to the Windows 8 Start Screen, as shown below.

Several other Web browsers are available in competition with Internet Explorer, such as Google Chrome and Mozilla Firefox. Microsoft offers a *Browser Choice* window, as shown on the next page. This allows users the opportunity to select a different browser instead of Internet Explorer, to comply with legal requirements imposed by the European Commission. The Browser Choice window is delivered to your computer over the Internet using the *Windows Update* feature. This places a tile for the Browser Choice window on the Start Screen, as shown on the right and in the Start Screen extract below.

Tap or click the **Browser Choice** tile to open the window shown on the next page.

Tap or click the **Install** button for the browser you wish to use. Internet Explorer remains a very popular Web browser, used by millions of people around the world. The latest version, Internet Explorer 10, contains many new features making it fast and easy to use. Internet Explorer 10 is used for the Web browsing examples throughout this book.

Search Engines

A Web browser such as Internet Explorer uses a program (or app) called a *search engine* to find Web pages containing specific *keywords*. The Windows operating system includes Bing, Microsoft's own search engine, shown below, ready to carry out a keyword search for information on, for example, the **peregrine falcon**.

Google is probably the world's most popular search engine, as discussed shortly. (The Google *search engine* is not to be confused with the Google Chrome *Web browser*).

Many people use the Google search engine while running Internet Explorer as their Web browser.

As discussed shortly, you can start using Google after typing **www.google.co.uk** into the address bar of your browser, such as Internet Explorer.

Launching Internet Explorer 10

Tap or click the tile on the Start Screen, as shown on the right. This launches Internet Explorer 10 so that a Web page fills the whole screen, as shown below.

Alternatively, tap or click the **Desktop** tile on the Start Screen and then tap or click the Internet Explorer icon on the Taskbar at the bottom of the screen, as shown on the right. This displays a Web page in the traditional way, with menus, tabs and icons across the top of the screen and the Taskbar along the bottom, as shown below.

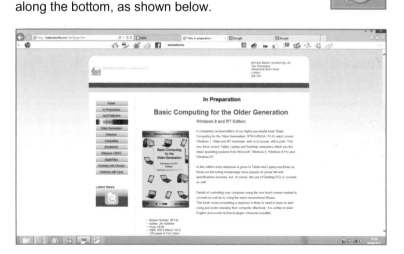

The Home Page

The Home Page is the first page you see whenever you start Internet Explorer, as shown in the example below.

Changing Your Home Page

To change your Home Page, tap or click the Desktop tile and launch Internet Explorer from its Taskbar icon, shown on the right. Tap or click the Tools icon, the gearwheel icon shown on the right of the three on the right. From the drop-down menu which appears select **Internet options** and then enter the Web address of your new Home Page in the box, replacing the Web address **http://uk.msn.com/** in the example below.

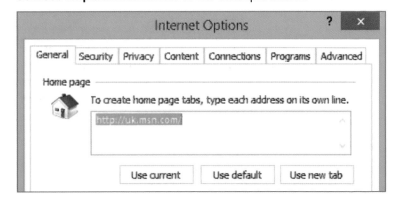

Surfing the Internet

The Internet is a collection of millions of Web pages stored on computers all round the world. These computers, known as *Web servers*, are provided by companies and organisations so that individual users can access information. A Web page usually contains text and pictures but multi-media content such as music, sound and video clips may also appear on a page.

There are various ways you can connect to a Web site on an Internet server computer; then you can move around the pages on the site. Methods of accessing Web pages and sites include:

- Clicking a *link* or *hyperlink* on a Web page. When you pass the cursor over a link, the cursor changes to a hand. A link may be a piece of text or a picture.

- Typing the unique address of a Web site, such as **www.babanibooks.com**, into the Address Bar at the top of the Internet Explorer screen.

- Entering *keywords* such as **red squirrel** into a search engine such as Bing or Google.

Clickable Links or Hyperlinks

Open Internet Explorer as described on page 145 to open the Home Page as shown on the previous page. (Your own Home Page may be different). Tap or click the headings to open a Web page. If using a mouse, when you move the cursor about the screen, you should see the cursor change to a hand when it is over certain pieces of text or pictures. In addition a piece of text may become highlighted or underlined when the cursor rolls over it. These are the clickable *links* or *hyperlinks* to other Web pages or Web sites. The blue text below is an example of a link.

Flash, Staffordshire. The highest village in the Peak District
www.peakdistrictinformation.com/towns/flash.php
Flash, Staffordshire is reputedly the highest **village** in England. It was once a hideout for footpads, highwaymen and counterfeiters. Prize fights took place at ...

When you tap or click the blue **Flash** village link shown at the bottom of the previous page, the Web site opens as shown below.

You normally find that the new Web page also contains lots of embedded links to other pages and Web sites. For example, the panel on the left above is a menu of links to other pages such as **Local Attractions** shown on the right.

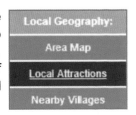

The photographs shown in the Web page above also act as links. Tapping or clicking a small "thumbnail" image on a Web page often opens a much larger edition of the image.

The **Forward** and **Back** buttons on the right allow you to revisit Web pages during a browsing session. These appear at either end of the address bar at the bottom of the Web page, as shown below.

Forward and back buttons may also appear in the middle of the left-hand and right-hand edges of the screen.

Typing in a Web Address

To use this method of navigating to a Web site, you obviously need to obtain the address, perhaps from an advertisement or newspaper article. Exact spelling and punctuation are important. Every Web site has a unique address, such as:

http://www.babanibooks.com/

This is entered manually into the Address Bar across the bottom of the Internet Explorer Web browser, as shown below:

http://www.babanibooks.com/ ×

In computing jargon, the address of a Web site is known as a *URL* or *Uniform Resource Locator*. In the above example, the meanings of the parts of the address are as follows:

http:

HyperText Transfer Protocol. This is a set of rules used by Web servers. *ftp* is another protocol used for transferring files across the Internet.

www.

This means the site is part of the World Wide Web.

mycompany.co.uk

This part of the Web address is known as the *domain name* and is usually based on the name of the company or organization owning the Web site.

co.uk

This is a Web site owned by a UK company. **co** is known as the *domain type*. More domain types are listed over the page.

Searching in the Address Bar

Simply type the keywords such as **barn owl**, for example, into the Address Bar and press Enter or tap or click the **Forward** button shown on the right.

Common Web Site Domain Types

.biz	Business
.com	Company or Commercial organization
.eu	European Community
.info	Information site or service
.me.uk	UK individual
.org	Non-profit making organization
.gov	Government
.net	Internet company
.jobs	Companies with jobs available
.pro	People in professions worldwide
.travel	Web sites related to travel and tourism
.tel	Internet communication services

In addition, some Web addresses include the code for a country, such as **fr** and **uk** as in: **http://www.mycompany.co.uk**

If you know the address of a Web site, enter this into the Address Bar in the Web browser as shown below. (In practice you can usually miss out the **http://www.** part of the address as this will be added automatically.)

www.babanibooks.com/   X   ⊙

When you press **Enter** or tap or click the right pointing **Forward** arrow shown above, your browser should connect to the Web site and display its Home Page on the screen. Then you can start moving about the site using the links within the page, as described earlier.

Finding Information — the Keyword Search

The *keyword search* is the usual way to find information on the Internet. Suppose you want to find out about the **barn owl**, for example. Start up Internet Explorer from its tile on the Start Screen, shown on the right. Now enter **barn owl** in the Bing search bar as shown below. (As discussed shortly, there are several other search engines, such as Google.)

Now click the **web search** button shown on the right above. Bing searches the Internet for any Web pages containing the words **barn owl**. Then a list of all of the relevant Web sites (over 2 million) is displayed, as shown in the sample below.

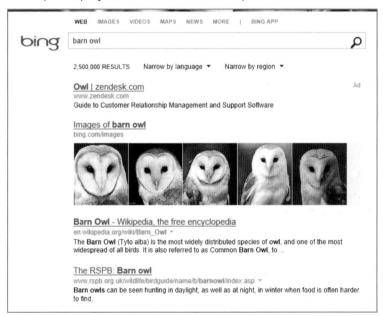

The search results shown below are extracts from Web sites containing the key words **barn** and **owl**. Tap or click the underlined blue links to open the Web sites.

Barn Owl - Wikipedia, the free encyclopedia
en.wikipedia.org/wiki/Barn_Owl ▾
The **Barn Owl** (Tyto alba) is the most widely distributed species of **owl**, and one of the most widespread of all birds. It is also referred to as Common **Barn Owl**, to ...

The RSPB: **Barn owl**
www.rspb.org.uk/wildlife/birdguide/name/b/barnowl/index.asp ▾
Barn owls can be seen hunting in daylight, as well as at night, in winter when food is often harde to find.

The **Barn Owl** Trust
www.barnowltrust.org.uk ▾
The **Barn Owl** Trust is a national registered charity based in Devon, UK dedicated to conserving **barn owls** and their environment.

As shown on the previous page, millions of results were found. Normally, if you're lucky, you find the information you want on the first page which should contain the most relevant results.

When searching for Web pages containing several keywords, the results may include pages which contain the keywords anywhere on the page, even if they are separated and in the wrong order as in "a short-eared **owl** made a nest in the **barn**". To exclude such unwanted search results, enclose the keywords in speech marks, as shown below.

This new search will only list Web sites where the words **barn** and **owl** appear next to each other and in the correct order.

When the search was repeated with inverted commas, as shown below, the number of search results dropped from 2,500,000 to 1,050,000.

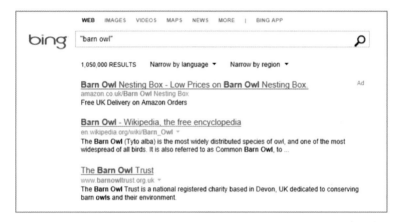

This decrease in the number of search results found occurred because the only Web sites listed now are those where the words **barn** and **owl** are next to each other on the Web page

Another cause of unwanted search results is the fact that the keywords used in a search may be found in a Web site which is irrelevant to the current search. For example, if you are a keen "twitcher" doing research, you are probably only interested in Web sites about the bird itself. You might not be interested in the Web sites of businesses who use **Barn Owl** in their company name or in their products, as shown below.

Barn Owl - Gloucester
www.barnowlpubquedgeley.co.uk
Welcome to the **Barn Owl!** Your fantastic 2 for 1 pub restaurant!

Fortunately the most relevant Web sites usually appear at the top of the list of results for the search.

Advertising on Web Pages

When you look at the results of a search, you will often see advertisements from companies, usually down the right-hand side of the Web page. These are for products or services which are relevant to the current search. For example, shown below are the results of a search displayed after entering **cruise holidays** into the Bing search bar, as previously described.

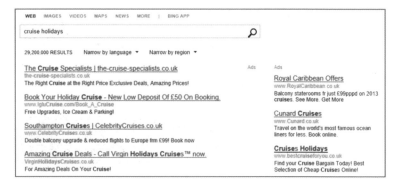

The results list is dominated by clickable links to the Web sites of companies who have paid to advertise on the search results page. So companies selling cruises, for example, are only one click away from individual users searching for cruise information.

Web-based search engines like Bing and Google and the Facebook social networking site are free to the individual user. This is possible because these Internet companies earn their revenue from targeted advertising. (Google is discussed shortly).

Click Through Rate

This is a measure of the success of advertising on Web sites. It is used in the calculation of the fees paid by the advertisers to the owners of the Web sites, such as Microsoft (owners of Bing), Google and Facebook. It is based on the number of times the advertisement is clicked to take an individual user through to the Web site of the company paying for the advertisement.

The Google Search Engine

Google is a highly acclaimed and freely available alternative to the Bing search engine provided with Windows. Google has a reputation for finding relevant results very quickly and is so popular that the verb "to Google" is now in common use.

To launch Google, enter **www.google.co.uk** into the Address Bar of Internet Explorer, as shown below.

In practice you can just enter **google** into the Address Bar and the full address **http://www.google.co.uk/** is completed automatically, as shown below.

When you press Enter or tap or click the **Forward** or **Go** button shown on the right, the Google search screen opens as shown below, ready for you to enter the keywords into the search bar. A Google search for Web pages containing **barn owl** is shown on the next page.

As shown below, the search can focus on various categories such as **News**, **Images** or **Maps**, for example.

Click the **Google Search** button shown on the right to find Web pages containing keywords **barn owl**.

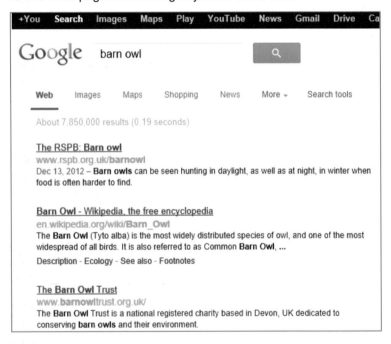

As shown above, Google found nearly 8 million Web results of Web pages containing the words **barn owl**. At the top of the results are links to a lot of high-quality information, images and audio and video clips showing barn owls in flight, such as the RSPB site shown on the next page.

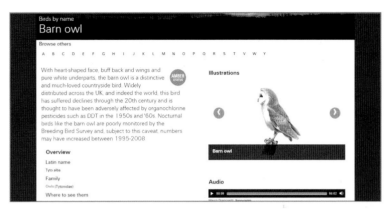

Web Pages Filling the Whole Screen

In the above screenshot, Internet Explorer 10 has been launched from the Start Screen. The Web page fills the whole screen and there are none of the menus, buttons, icons etc., which are always present in other versions of Internet Explorer.

Displaying Buttons, Tabs and the Address Bar

In the Start Screen version of Internet Explorer 10, you can display the menus and icons shown below by swiping up from the bottom or down from the top or by right-clicking with a mouse. The small "thumbnail" Web pages across the top of the screenshot below are known as *tabs* and are discussed shortly.

On the Address Bar at the bottom left of the screenshot on the previous page, you can see the Back button and the address of the current Web page.

On the right of the Address Bar at the bottom of the previous page, the following buttons appear.

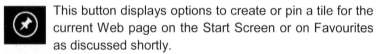

On the extreme right above is the Forward button, as discussed previously. The other buttons have the following functions:

Tapping or clicking this button refreshes the Web page with the latest up-to-date information.

This button displays options to create or pin a tile for the current Web page on the Start Screen or on Favourites as discussed shortly.

This button has options to search for and highlight certain words in a long document. You can also view a Web page in the traditional Windows Desktop.

Pinning a Web Site to the Start Screen

If there is a Web site which you frequently use, you can pin a tile for the site on the Start Screen. Then you can launch the Web site very quickly with a single tap or click whenever you want.

Tap or click the pin button shown above and on the right in the middle. Then select **Pin to Start** as shown above.

Then the window on the right appears giving a preview of the tile. You can also change the caption which appears on the tile, in this example **The RSPB: Barn owl**. Finally tap or click **Pin to Start** as shown on the right, to pin a tile for the RSPB Web site on the Start Screen, as shown in the centre of the extract below.

Tap or click this tile on the Start Screen to launch the Web site at any time.

Removing a Tile for a Web Site from the Start Screen

If you no longer need a tile for a Web site on your Start Screen, this can be unpinned as follows. First the tile must be selected as shown on the right, highlighted with a tick. To select a tile on a touch screen, gently drag the tile downwards a few millimetres and then release upwards. If using a mouse, right-click with the cursor over the tile.

Then tap or click the **Unpin from Start** icon which pops up at the bottom left of the screen. The tile will now be removed from the Start Screen.

When you select a tile as described above, the toolbar which appears along the bottom of the screen contains various tools, depending on whether the tile represents a Web site or program.

Tabs in Internet Explorer 10

When you launch Internet Explorer 10 from the Start Screen, the icons, buttons, etc., are hidden and the Web page itself fills the whole screen, as shown on the top screenshot on page 157. Then when you swipe in from the top or bottom of the screen or right-click the mouse cursor over the Web page, the Address Bar and various icons, buttons, etc., are displayed, as shown in the lower screenshot on page 157. Also shown across the top of this screenshot are the small "thumbnail" views of Web pages, shown below.

The row of thumbnails above is known as the *Tabs Bar* and provides a very fast way of switching between Web pages that are currently open. Tap or click the thumbnail miniature to open the full-size Web page on the screen. Alternatively, click the Close Tab button shown on the right and on the tabs above to close the Web page.

On the right of the thumbnails across the top of a Web page, there are two buttons as shown on the right.

Tap or click the lower button to display the small menu shown on the right. Turning on InPrivate Browsing prevents Internet Explorer from saving details of your browsing activities.

Alternatively tap or click the lower option shown on the right to close all currently open tabs and Web pages.

New InPrivate tab

Close tabs

Creating a New Tab

The New Tab button shown on the right appears on the top right of the Web page as shown on the lower screenshot on page 157. One result when you tap or click this button is, not surprisingly, to create a new tab on the top of the screen as shown on the right. However, you can also set
the New Tab button to open your Home Page. A Web page can be opened in the current tab or in a new tab.

To change these settings, open the Desktop from the Start Screen. Then tap or click the Internet Explorer icon shown on the right, on the bottom of the screen. Tap or click the gearwheel Tools icon shown on the
extreme right and then select **Internet Options** from the drop-down menu. From the Internet
Options window, tap or click the **Tabs** button, shown on the right. The Tabbed Browsing Settings window opens, allowing you to alter the actions for the New Tab button and new pages when they are opened.

When a new tab is opened, open:

| The new tab page ⌄ |

When a pop-up is encountered:

◉ Let Internet Explorer decide how pop-ups should open

◯ Always open pop-ups in a new window

◯ Always open pop-ups in a new tab

Open links from other programs in:

◯ A new window

◉ A new tab in the current window

◯ The current tab or window

Opening a Web Page in a New Tab from a Link

Press and hold the link or right-click with a mouse. From the small menu which appears tap or click **Open link in new tab**.

| Copy link |
| Open link in new tab |
| Open link |

If using a mouse and keyboard, hold down the Ctrl key while clicking the link with the mouse.

Revisiting Web Pages

As mentioned previously, when you launch Internet Explorer 10 from the Start Screen (rather than the Desktop) the various menus, tools and button are hidden. This enables the content of the Web page itself to be viewed on the full screen. Swiping in from the top or bottom or right-clicking with a mouse reveals the Address Bar at the bottom of the screen and the Tabs Bar across the top as shown at the bottom of page 157.

If you now tap or click in the Address Bar at the bottom of the screen, a row of tiles appears as shown below.

The left-hand group of three tiles shown above are those that the user has **Pinned** to the Start Screen as described at the bottom of page 158. The **Frequent** group of tiles are links to Web sites that have been visited recently. The tile on the extreme right above has been designated as a **Favourite**, as shown on the right. Tap or click any of the tiles above to quickly return to the relevant Web site.

Clearing Your Browsing History

After a while you may find you have too many tiles in the **Frequent** section shown on the previous page. A tile can be removed after pressing and holding the tile or right-clicking over it. Then tap or click **Remove** as shown on the right.

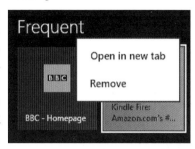

Alternatively to remove all of the tiles you've visited, with Internet Explore 10 launched from the Start Screen, swipe in from the right or click in the top or bottom right-hand corner of the screen, then tap or click the **Settings** charm shown on the right. Under

Settings shown near the top right of the screen, tap or click **Internet Options** as shown on the right below. (**Internet Options** only appears under **Settings** if you have opened Internet Explorer from the Start Screen, not from the Desktop.)

Now click the **Delete** button as shown on the right below to remove the tiles under **Frequent** as shown on the previous page, representing the Web sites you have visited recently. You need to restart Internet Explorer before the

tiles for the Web sites actually disappear from the **Frequent** section shown on page 162.

Using Internet Explorer from the Desktop

The previous pages have mainly described Internet Explorer 10 after it has been launched from its tile on the Start Screen. It was also shown that some settings such as the Tabbed Browsing Settings window shown at the bottom of page of page 161 need to be accessed after launching Internet Explorer 10 from the Desktop. Users of earlier versions of Windows such as Windows XP and Windows 7 will be familiar with the Desktop version of Internet Explorer.

You can use the Desktop version of Internet Explorer to view your browsing History and Favourites as an alternative to the Frequent and Favourites tiles displayed in the Start Screen version shown on page 162.

Tap or click the Desktop tile on the Start Screen and, from the Taskbar at the bottom of the screen, tap or click the Internet Explorer icon shown on the right.

Tap or click the star icon shown on the top right below to open the **Favourites**, **Feeds** and **History** window shown below. The **History** tab shown selected on the right gives a detailed record of all the sites visited. This is more detailed than the tiles listed under **Frequent** as shown on page 162 Tap or click the name of the site to open it on the screen. The **History** list can be arranged in various ways such as date visited or alphabetical.

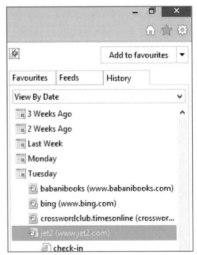

Tap or click the **Favourites** tab to open the sites you have added to your **Favourites** list. These are the same sites as the tiles under **Favourites** in Internet Explorer in Start Screen mode.

Internet Security

By enabling millions of computers to communicate with each other around the world, the Internet has created opportunities in work, education, communication and entertainment, etc., that previous generations could never have imagined. Unfortunately, in addition to these legitimate activities, the Internet provides skilful *hackers* with opportunities for a range of criminal acts. Unlike conventional crime, there is no burglary or violence and the criminal may be thousands of miles from the crime scene — which might be the computer in your home.

A major type of Internet crime is *malware*, i.e. malicious software. This is the use of specially written programs designed to damage or invade your computer and its files. These include *viruses*, *worms* and *Trojan horses*. Viruses may be attached to e-mails or software and are designed to spread, cause damage to files and slow down computer systems and networks. Worms can spread without being attached to a program. The Trojan Horse poses as a legitimate piece of software but has an illegal purpose such as to give a hacker access to your computer. *Spyware* uses *phishing* to try to find out personal and financial information, such as your bank account details.

Windows 8 and Windows RT provide a wide range of security software to combat these threats. These are turned on by default but it's worth checking they are up-and-running and up-to-date.

Open the Control Panel, as discussed on page 99, and under **System and Security**, select **Review your computer's status**. In the **Action Center** shown below, tap or click the arrow to the right of the word **Security**.

This displays a drop-down list of the main security tools and their status, **On** or **Off**, as shown below.

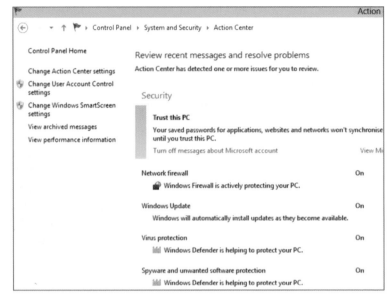

To change the **On** or **Off** status of any of the security messages, tap or click **Change Action Center settings** shown at the top left of the **Action Center** shown above. Then tap or click the check box to add or remove a tick from a security tool.

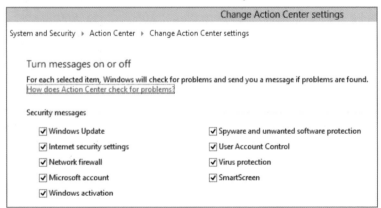

Windows Firewall

The **Windows Firewall** shown on the previous page is a barrier designed to stop hackers and malicious software such as worms from entering your computer. The firewall can also prevent malware being sent out from a computer to the Internet.

Windows Update

Windows Update downloads and installs the latest software upgrades from Microsoft, frequently intended to fix security problems. This is usually done automatically or you may be asked to choose whether or not to install a particular update. The Browser Choice window (discussed earlier) may be downloaded as a Windows Update. A log of all your recent updates is kept in the **View update history** window shown below. This is displayed after selecting **Windows Update** at the bottom left of the **Action Center** shown at the top of the previous page. Then tap or click **View update history** at the top left of the **Windows Update** window.

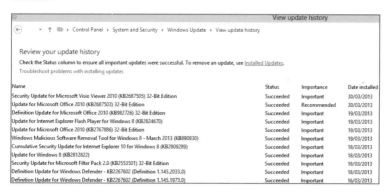

Many of the updates downloaded by Windows Update are *virus definitions*. These allow anti-virus software such as Windows Defender to detect and eradicate the latest viruses. Windows Defender is listed in the Action Center at the top of the previous page and discussed on the next page.

Windows Defender

This software is included in Windows 8 and RT and should always be **On**, as previously discussed. The window shown below can be quickly launched by swiping up from the bottom of the Start Screen or right  clicking to display the **All apps** icon shown on the above right. Then scroll across the All apps screen and tap or click **Windows Defender** or its icon.

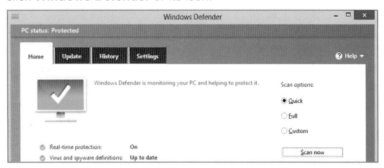

Windows Defender continually monitors your computer for viruses, spyware and malware. You can also launch a manual scan whenever you wish, using **Scan now** shown in the bottom right-hand corner above. Viruses are continually being developed, so the latest virus and spyware definitions are regularly updated automatically to Defender.

SmartScreen

The SmartScreen feature listed on page 166 detects e-mails, etc., from sources which can't be detected by normal antimalware software. SmartScreen issues alerts about unsafe Web sites which may be "phishing" for your bank details, etc.

Internet Activities

Introduction

Previous chapters discussed the setting up of an Internet Connection and the methods used to find Web pages containing the information you require. This chapter describes some of the Web sites which we find particularly useful ourselves. In this context, the terms Web site and Web page are interchangeable, since a Web site is simply one or more Web pages or documents.

It may be helpful at this point to recap on the methods by which you can arrive at a particular Web site, as discussed in more detail in the previous chapter.

- Typing the unique address or URL of a Web site, such as **www.babanibooks.com**, into the Address Bar then pressing Enter or tapping or clicking the Forward button.

- Entering *keywords* such as **barn owl** into a search engine such as Bing or Google or into the Address Bar of Internet Explorer. Then tapping or clicking a link to a Web site in the list of search results.

- Tapping or clicking a *link* or *hyperlink* on a Web page.

- Tapping or clicking a Web site in the *Favourites* tiles you have created or in the *Favourites* list in the Desktop version of Internet Explorer.

- Tapping or clicking a Web site in the *Frequent* tiles or the *History* list in the Desktop version of Internet Explorer.

Searching Google Categories

Launching Google is discussed on page 155. Google allows you to concentrate a search on various categories such as **Images**, **YouTube**, **Maps** and **News** shown in the extract below.

Search	Images	Maps	Play	YouTube	News

Searching in Google Images

If you select **Images** and then enter **Barn Owl**, for example, in the Google Search Bar, the search produces an array of thumbnail images as shown below.

Tap or click any of the thumbnails above to display a larger version of the image.

Searching in Google Maps

Select Maps from the bar across the top of the Google window and enter the name of a place you wish to find in the search bar. For example, if you enter Entrevaux, an ancient village in Provence, a drop-down menu appears with a number of suggestions, as shown below.

Tap or click to select the place you want and tap or click the search icon (magnifying glass). A map is quickly displayed with the place you require pinpointed as shown on the right and below.

As shown above, there are controls to pan around the area and to zoom in and zoom out. You can also find out more about the area by tapping or clicking to enlarge the thumbnail photos on the left and also by tapping or clicking the link to **Explore this area**.

Google Earth and Google Street View

Google Earth provides high-quality maps based on satellite images and aerial photographs of the world with the ability to search for a particular location. This includes zooming in to get a close-up view. The most extreme zoom leads to Google Street View which gives 3-D images of a neighbourhood including panoramic views of houses, gardens and any people and vehicles present at the time the area was photographed.

You can download a copy to your computer after entering Google Earth into the Google search engine as shown below. Google Earth is free but not currently available for Windows RT.

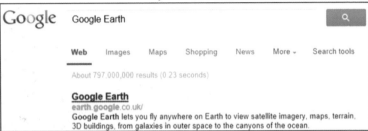

Tap or Click the link **Google Earth** shown above and then tap or click the **Download Google Earth** button. Follow the instructions on the screen to install Google Earth. This places an icon on the **All** **apps** screen as shown on the right. Swipe in from the bottom of the screen or right-click then tap or click the **All apps** icon. Scroll through the apps and then press or right-click the Google Earth app. Then tap or click the **Pin to Start** button at the bottom left of the screen to place a tile for Google Earth on the Start Screen as shown in the centre of the extract below.

Google Earth opens showing an image of the entire globe. Enter the name of a place you want to look at then tap or click **Search** or press Enter and Google Earth descends from the global image and "flies to" the location you've chosen.

Buttons on the right of the screen allow you to zoom in or pan around an area. If you zoom in as far as possible, Google Earth opens in *Street View*, as shown below. Drag to explore the area.

Shopping Online

We have been shopping online and carrying out financial transactions such as banking and paying bills for many years. Obviously there is a concern about security when you enter your account details online but so far we have never lost a penny. One of the first and most successful Internet companies is Amazon, which started in America in 1995 as an online bookstore. Since then it has diversified into a global online retailer of a wide range of goods, especially electronics.

Online retailers like Amazon have several advantages:

- You can view the products and order them from the comfort of your own home without travelling to shops.
- Comprehensive details and specifications of products are given online, which you can digest at leisure, unlike shopping in the hustle and bustle of the High Street.
- Many items may be reviewed online by other customers, giving you unbiased opinions rather than those of sales staff in a shop who may be trying to earn commission.
- It's easier to visit various online retailers to compare prices rather than physically visiting High Street shops.
- The online retailer can despatch goods from a central warehouse without maintaining an expensive High Street presence. So online goods should be cheaper.
- If you are a repeat customer with Amazon, your details are remembered so an item can be purchased with literally one click of the left-hand mouse button.
- In the case of Amazon, goods may be received within a day of placing the order and delivery may be free.
- An online bookseller like Amazon can have millions of books in stock, unlike the smaller High street retailer who may have to order a book from their distributor.

Log on to Amazon by entering its address into the address bar of your Web browser such as Internet Explorer, and press Enter.

The Amazon Web page opens showing the range of departments down the left-hand side. As well as books, the range of goods now includes clothes, electronics, hobbies, groceries and DIY.

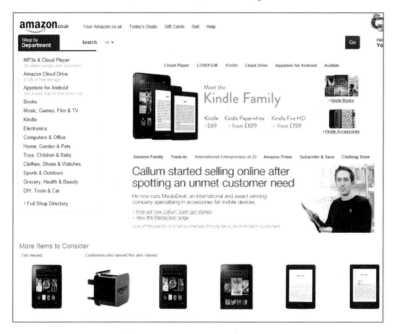

Amazon has enjoyed considerable success with its Kindle, a hand-held electronic device used for downloading and reading books from the Internet and known as an *e-book reader*. The Kindle image shown above is a link to another page on the Amazon Web site, as shown on the next page.

On the left of the screen shown above is a link to a **Quick Tour**, a video describing the product. In the centre are some technical details. A search bar at the top allows you to look for specific products or you can use links to browse through different departments. If you wanted to buy an item you would click **Add to Basket** shown on the right before proceeding to the checkout to complete your personal details such as name, address and bank

details, completing the purchase and choosing a delivery option. New customers create a new account with their e-mail address and password. Existing customers can sign in with their stored e-mail address and password. Then they can tap or click **Buy now with 1-Click** and the transaction is completed and delivery arranged with no further input from the customer.

Online Newspapers

Many national and local newspapers can now be read online. The Internet version of a newspaper can be found with a simple search in Bing or Google, for example, as shown below.

After tapping or clicking the newspaper's link in the results list, you may see the entire paper straightaway. Many of the online tabloids and local papers are free. Alternatively you may need to sign up as a subscriber with your e-mail address and password. For example, you might need to pay around £2 a week for one of the heavyweight newspapers, obviously much cheaper and more convenient than buying a daily printed edition of the paper.

The online version of a newspaper can show breaking news throughout the day and there is no paper to recycle.

Tracing Your Family History

Finding out about your ancestors used to be a very time-consuming job — visiting churchyards and searching through old parish records and county archives. Or you could pay a professional genealogist to carry out the work. The Internet has greatly simplified the task of tracing your forebears since millions of records have been made available on the Internet. Nowadays records can be retrieved with a search engine like Google or Bing, or by using dedicated genealogy Web sites.

Genealogy online is now extremely popular and as a result there are many specialist Web sites such as **findmypast.co.uk**, and **Ancestry.co.uk**. These genealogy Web sites allow you to access millions of records from the Civil Registrations of births, marriages and deaths and the National Censuses. The Web sites have built-in facilities to search for people. Shown below is a search using findmypast.co.uk to find a marriage, after entering the person's name and approximate year of the marriage.

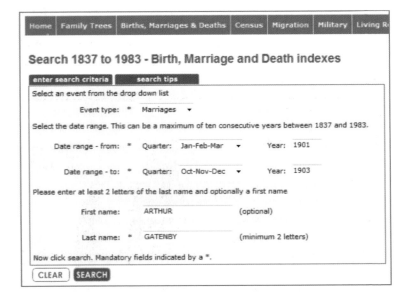

The results are presented in normal text on the computer screen but you can also view and print a copy of the original document, which may have been handwritten or produced on a manual typewriter, as shown below.

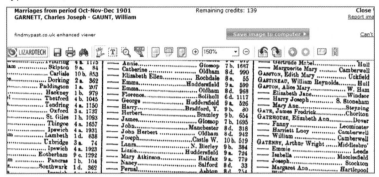

Web sites like findmypast.co.uk also include options to order copies of official Birth, Marriage and Death Certificates, to be delivered within a few days by the traditional post.

Ancestry.co.uk has one of the largest collections of family records and has sponsored the transcribing of millions of handwritten Birth, Marriage and Death records into a format searchable by computer. The ancestry.co.uk Web site also has facilities to enable you to create, save and print your family tree.

Another major source of family records is the U.K. National Censuses available every 10 years from 1841 to 1911. These give the name, sex, age and occupation, etc., of everyone living in a household on the night of the census, as shown below.

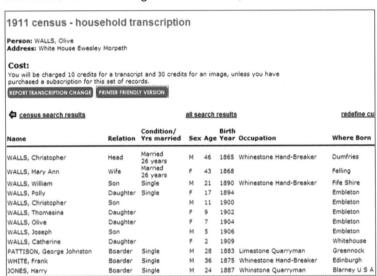

1911 census - household transcription

Person: WALLS, Olive
Address: White House Ewesley Morpeth

Cost:
You will be charged 10 credits for a transcript and 30 credits for an image, unless you have purchased a subscription for this set of records.

`REPORT TRANSCRIPTION CHANGE`   `PRINTER FRIENDLY VERSION`

◁ census search results   all search results   redefine cu

Name	Relation	Condition/ Yrs married	Sex	Age	Birth Year	Occupation	Where Born
WALLS, Christopher	Head	Married 26 years	M	46	1865	Whinstone Hand-Breaker	Dumfries
WALLS, Mary Ann	Wife	Married 26 years	F	43	1868		Felling
WALLS, William	Son	Single	M	21	1890	Whinstone Hand-Breaker	Fife Shire
WALLS, Polly	Daughter	Single	F	17	1894		Embleton
WALLS, Christopher	Son		M	11	1900		Embleton
WALLS, Thomasina	Daughter		F	9	1902		Embleton
WALLS, Olive	Daughter		F	7	1904		Embleton
WALLS, Joseph	Son		M	5	1906		Embleton
WALLS, Catherine	Daughter		F	2	1909		Whitehouse
PATTISON, George Johnston	Boarder	Single	M	28	1883	Limestone Quarryman	Greennock
WHITE, Frank	Boarder	Single	M	36	1875	Whinstone Hand-Breaker	Edinburgh
JONES, Harry	Boarder	Single	M	24	1887	Whinstone Quarryman	Blarney U S A

As shown below, ancestry.co.uk, provides records from the National Censuses, the Births, Marriages and Deaths Registers, Military Records from World Wars I and II, and immigration, ships' passenger lists and parish and criminal records.

Our records hold the key to your family history...

Census records
Censuses are perhaps the most important genealogy records — and we have the most complete online collection. Move back through the generations with details such as addresses, ages and occupations.

Birth, marriage & death indexes
Build a timeline of your ancestors' lives with our complete birth, marriage and death indexes from 1837 to 2005. Discover where and when each event happened, then order full certificates for even more

Military records
Trace the war heroes in your family with millions of military records. We have the largest online collection of World War I records, plus comprehensive collections for World War II and many earlier conflicts

Plus much more!
Discover your ancestors' stones and build your family tree with immigration records, parish records, criminal records, the National Probate Calendar and over 6 billion other records from all over the world!

More detailed coverage of Ancestry is given in our book BP 720 How to Trace Your Ancestors Using a Computer for the Older Generation. (978-0-85934-720-4)

Arranging a Holiday

You can make all your holiday arrangements online without having to leave home to visit a travel agent. Prices on the Internet are usually cheaper than traditional methods of booking and you can compare prices easily and get last-minute deals.

Finding Out About a Destination

A quick search with Google or Bing will provide lots of useful information about a place you are thinking of visiting.

The search results will include links to the main travel companies offering holidays to the area. There will also be official Web sites giving details of resorts and tourist attractions. The link to the free online encyclopedia Wikipedia will also give a lot of useful background information about the history of a place. Entering something like **weather Tenerife** into your search engine such as Google should produce current weather details, weekly or longer forecasts and year round averages, as shown overleaf.

Today's weather in Tenerife	5 day forecast in Tenerife				
	Tuesday 02/04/13	**Wednesday** 03/04/13	**Thursday** 04/04/13	**Friday** 05/04/13	**Saturday** 06/04/13
21°C Clear	Clear	Scattered Clouds	Scattered Clouds	Clear	Clear
Local Observation Time Currently unavailable 6 Visibility N/A Humidity 66%	**24°C** High Temp.	**23°C** High Temp.	**24°C** High Temp.	**24°C** High Temp.	**23°C** High Temp.

Webcams

Many hotels and resorts have set up *webcams* to take pictures which are updated regularly. For example, to get views of Tenerife, enter something like **Tenerife webcams** into a search engine such as Bing or Google.

Then tap or click the links in the list of search results to view the various webcams, as shown in the Tenerife example below.

Webcam Playa Valle

Island: La Gomera
Province: Santa Cruz De Tenerif
Region: Canary Islands
Country: Spain
Description: Camera live, sight
Webcam beaches showing weath
Landscapes real time web cams.

Las Americas Golf
www.golfholidays.com/LasAmericas
Best Available Rates at Las Americas & L
Madrigueras   Gestión anunci

(13) webcam La Gomera (island) | (30) webcam La Palma (island) | (95) webcam T
webcam Las Palmas (province) | (138) webcam Santa Cruz De Tenerife (province) |
Canary Islands (region) | See more webcam Spain (country) |

Booking a Hotel

After carrying out a search for a destination, there will be lots of links to firms offering deals including hotels and flights, including special last-minute

Cheap Hotels in **Marbella**
www.laterooms.com/**Marbella**-Hotels
laterooms.com is rated ★ ★ ★ ★ ⊀
Cheap 4* Hotels in **Marbella**.
With Up to 50% Off! Book Online.

offers. You may find that a link to the TripAdvisor Web site appears after a search for a hotel. For each hotel there should be a large number of reviews by previous guests.

The hotel Web site normally includes the room prices. There may be sample menus and views of the different types of room. Some hotels include a virtual tour or video of all of the facilities of the hotel including the restaurant, bars and swimming pool.

Search Hotels

Destination/hotel name:
Edinburgh

Check-in date
Day ▾ Month ▾

Check-out date
Day ▾ Month ▾

☐ I don't have specific dates yet
Rooms   1 ▾
Adults   2 ▾
Children   0 ▾

Search

The hotel Web site allows you to check room availability for your dates, as shown on the right. Then you can proceed to make an online booking. You may be required to pay straightaway or at the end of your stay. (A credit card gives greater protection for an online payment than a debit card).

Arranging Flights Online

You'll probably know which airport you'd like to use for your trip. Enter the airport name into a search engine like Google. The airport site will have links to its flight destinations and time-tables. From these you can find out if there are any flights to your chosen destination. If suitable flights are available, you can enter your required dates and obtain prices.

Before making an online booking to purchase tickets, you may be able to compare prices with other airlines, perhaps operating out of different airports. Where we live in Derbyshire people regularly fly from Birmingham, Manchester, Gatwick, Heathrow Luton and East Midlands. The Internet makes it easy to compare prices and match your travel requirements such as destinations, dates and times.

Several Web sites are designed to help you to find cheap flights and compare prices. You could type one of the following into the Address Bar of your Web browser such as Internet Explorer:

www.cheapflights.co.uk   www.travelsupermarket.com

Alternatively enter the keywords **cheap flights** into your search engine and follow the links in the results to the various Web sites.

Some airlines now allow you to *check in* online. This can save a lot of queuing at the airport, answering questions and waiting for your boarding pass to be printed. Instead you print your boarding pass at home on your own computer, together with confirmation documents that act as your tickets. You may also be able to choose where you sit on the plane (for an additional charge).

Tracking Flights in Real Time

You can use your computer to check flights in real time, even if the planes are hundreds or thousands of miles away. This might be useful if you're waiting for a friend or relative to arrive. Enter the keywords **flight tracking** into your search engine.

Numerous links to flight tracking Web sites are produced, including **flightradar24.com**. This site is free to use and can be launched by entering the following into your Address Bar:

www.flightradar24.com

Select the **Planes** tab on the left of the screen and scroll down to the flight number of the aircraft, such as **UAE17** for example. Then tap or click **Show on map** to see the plane's position.

The map below shows that flight **UAE17** (highlighted in red) is currently over the Netherlands. The left-hand panel shows it is a United Arab Emirates Airbus A380 travelling from Dubai to Manchester at an altitude of 40000ft and a speed of 481mph.

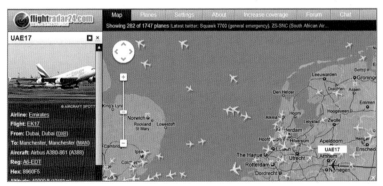

To see the details of planes currently flying overhead in your area, scroll the map to show your area and tap or click on the icons for each of the planes in turn. Buttons on the left allow you to zoom in and out and move in any direction.

Buying and Selling on eBay

If you are thinking of downsizing or simply want to get rid of some "clutter", *eBay* allows you to offer your items to a nationwide or worldwide audience of millions of potential customers. The range of goods offered for sale on eBay is enormous, from jewellery, antiques, porcelain and collectable items through to motor vehicles and even real aircraft. Open the Web site by entering the following into the Address Bar of your Web browser.

http://www.ebay.co.uk/   ✕   ➔

As shown below, each item is listed with a photograph and a brief description.

Vintage Bracket Mantle   8 Bids   £114.99 +£39.00   10h 40m
Clock moonphase
WARMINK oak stri...

A time limit for the sale, usually several days, is set by the seller and eBay displays a running total of the number of bids, the highest bid received so far (**£114.99** in the example above) and the amount of time left for bidding. The cost of posting (e.g. **£39.00** above) is also shown. At the end of the time allowed, the item is sold to the highest bidder who then pays the seller before the seller arranges delivery. Obviously in the case of very large items like cars or furniture, for example, buyer and seller must liaise to make arrangements for collection.

PayPal is a security system used by eBay to protect the purchaser's payment against the goods not being delivered and also ensures that the seller receives their payment instantly. **Seller information** allows you to check the seller's record, including a rating based on feedback from purchasers.

Useful Web Sites

There are many Web sites specializing in useful information of particular interest to older people. The following Web addresses can be typed straight in after tapping or clicking in the Address Bar. You don't need to enter **http://** and in most cases **www.** is not needed either as these are added automatically. Most of the Web sites give advice and information on topics such as health, finance, shopping and travel for the over 50s.

www.ageuk.org.uk Support for older people.

www.agepartnership.co.uk Equity release specialists.

www.aarp.org Discounts, magazine and online information.

www.cennet.co.uk Holidays for the over 50s.

www.gov.uk Guide to government services.

www.dwp.gov.uk Advice on benefits, work and pensions.

www.equityreleasecouncil.com Release some of the capital tied up in your home.

www.facebook.com Rekindle old friendships and make contact with people having similar interests to yourself.

www.fiftyplus.co.uk Fashion catalogue for people over 50.

www.friendsreunited.com Catch up with old school friends.

www.digitalunite.com Computer training for the over 50s.

www.kelkoo.co.uk Price checks on Internet goods for sale.

www.laterlife.com Promotes a fuller life for the over 50s.

www.neighbourhoodwatch.net Promotes home security.

www.nhsdirect.nhs.uk Advice and help with illness.

www.opin.org.uk Older People's Information Network.

www.overfiftiesfriends.co.uk Senior social networking.

www.rias.co.uk Insurance for over 50s.

www.saga.co.uk Wide range of services for older people.

www.seniority.co.uk Internet community for over 50s.

www.seniorsnetwork.co.uk News and information.

www.silversurfers.net Provides links to an enormous range of Web sites relevant to over 50s in particular.

www.sixtyplussurfers.co.uk Online magazine for over 60s.

www.theoldie.co.uk A witty magazine for *all* ages.

www.thewillsite.co.uk Help in making your own will.

www.thisismoney.co.uk Guide to savings and loans.

www.twitter.com Send and receive text messages up to140 characters long.

www.uswitch.com Look for cheapest gas, electricity and telephone, etc.

The next chapter looks at Web sites designed to help people to share news and information with friends, family and acquaintances, the phenomenon known as *social networking*.

Social Networking and Communication

Introduction

While *electronic mail* is a well-established method of Internet communication, social networking is a relatively recent phenomenon that has developed in the last few years and now involves hundreds of millions of people around the world. Social networking Web sites allow people to exchange news, information and photographs. Well-known sites such as Facebook and Twitter are free to use and make their money from advertising. Free world-wide telephone calls using the *Skype* Internet service were discussed on page 11. The following Internet services are covered in this chapter:

Electronic Mail or E-mail

Users send longer messages, including documents and pictures, to one or more people via their e-mail addresses.

Facebook

Users create or renew friendships online to exchange news, photographs and detailed biographical information.

Twitter

Members post small text messages or *tweets* about their current activities. Other people (*followers*) can read and reply to the tweets of anyone they choose to follow.

Electronic Mail

E-mail was one of the first applications of the Internet and is still one of the most heavily used methods of communication. While perhaps not as versatile as the new social networking sites such as Facebook and Twitter, discussed shortly, e-mail has many advantages for both personal and business use.

- The message is delivered almost instantly.

- The same message can be sent to many recipients, easily selected from an electronic address book.

- It is very simple for recipients to *reply* or *forward* the message to someone else.

- An e-mail can have large files attached, such as text documents, spreadsheets, video clips or photographs.

- Messages can easily be deleted or saved in an organised structure of folders, for future reference.

- E-mail can be used for long messages. Social networks like Twitter are limited to very short messages.

Electronic mail can be used to keep in touch with relatives around the world. Documents, photos and other files can be "clipped" to the message and are known as *attachments*. The text in the body of the e-mail can be used to create quite long documents. You can also "cut" and "paste" text and pictures into an e-mail and embed a *link* to a Web site. A contact receiving the e-mail can tap or click the link to launch the Web site.

In order to use e-mail you need a unique e-mail address such as **samueljohnson@hotmail.com**. Creating a new e-mail address is discussed on page 192. Once created, your e-mail address can be used to join Social Networking sites such as Facebook and Twitter and to create an online diary or *blog*, as discussed later in this chapter.

The Windows Mail App

Windows 8 and Windows RT have their own e-mail app, known as *Windows Mail* or simply *Mail*. This is launched by tapping or clicking its tile on the Start Screen, shown in the extract below.

In this example I have sent a simple e-mail to myself, as shown below. When you receive an e-mail, a notification appears on the **Mail** tile on the Start Screen. The **Mail** tile below shows the sender's name, the title, the first few words of the message and the number of unread messages.

Tap or click the tile to read the full message as shown below.

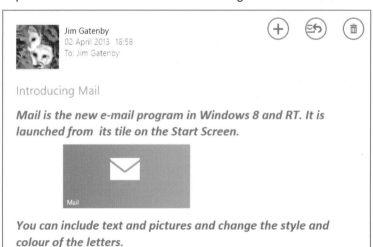

Creating an E-mail Address

An e-mail address will also allow you to sign in to Facebook, Twitter and a blog as well as the Lock Screen. From the **Settings** charm discussed on page 95, select **Change PC settings**, then **Users** and **Add a user**. Here you can sign up for a new

Microsoft user account, including an e-mail address and password. Or you can select **Sign up for a new e-mail address**, to create an additional e-mail account.

You will need to modify your name if someone else is already using it. Complete the form with your chosen password, which must contain upper-case and lower-case letters and a number. Then select a security question from the drop-down list and enter your answer to it. The new e-mail address can be used to sign into Windows 8 and RT via the Lock Screen and to various Windows apps and also Facebook and Twitter.

When you start the computer, the Lock Screen is displayed. Swipe or click the screen and enter your password as discussed above and on page 85. The Start Screen is displayed including the **Mail** tile. Tap or click the **Mail** tile to open the **Mail** app on the screen, as shown on the next page.

The left-hand of the Mail page above shows the various folders used to organize your e-mails, such as the **Inbox**, **Drafts**, **Sent Items**, **Outbox**, **Junk** and **Deleted Items**.

The middle panel above shows a list of the recent e-mails, with the names of the senders and the time or the day they were sent, including a tick if they've been read.

The right-hand panel in the top screenshot shows the text of the e-mail and any images. Also shown at the top of the message is the sender's name, the time and date it was sent and the title.

The row of three icons shown on the right and at the top right of the upper screenshot are used (reading from left to right) to create a **New** e-mail, **Respond** to a selected e-mail or **Delete** a selected e-mail. Tapping or clicking the **Respond** button displays the options shown on the right. **Reply all** sends a reply to all other recipients of the original message. **Forward** sends the message on to someone else.

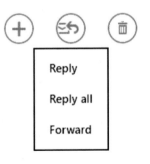

There may also be one or more icons at the top of the message representing *attachments* such as photos or documents of different types, as discussed shortly.

Sending an E-mail

Tap or click the **Mail** tile on the Start Screen shown on page 191. Then tap or click the **New** icon shown on the right and on the previous page.

A new blank e-mail window opens ready for you to enter the text of the message. First enter the e-mail addresses of the main recipients in the **To:** slot, pressing **Enter** after each one.

The **Cc:** slot above is used to send a (carbon) copy to other people who may be interested. The small icon as shown here on the right and on the right of the **To:** slot above is used to add people from your contacts list to the recipients of the new message. People are added to your contacts list automatically when you receive mail from them.

Next give a title to the message, replacing the words **Add a subject** shown above. It's now time to start entering the main body text under the horizontal line on the right-hand side shown above. Swipe in from the top or bottom or right-click with the mouse to display the formatting toolbar along the bottom of the screen, as shown below. The formatting features include different font styles, sizes and colour of letters and bold and italics, etc.

The above toolbar also appears when you highlight a piece of text.

As shown on the toolbar at the bottom of the previous page, there are buttons to change the font style, size and colour of the text. You can also insert *emoticons* — small cartoon-like images intended to express feelings or cause amusement, as shown on the right.

Bantam Moves Into Angry Cat's Basket

Hello Jill

Thought you might be interested in this picture showing our cat Bop trying to repossess his basket after it had been occupied by one of the bantams.

Copying and Pasting an Image or Text

In the above example, the image has been placed in the body of the e-mail by "copying" and "pasting". This is done by pressing and holding or right-clicking over an image (a piece of text) in another program and then selecting **Copy** from the menu which pops up. Swipe in from the top or bottom or right-click and then tap or click the **Paste** button at the bottom left of the screen, shown here on the extreme right.

When the e-mail is complete, tap or click the button shown on the right to **Send** the e-mail on its way.

It is usual to send large text documents, spreadsheets and photographs, etc., as *attachments* to an e-mail, as discussed over the page.

Adding an Attachment

Attachments are often photos sent with an e-mail, to share with friends or colleagues. In fact the attachment can be any sort of file such as a word processing or spreadsheet document, or a video or music clip. Some e-mail services set a limit on the size of attachments sent with an e-mail, such as 10 or 20MB. Also, if you have a slow broadband service, files can be very slow to upload to the Internet. Even so, you should be able to send several photos with an e-mail, especially if you use a facility to reduce the size of the file before sending.

An attachment can be added to an e-mail from the main screen used for typing the text. Swipe up from the bottom or right-click  with the mouse. Then tap or click the **Attachments** button shown above, located at the bottom left of the screen. You then browse the discs, flash drives, cameras, camera cards, etc., attached to your computer, where you know the required photo is stored.

When you've located the file or photo to send, tap or click the **Attach** button shown above. A thumbnail of the file appears at the top of the e-mail, as shown on the next page. There is an option to send the file to *SkyDrive* rather than as an attachment. SkyDrive is a Microsoft Internet Storage location in the "clouds". You can use it to save files so that friends and colleagues can share them. In Windows 8 and RT, you have a SkyDrive tile on the Start Screen and a SkyDrive folder in the File Explorer into which you can "drop" files to be uploaded to the clouds.

Return of the Salmon

1 file attached   Send using SkyDrive instead

Hi Stella

After an absence of many years, salmon have returned to the River Dove in Staffordshire and Derbyshire. The attached photo was taken below the weir at <u>Norbury</u>.

Considering the length of the rivers inland from the North Sea to <u>Norbury</u>, this represents an epic journey by any standards.

Sent from Windows Mail

The e-mail is sent together with any attachments by tapping or clicking the **Send** button shown above and on the right. When the recipient opens the e-mail in their Inbox, they tap or click the thumbnail for the attachment. They are then given a choice to open the file in a suitable program or save it on a local disc, solid state drive or flash drive, etc.

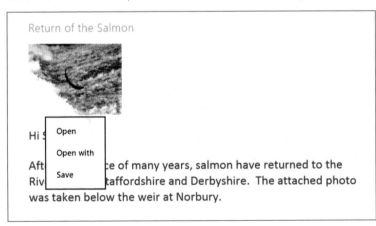

The Facebook Social Network

This is probably the most popular social networking site, with over a billion users. Although originally started by college students in America, it is now used by people of all ages; Facebook is becoming increasingly popular with older people especially if they have children and grandchildren on the other side of the world. Businesses and celebrities also use Facebook for promotional purposes, enabling them to reach a very large audience with their latest news and information.

Facebook Friends

Facebook is based around the concept of having lots of *friends*. These may include close personal friends and family but may also include people you have never met in the real world. Some people have thousands of "friends" on Facebook.

These virtual friends on Facebook are people with whom you have agreed to share information across the Internet. Facebook identifies people who you might want to invite to be your friends, perhaps because they are in the list of contacts in your e-mail address book and are already members of Facebook. When you join Facebook you can enter a personal profile giving details of your education, employment and interests, etc. This information allows Facebook to suggest people who you might want to invite to be a friend. They can either accept or decline this invitation.

Confidentiality and Security

Facebook provides a platform for you to post on the Internet a great deal of personal and biographical information. The Internet enables this information to be viewed by a potential audience of millions of people. Facebook has *privacy settings* to allow you to restrict the viewing of certain types of information to specific groups of people. It's advisable not to put confidential information on Facebook unless you are thoroughly conversant with the privacy settings. You are also advised not to accept complete strangers as Facebook friends or arrange to meet up with them.

Joining Facebook

Signing up to Facebook requires you to be at least 13 years of age, with a computer connected to the Internet and a valid e-mail address. The sign up screen appears after you enter **www.facebook.com** into the address bar of your Web browser.

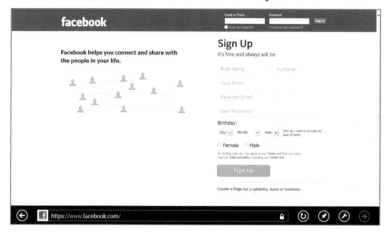

From your e-mail address, Facebook checks your list of e-mail contacts and produces a list of potential friends who are already on Facebook. You can then invite them to be your Facebook friends. Any of your e-mail contacts who are not members of Facebook may be sent an invitation to join the social network.

Your Facebook Profile or Timeline

You are then asked to start entering your *Profile* information, also called your *Timeline*. The profile or timeline contains details such as your education, employment history, hobbies and interests, address and contact details.

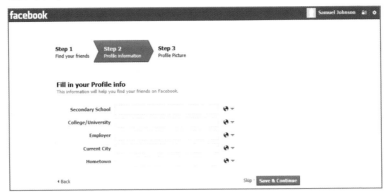

You can also add a profile picture, allowing friends to identify you after a search on Facebook, which may have produced a lot of people with the same name as you. If you have a suitable profile picture stored on your computer, it can be uploaded to Facebook, after clicking **Upload a photo**, shown below. Otherwise, if you have a *webcam* on your computer, you can take a picture and upload it directly to Facebook using **Take a photo** shown below.

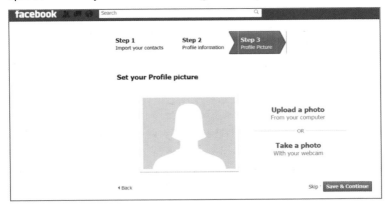

You don't have to fill in every part of your profile or timeline during the sign up process — you can return to edit it later.

At the right of some pieces of the information is the *inline audience selector* icon shown on the right. Click this icon to open the menu shown above. This allows you to select the audience for the item of information, e.g. **Public**, **Friends** and **Only me**, etc.

Communicating With Others Via Your Wall

You can type text and add photos in the **Status** box shown on the right and **Post** updates to a "noticeboard" known as your **Wall**. Other people can view your Wall according to the  privacy settings such as **Friends** or **Close friends** on the menu shown on the right.

You may also be interested in book BP 734 Social Networking for the Older Generation. (978-0-85934-734-1)

Tweeting With Twitter

Twitter is another very popular social network with over 500 million users worldwide. Although there are some similarities with Facebook, Twitter is also different in many ways.

What is a Tweet?

One of the main features of Twitter is that messages or *tweets* can be no more than 140 characters long. This makes Twitter suitable for brief text messages like SMS phone texts. As well as PC and Apple computers, Twitter can also be used on the latest smartphones such as the iPhone and the Blackberry.

Whereas e-mail messages are sent to the unique e-mail addresses of known contacts, tweets can be read by very large numbers of people who may be complete strangers to the tweeter. Twitter is based on the idea that users will want to follow the regular pronouncements of other people such as friends, family, celebrities, politicians, reporters or companies and other organisations.

Followers on Twitter

Regular tweeters may post messages several times a day, such as the actor and writer Stephen Fry, who has millions of *followers*. Some users of Twitter will be followers who only read other people's tweets, rather than posting their own. You need to be sufficiently well-known for lots of other people to want to read what you have to say in your tweets, or find ways of encouraging people to become your followers.

You can choose to follow anyone you like on Twitter, but you can't choose who follows you. You can read all the tweets of the people you follow and send a reply if you wish. On Facebook, although some information such as photos and educational details are available for all to see, interaction is usually between people who have agreed to be Facebook "friends". Facebook has privacy settings to control who can see what information.

Hashtags

A hashtag is a word or phrase, etc., preceded by the hash sign (**#**) and placed in a tweet, e.g. **#BBCQT**. (BBC Question Time in this case). Clicking on a hashtag which appears in a tweet allows you to read all the tweets on that particular topic. You can also find all the relevant tweets by entering the hashtag in the search bar at the top of the Twitter screen as shown below.

Hashtags allow anyone on Twitter to participate in online forums on current news issues or television programs, for example

Twitter in Use

Whereas Facebook relies heavily on detailed personal profiles to bring together people sharing similar backgrounds and interests, Twitter only accepts about a paragraph of biographical information, as shown below under **findmypast.co.uk**.

Many companies, such as the family history Web site, **findmypast.co.uk**, include a link to Twitter on their main Web site. Clicking this link opens the
Twitter Home page of **findmypast.co.uk** as shown below.

The latest tweets from **findmypast.co.uk** are displayed down the right-hand side of the screen as shown in the example below.

When you roll the cursor over a tweet, the whole tweet is highlighted in blue as shown above. An extra line of blue text appears along the bottom of the tweet, starting with the time or date the tweet was sent. As you can see above, there are links enabling you to **Reply** to a tweet or to **Retweet**, which means to forward a tweet to your followers. There is also a **Favorites** folder in which to place tweets for future reference.

Shown above is the top of the Twitter page for **findmypast.co.uk**, also shown on page 203. This includes brief details of the company and a link to its Web site. The **Follow** button on the right allows you to become a follower of **findmypast.co.uk**. When you are a follower of a person or organisation on Twitter, their tweets appear on the timeline or list of tweets on your Twitter Home page. The figures show total numbers of tweets, the number of people or organisations that **findmypast.co.uk** is following and the number of followers of **findmypast.co.uk**. A tweet appears on the timeline of all your followers.

Signing up for Twitter

Log on to the Twitter Web site by entering **www.twitter.com** in the Address Bar of your Web browser, such as Internet Explorer and pressing Enter.

Fill in the box shown on the right, including a valid e-mail address and a password. Then click **Sign up for Twitter**, as shown on the right. Your username, **@samueljohnson** for example, and Twitter account are then created. Then the Twitter Teacher gets you

started by providing a list of people for you to follow. When you click the **Follow** button against a person's name and photo, as shown below, their messages appear on your tweet page.

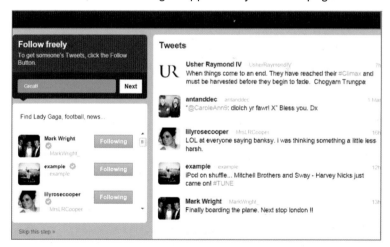

You can also search your e-mail address list for people to follow on Twitter. An image of yourself can be added with a short text profile. An e-mail is sent to you by Twitter and you click on a link for confirmation. You can now begin tweeting.

Posting a Tweet

Start Twitter by entering **www.twitter.com** in the Address Bar of your Web browser and pressing Enter. Sign on to Twitter with your username and password then type your message in the box under **What's happening?** The number **99** shown on the lower right below is the number of characters still available to be used out of the maximum of 140. (You don't have to use all 140 characters).

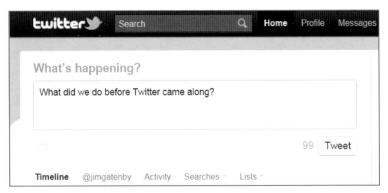

Click the Tweet button shown above to post the tweet.

Reading Tweets

The message is posted and is immediately available on the *timeline* or list of tweets of anyone following you, as shown below. This shows a tweet posted one minute previously by me to anyone following me. My username **@jimgatenby** is shown below. In this case the follower is Christopher Walls, username **@christowalls** — the change in spelling needed because the full name was already taken by another Twitter user.

Including an Image or Photograph with a Tweet

The icon on the right and on the lower left below allows you to add an image stored on your computer to a tweet. Click the camera icon then browse your computer and select the required image. Photos should be less than 700 kilobytes in size for posting on Twitter. A thumbnail of the image appears on the tweet as shown below. Then click the **Tweet** button to post the message.

The tweet will be available to be read by your followers almost immediately, as shown below for my follower Christopher Walls.

Twitter has embedded a link to the photograph in the tweet received by Christopher (**christowalls**). The link is the line of text **pic.twitter.com/gRT61Sk8**. (The creation of this link is done automatically for you by Twitter).

Click on the link to display the picture full size, together with the text of the tweet, as shown on the next page.

A Tweet Including a Link to a Photograph

Reducing the Size of a Photo for Posting on Twitter

As shown above, Twitter provides a very fast and easy way of sending a concise text message, together with a photograph or another sort of image. The image must be stored on your hard disc drive or removable storage device such as a flash drive or CD/DVD. As with other forms of image transfer across the Internet, very large files can cause problems, so photos should be reduced to a file size of less than 700 kilobytes. Photos can be reduced in size using programs like the freely-available Windows Live Photo Gallery or by purchasing software like the popular Adobe Photoshop Elements.

Microsoft Office

Introduction

Microsoft Office is probably the most widely used business software in the world. The Office Home and Student edition comprises several programs (or apps), as follows:

Word: a *word processor* used for letters, reports, theses, etc. and also providing many features traditionally found in dedicated desktop publishing software.

Excel: A *spreadsheet* program used for accounts, calculations on tables of figures, graphs and charts.

OneNote: A virtual notebook which allows you to collect notes and all types of information — photos, videos, Web links, etc.

PowerPoint: Software used to illustrate presentations, with "slide shows" including text, photographs and other images.

If your computer is using Windows 8 or Windows 8 Pro (but not Windows RT) you can run the retail version of Microsoft Office Home and Student Edition costing under £70. Windows RT is supplied with special built-in versions of Word, Excel, PowerPoint and OneNote, designed to work with the ARM processor used in some tablet computers. Shown below is part of the Taskbar on the Desktop of a Microsoft Surface RT tablet. The icons **N**, **P**, **W** and **X** represent OneNote, PowerPoint, Word and Excel respectively.

This chapter discusses two of the most important Microsoft Office programs, Word and Excel, which are invaluable to both the home and professional user alike. Competence in their use is an essential requirement in many occupations.

Microsoft Word

Word processing has been one of the most prevalent applications since personal computers were first introduced. It greatly increases office productivity because documents can be edited on the screen without the need for complete retyping.

Initially the word processor was used for the production of plain text without any special effects. If a document had to be formatted with special effects such as a newspaper style layout with text in columns and pictures, for example, the text from the word processor had to be imported into a separate *desktop publishing* program.

Nowadays the word processor has many of the features of the desktop publisher, such as text in columns and the ability to include pictures and other design and page layout features. Microsoft Word is part of the Microsoft Office suite of software and is probably the most commonly used software for producing anything from a simple letter to a book such as this one.

For many years I have used Microsoft Word for the production of books. Word is capable of all the necessary typesetting features such as headers, footers, insertion of pictures and clip art and manipulation of text. You can also save a Word document in the popular *PDF* format (Portable Document Format) which commercial printers work from. I use the sister program Microsoft Publisher for colour books such as this one, because Publisher has a specialist commercial colour printing capability (known as *CMYK*) not available in Microsoft Word. However, in other respects Microsoft Word is more than capable of the most demanding of tasks and easily satisfies the word processing and desktop publishing needs of most people.

Dedicated desktop publishing software may provide additional features for more specialist tasks such as glossy coloured leaflets, for example. For the home and small office user, Serif PagePlus and Microsoft Publisher are available for under £100.

Shown below is an extract from a 320-page book, typeset ready for the printers and produced entirely in Microsoft Word.

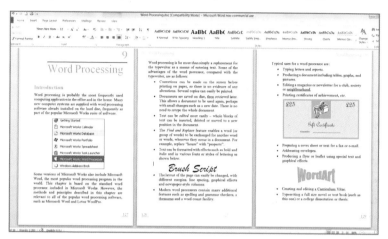

As you can see above, Microsoft Word allows you to produce documents including text in various *fonts* or styles of lettering such as **Brush Script** shown above. There are dozens of fonts to choose from after tapping or clicking the arrow to the right of the words **Times New Roman** shown below highlighted in blue.

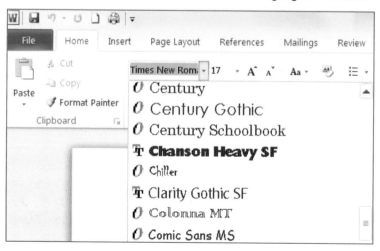

Bullets or dots are used to highlight items in a list. The extract on the previous page also shows that pictures or images such as the Gift Certificate on the right-hand page can be inserted into a document. Images can also be moved around and resized by dragging with the finger or with the left mouse button held down.

WordArt on the previous page is a feature in Microsoft Word and Microsoft Publisher which allows words to be manipulated and distorted into various shapes as shown below.

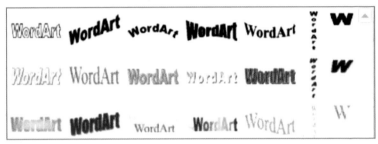

The Tabbed Ribbon

In later versions of Microsoft Office, from Office 2007 onwards, the traditional drop-down menus such as **File**, **Edit** and **View**, etc., have been replaced by a *tabbed ribbon* as shown below. Similar ribbons are also used in the Microsoft Excel spreadsheet and the Publisher desktop publishing program.

All of the usual tools are still available – it's just that they are presented in a different layout. There is a new **File** tab with options, for example, to **Open**, **Save** and **Print** a document, as shown on the next page.

The File Tab

When you click the **File** tab shown below, a menu appears with options to carry out major tasks such as saving and printing a document. As shown below, when you click **New**, a choice of *templates* is presented, providing ready-made formats and designs appropriate to the new document you wish to create.

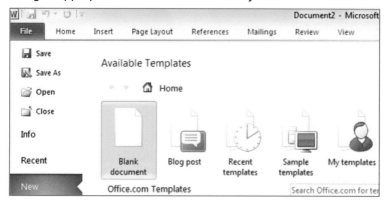

There are various other tabs on the ribbon such as **Home**, **Insert** and **Page Layout**, as shown above. Icons for related tasks are grouped together, such as the **Font** group for changing the style and size of letters. The text formatting tools such as indentation, centering, justification and line spacing are displayed in the **Paragraph** group shown on page 212.

As you change to a different task, the tools on the ribbon change automatically. For example, if you select or highlight a picture in a Word document, the **Picture Tools Format** tab appears, as shown below. Clicking this tab displays a complete set of tools for formatting a picture. An extract from the ribbon with the **Picture Tools Format** tab selected is shown below.

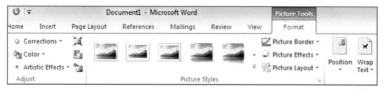

Saving a Document in Word

Save and **Save As** shown on the **File** menu on the previous page are used to make a permanent copy of your work, such as a letter about travel insurance, for example. Tapping or clicking **Save As** opens the dialogue box shown below.

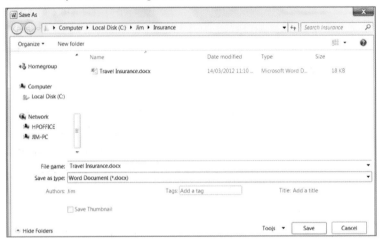

You can browse to find a folder on your computer in which to save a document, by tapping or clicking in the left-hand panel shown above. The folder may be on your hard disc drive (usually drive **C:**) or you might select a folder on a removable device like a flash drive (memory stick), usually drive **E:** or **F:**. Or you can create a new folder if you wish after selecting **New folder** shown above. In this example the document has been given the file name **Travel Insurance.docx**. The file type **.docx** is the latest Word format. If you click the arrow on the extreme right of **Save as type:**, you can save a file in the **.doc** format used by Word 97 -2003. You can also save in the **.pdf** format (Portable Document Format) acceptable to most computer systems and the Internet. Click the **Save** button shown above to save the **Travel Insurance** document in the selected folder, **Insurance**, within the folder **Jim** on the **C:** drive (hard disc drive). The full path is:

C:\Jim\Insurance\Travel Insurance.docx

Microsoft Word Facilities

- Text can appear in different sizes, styles and colours.
- Text can be arranged in newspaper style columns.
- Photographs, tables, graphs and images can be inserted.
- Ready-made templates with professional looking page designs can be modified by inserting your own content.
- Vast libraries of free "clip art" images are available.
- Sentences, paragraphs and whole pages can be inserted, deleted or moved about by "cutting and pasting".
- Documents can be corrected and amended on the screen without any evidence of the alterations on paper.
- *Mail merge*: Multiple copies of a standard letter infilled automatically with different names and addresses, etc.

Word Processing and DTP Output

- Letters, reports, newsletters, magazines, etc.
- Complete books — academic, technical, novels, theses.
- Leaflets, flyers, brochures and other publicity materials.
- Business cards, greeting cards and certificates.
- PDF (Portable Document Format) documents — standard format used for documents downloaded from the Internet. Compatible with most types of computer.

Word Processing and DTP Software

Home and small business users should find that most of their desktop publishing needs can be met using Microsoft Word. For very specialised tasks such as commercial colour printing, DTP software such as Microsoft Publisher and Serif PagePlus are available for under £100. Professional users may choose to pay several hundred pounds for an industry standard package such as Adobe InDesign.

The Excel Spreadsheet

Like the word processor, the spreadsheet program was one of the first applications of computers. The spreadsheet takes the hard work out of lengthy, repetitive and complex calculations. Microsoft Excel is probably the most widely used spreadsheet in the world; it is extremely powerful yet easy to learn and use. As mentioned earlier, Excel is included with Microsoft Word in the Microsoft Office Home and Student Edition.

Microsoft Excel is a worldwide standard tool for preparing accounts in business and is also very suitable for the home user wishing to keep a tight rein on their finances. In fact the spreadsheet can be used wherever calculations are required on rows or columns of figures. Shown below is a simple spreadsheet based on plant sales in a small business.

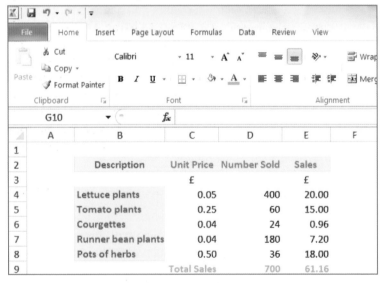

As you can see above, the spreadsheet uses a very similar tabbed ribbon to the one used in Word. This allows the spreadsheet to be formatted with different styles of text and colour. The **File** tab above is used for saving and printing.

The spreadsheet consists of a table of *cells* identified by "grid references" such as **C4** and **D4** shown below. A cell can contain text or numbers or a *formula* to carry out a calculation. Many of the formulas such as **Sum** or **Average** can be selected from the ribbon by tapping or clicking with the mouse. Others can be typed directly into a cell, preceded by an equals sign, as in **=C4*D4** shown below. (* is used for multiplication).

	A	B	C	D	E	F
1						
2		Description	Unit Price	Number Sold	Sales	
3			£		£	
4		Lettuce plants	0.05	400	=C4*D4	
5		Tomato plants	0.25	60	15.00	

Replicating a Formula

One of the great strengths of the spreadsheet is that you only have to enter a formula once at the top of a column or at the beginning of a row. Then you drag a small cross from the corner of the cell containing the formula all the way down the column or along the row. This applies the formula to all the other cells in the row or column. A big spreadsheet could have many more rows or columns than the small example shown on the previous page. This *replication* of formulas can save a great deal of work

Recalculation

Another very important facility of the spreadsheet is the ability to carry out "what if?" speculations. For example:

- What if inflation reached 7%?

- What if petrol were to cost £2.00 a litre?

- What if savings interest rates were 3%, 4%, or 5%, etc.?

The spreadsheet program makes it very easy to feed in variables like these and automatically recalculates a very large table in seconds, helping to predict possible future scenarios.

Spreadsheet Graphs and Charts

The spreadsheet program makes it easy to turn columns of figures into graphs and charts, by simply dragging over the required rows or columns and then selecting the type of graph from the Excel tabbed ribbon, shown in the extract below.

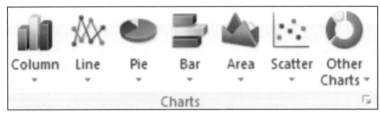

Multiple columns or rows can be selected for use in the graph by holding down the **Ctrl** key while dragging the cursor over the relevant cells with the left-hand mouse button held down. As shown in the example below, the spreadsheet program works out the scales and labels the axes automatically, tasks which are very time-consuming by traditional "manual" methods.

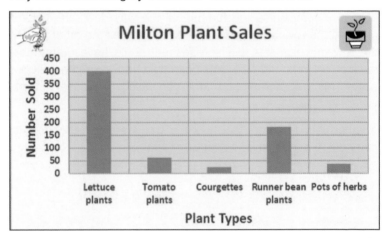

Microsoft Excel is covered in more detail in our book An Introduction to Excel Spreadsheets. (978-0-85934-701-3)

Printing from Applications

Despite talk over many years of the paperless office, in lots of situations it's still essential to be able to print hard copy on paper.

In all versions of Windows 8, including RT, there are two quite different methods of printing, depending on the application.

- Applications such as Word and Excel which run in the **Desktop** (with the traditional Taskbar along the bottom) use **File** and **Print** as in earlier versions of Windows.

- Applications such as Mail and Internet Explorer 10 (when running in the Modern User Interface, i.e. without the Taskbar as in the Desktop) print from the Devices charm, as discussed on the next page.

File and Print

From an application such as Word or Excel, tap or click **File** then **Print** on the left. If you have several printers, make sure the correct one is selected. Set the number of copies and the pages to be printed, etc., and then tap or click the **Print** icon near the top of the screen, as shown below.

Printing from Apps Designed for the Modern User Interface

Modern apps such as **Mail** don't have the **File** and **Print** options discussed on the previous page. Instead you need to swipe in from the right or hover the cursor in the top or bottom right-hand corner of the screen, then tap or click the **Devices** charm as shown on the right and on page 93.

The **Devices** panel opens to display any printers available to your computer. This information is not displayed if you're running in Desktop mode, although the Devices charm is still available. Tap or click your printer such as the **HP Photosmart Wireless B109** listed on the right. The following window appears, with

options to set the orientation, paper size, quality and number of copies. Then tap or click the **Print** button shown at the bottom right below.

Multimedia Activities

Windows 8, Windows 8 Pro and Windows RT

Three new apps have been introduced for viewing photos and playing music and videos. These apps can be launched from their own tiles, included by default on the Start Screen in Windows 8, Windows 8 Pro and Windows RT, as shown below.

Windows 8 and Windows 8 Pro (but not RT)

Windows 8 and Windows 8 Pro include the *Windows Media Player* to play music and video and the *Windows Media Center* to watch DVDs. The Media Center can also be used with a *TV Tuner* (a plug-in USB dongle or an internal expansion card) to watch live and recorded television. Users of Windows 8 and Windows 8 Pro can also use the *Windows Live Photo Gallery* to import, edit and organize photographs.

Both Windows Photo Gallery and Windows Media Center are available for Windows 8 and Windows 8 Pro as downloads from Microsoft at **windows.microsoft.com**. The Windows Media Player is installed as an integral part of Windows 8 and Windows 8 Pro.

The rest of this chapter discusses the new **Photos**, **Music** and **Video** apps shown in the above extract from the Start Screen.

More multimedia apps can be downloaded from the Windows Store, as shown on page 84. Some of these apps are free.

The Music App

The Music app allows you to listen to your favourite music in two ways. With *streaming* you listen to the music while it is being transmitted over the Internet, without actually saving it on your computer. You may, however, have to listen to some advertising. Alternatively you can purchase, *download* and save tracks which can be played offline at any time. This is useful in places where you can't use the Internet. You can also create *playlists* or sets of your favourite tracks.

The **xbox music** window shown below is launched by tapping or clicking the **Music** tile on the Start Screen, shown on the right.

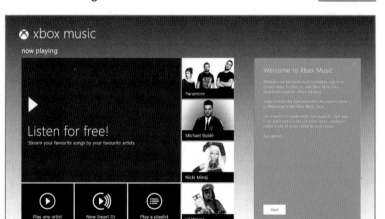

If you select **Play any artist** as shown on the right and above, a search bar appears, as shown below, allowing you to enter the name of any artist.

Enter artist

After tapping or clicking the button shown on the bottom right of the previous page, the Music app starts playing a song by your chosen artist. While the track is playing, pictures of the artist appear in the window. Swiping in from the bottom or right-clicking with a mouse displays the toolbar shown below, with buttons to pause, control the volume or change to another track.

Buying and Downloading Music

Display the Search charm as described on page 93,and, with **Music** selected, enter the name of the artist in the search bar. Then select the album you wish to download and select **Buy album** on the left of the window. You will then be asked for your

Microsoft password before entering your bank card details and starting the download. The titles and album covers of the

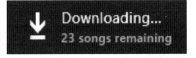

music on your computer can be viewed on the left of the **xbox music** window under **my music**, as shown below.

Purchasing an Xbox Music Pass (£8.99 a month or £89.90 for 12 months) gives unlimited streaming or downloading of millions of tracks, played as often as you like on up to four computing devices, which can include a Windows Phone.

The Music Library

When you download music it's automatically saved on your computer's hard disc drive or SSD in the *Music Library* in the File Manager. To look at the Music Library, tap or click the **Desktop** tile on the Start Screen, then tap or click the File Explorer icon on the Taskbar at the bottom left of the Desktop, as shown on the right and below.

The File Explorer window opens, as shown below. Double-tap or double-click **Libraries** on the left-hand side shown below, then tap or click **Music** and **My Music** to see your folders. Open the folders by tapping or clicking, to see the list of tracks.

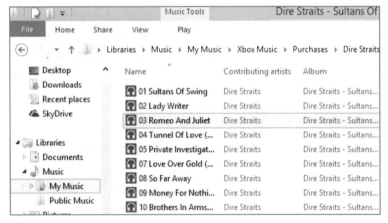

Then select **Play** under **Music Tools** shown above and below and then select **Play** again on the left of the icons shown below to play the track in the Music app.

The Video App

This application allows you to view details of commercial videos and buy them if you wish. As shown on the left below, any videos which you've imported also appear, under **my videos**.

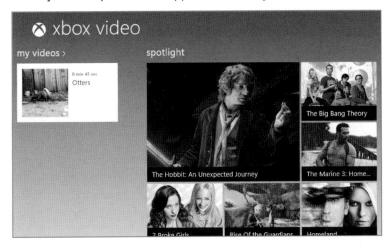

In the example on the left above, I have imported a video clip from my digital camera. Tap or click the small image above to play the clip on the full screen in the **Video** app. Swipe in from the bottom or right-click, to display the control buttons along the bottom, such as **Pause**, **Next**, **Previous** and **Volume**.

Commercial Videos

These are classified under **spotlight**, **movies store**, shown below and also **tv store**. Tap or click the image of a video to obtain a description and details of the cost to buy or rent.

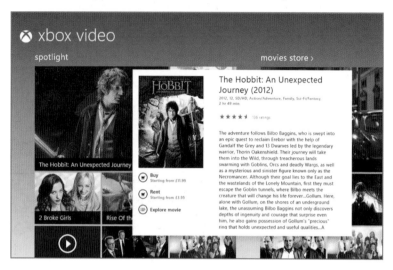

You can stream the video for immediate viewing or download it and save it on your hard disc drive or SSD. Both SD (Standard Definition) and HD (High Definition) versions are available.

The Videos Library

Videos saved on your computer appear in the *Videos Library* in the File Explorer. The Videos Library is opened by tapping or clicking the File Explorer icon shown on the right. This appears on the left of the Taskbar at the bottom of the screen after tapping or clicking the **Desktop** tile on the Start Screen. You may need to scroll up or down in the left-hand panel to see the **Videos Library** as shown below on the left.

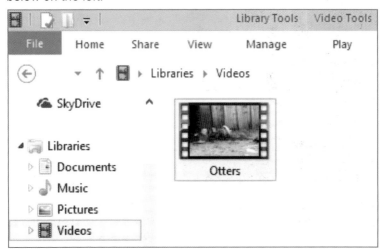

Playing a Video in the Videos App

Tap or click the icon to select it, as shown above, then tap or click **Play** under **Video Tools**. Then tap or click **Play** again from the small toolbar which appears, as shown below.

The Photos App

This application can be used to view all of your photos, wherever they are stored. The **Photos** tile is live, displaying small images of your photos which change regularly.

When you tap or click the **Photos** tile shown on the right above, the following screen appears. The **Photos library** shown below is similar to the Music and Videos libraries just discussed. Photos (and videos) imported from a digital camera or memory card are automatically saved in the Photos library.

SkyDrive is the Microsoft document and photo storage space in the "clouds" (on the Internet). Users have up to 7GB available. You can send photos to SkyDrive by dragging them from the Photos library and dropping them into the SkyDrive folder, which is built into the File Explorer in Windows 8. SkyDrive can be accessed by any computer connected to the Internet, making it easy to share your photos with friends wherever they are. Facebook and Flickr can also be used to share photos but if you don't use them there is an option to **Hide** their tiles as shown on the right.

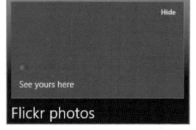

Tap or click the **Pictures library** tile shown on the previous page, to display all of your photo folders as shown below. Scroll horizontally with a finger or drag the horizontal scroll bar to see all of the folders. The scroll wheel on a mouse may also be used.

Tap or click a folder to display the images inside in a continuous display which can be scrolled horizontally. Tap or click an image to make the image fill the entire screen.

Swipe in from the bottom or right-click to display the toolbar shown at the bottom left above, with options including **Delete**, **Rotate**, **Crop**, **Slide Show** and using the photo for your Lock Screen as discussed on page 103.

The Pictures Library

Photos and video clips imported from a digital camera are automatically saved in the Pictures Library. (Unless you use the **New Folder** option in the **File Explorer** to create new folders and sub-folders of your own). To view the libraries, tap or click the **Desktop** tile on the Start Screen, then tap or click the File Explorer icon shown on the right. Select **Libraries**, as shown below on the left of the File Explorer, to display the **Pictures Library**. Double tap or double-click a folder to display the individual photos.

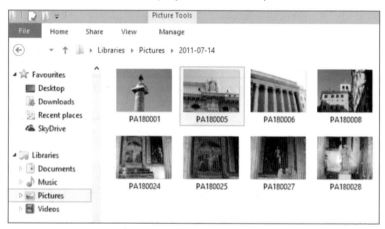

The menu bar across the top of the File Explorer has various ribbons such as **Home** shown below and also **Share**, **View** and **Manage**. These allow you to perform many tasks on your photos, such as copying, deleting, moving, renaming, creating new folders, e-mailing to friends and burning to a CD/DVD.

Importing Photos and Videos

The USB ports discussed in Chapter 5 can be used to connect a digital camera via a USB cable. Alternatively the memory card can be removed from your camera and inserted into a USB card reader as shown on page 54. Some computers and printers have a built-in card reader in the form of a slot which accepts various memory cards. You may also wish to transfer photos, etc., stored on a USB flash drive.

As soon as the camera, memory card or flash drive is connected to the computer, it is detected. Depending on certain optional settings, the following message may appear.

KINGSTON (D:)
Tap to choose what happens with mixed content.

The AutoPlay Menu

When you tap or click the notification as shown above, the AutoPlay window opens similar to the one on the right. In this example a Kingston USB flash drive contains the photos, which can be imported using the **Photos** app or viewed in the **File Explorer**. The images on the memory card are then displayed. Initially all of the images are ticked for importing. **Clear selection** allows you to remove all the ticks then just tap or click to tick certain images that you wish to import. Tap or click the **Import** button to copy the selected photos to the Pictures Library as discussed on the previous page.

KINGSTON (D:)

Choose what to do with mixed content.

Import photos and videos
Photos

Open folder to view files
File Explorer

There is also a button icon to start the import process on the main Photos start up screen. Swipe up from the bottom or right-click to display the button shown on the right.

Managing Files in the File Explorer

The File Explorer is used to manage photos and other files in the Pictures Library or in folders which you may have created.

Open the Pictures Library as discussed on page 230 and press and hold or right-click to display the menu shown in part below.

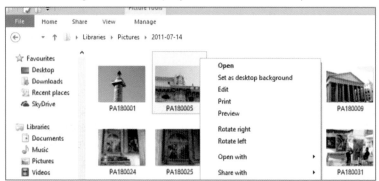

This has many file management options such as to **Copy**, **Delete**, **Rename**, **Prin**t, **Rotat**e, **Send to** a DVD or e-mail recipient, etc. **Open with** shown above presents a choice of programs or apps in which to launch the file, in this case a photo.

The above Windows 8 Pro example has quite a lot of programs to choose from, including traditional ones such as **Photo Gallery**. If running Windows RT you may only see **Photos**, **Paint** and **Windows Photo Viewer**, unless you've downloaded some photo apps from the Windows Store. Double tapping or double-clicking a file icon launches it in the *default program*.

Useful Software Tools

This chapter looks at some of the utility programs available to manage your computer and keep it working properly. Most of these are installed on your hard disc as part of the Windows operating system or alternatively they can be freely downloaded.

Windows Easy Transfer

This program is used to simplify the task of copying your essential files from one computer to another. For example, you buy a new Windows 8 or RT computer and want to copy to the new machine all of your documents, e-mails, videos and photos, etc., from an older machine running Windows 7, for example.

Easy Transfer copies your personal files, not programs, to the new machine. Programs have to be installed from their original CDs or by downloading from the Internet.

Easy Transfer has to be installed on both computers. It is automatically installed as part of Windows 8 and Windows RT and users of other versions of Windows can download a free copy from:

www.microsoft.com/download

Type **Easy Transfer** into the search bar then follow the instructions to download a copy for your version of Windows.

There are three physical methods of making the transfer:

- Connecting the two machines using a special Easy Transfer USB cable, available from computer stores. This package includes software for the cable on a CD.

- Transferring files across a network to which both computers are connected.

- Copying all of the files to a single Easy Transfer file on an external hard disc drive. For a smaller quantity of data a removable USB flash drive may be adequate.

In this section "old" and "new" refer to the source and destination computers. Easy Transfer can also be used when a single computer is being upgraded, say, from Windows 7 to Windows 8. In this case an external hard disc drive would have to be used.

It is recommended that you start by running Easy Transfer on the new machine. Easy Transfer can be launched in Windows 8 and RT by tapping or clicking its icon on the **All Apps** screen as discussed on page 90. If using an Easy Transfer cable, don't  connect it until instructed. On Windows 7 the program can be launched by clicking the **Start** button and entering **Easy Transfer** in the *Search programs and files* bar at the bottom left of the screen. First you are asked to select the method to be used — Easy Transfer cable, network or external hard drive/flash drive as mentioned above.

When Easy Transfer is running on both machines you are asked to connect them using the Easy Transfer cable or alternatively plug in the external hard disc drive or flash drive on the old machine. If using an external hard disc drive or flash drive a single Easy Transfer File is created and this contains all the files in the transfer. You are told to browse to the location where the Easy Transfer File is to be saved.

If you are using Easy Transfer across a network you are asked to start the program on the new machine first. Then, when instructed, start Easy Transfer on the old machine and note the *Easy Transfer key* which is generated. This is then entered in the new machine to complete the Easy Transfer network connection.

> **Windows Easy Transfer key:**
>
> **545-696**

With the two machines connected and running Easy Transfer, or with the old machine connected to the external hard disc drive or flash drive, the old computer is scanned. A default selection of files to be transferred is displayed by Easy Transfer. You can modify this list of files after clicking **Customize**, as shown below.

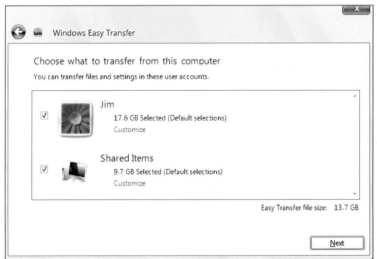

If using an Easy Transfer cable, after you click **Next** the files are transferred directly to the new computer.

Alternatively the files are saved to the external hard disc drive or flash drive as a single Easy Transfer file in the .MIG format. An optional password may be added. You are advised to write down the location of the transfer file so you can open it in Easy Transfer on the new machine.

If using an external hard disc drive or flash drive, start up Easy Transfer on the new Windows 8 or Windows RT machine by tapping or clicking the Easy Transfer icon on the **All apps** screen. Alternatively, if  using a keyboard, type **Easy Transfer** while the Start Screen is displayed.

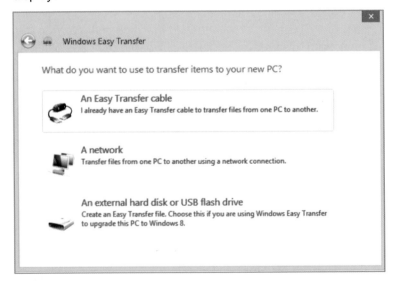

On the new machine, select **external hard disk or USB flash drive** as shown above. Then select **This is my new PC** from the next window which is displayed..

Next tap or click **Yes** to say that Easy Transfer has saved the files from your old computer to a hard disc or flash drive. You are then required to plug in and browse the hard disc or flash drive to find the Easy Transfer file.

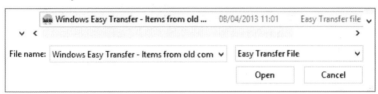

Tap or click **Open** shown above, then tap or click **Transfer** and wait for the files to be copied. The following window opens showing that the transfer of files to the new machine is complete.

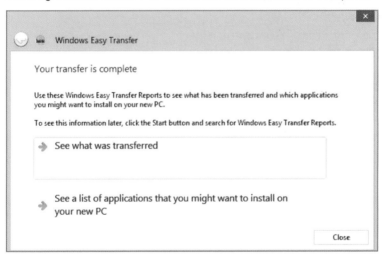

Tapping or clicking the text in blue above allows you to see what files have been transferred and where they are located on the new computer. You can also check on the details of the transfer by selecting  **Windows Easy Transfer Reports** on the **All apps** screen.

Using File History to Protect Your Files

It's not uncommon for someone to lose the entire contents of their hard disc drive or SSD. This might include irreplaceable photos, important documents or your almost complete memoirs. The solution is to make *backup copies* of your important files on a separate external hard disc drive or USB flash drive.

When you plug a device into a USB port on the computer (as discussed on page 52) you are asked to tap (or click) to say what

happens with removable drives. Then the window shown on the right appears. In this example, the backup device is a **KINGSTON** flash drive, designated drive **(E:)**.

Tap or click **Configure this drive for backup File History** as shown on the right. The **File History** window opens as shown below. If you have upgraded a computer from Windows 7 to Windows 8 you may need to click a link and switch off the Windows 7 backup facility.

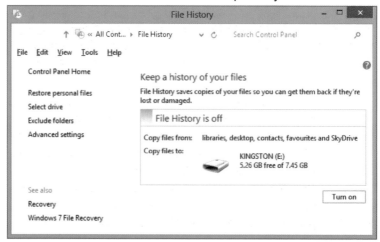

The **File History** window can also be displayed from the **System and Security** section of the **Control Panel**, which can be opened as discussed on page 99. As shown on the previous page, you need to tap or click **Turn On** to start File History.

File History is on

Copy files from:	libraries, desktop, contacts, favourites and SkyDrive
Copy files to:	KINGSTON (E:) 5.26 GB free of 7.45 GB

File History is saving copies of your files for the first time.

The backup process starts straightaway, with backup files copied to the secondary storage every hour by default. It is normal for files to be backed up if they have changed since the last backup. You can change the time between backups after selecting **Advanced settings** as shown on the left of the File History window on the previous page. When you plug in a flash drive or the USB cable for an external hard drive, this drive is automatically selected as the destination for the backup files. However, if you have more than one secondary drive that can act as the backup medium, this can be chosen after tapping or clicking **Select drive** as shown on the left of the **File History** window on the previous page.

A flash drive as shown above can be used to back up selected folders after tapping or clicking **Exclude folders** shown on the **File History** window on the previous page. Then add the unwanted folders to the list in the **Exclude Folders** window. For a full backup of a hard drive or SSD you would need an external hard drive with a USB cable and a capacity of, say, 1 or 2TB. (1TB or *terabyte* is about 1,000GB, as discussed on pages 45 and 46). Currently a 1TB external USB drive costs around £60.

Recovering Backed Up Files

The folders and the files within them are backed up in a folder called **FileHistory**, automatically created on the backup medium. This may be all of your files and folders backed up onto an external hard drive or a selection backed up onto a flash drive.

There are various events which can cause you to lose files and folders from your hard drive or SSD. You may accidentally delete files or overwrite them during a copying operation or files may be corrupted by a virus or technical fault. It's not too unusual for Windows itself to be corrupted and have to be re-installed. This can involve wiping or formatting the hard disc drive so that all of your personal files and folders are lost. Or your computer might be severely damaged by a fire or flood. Fortunately, if you've made backup copies and stored them in a secure place, these can be restored to the original location on your computer or onto a different computer.

To restore the backup files and folders open the **File History** window as discussed on page 238, then select **Restore personal files** in the left-hand panel of the window. Press and hold over a folder and select **Restore** to copy a folder to its original location. **Restore to** lets you select a new location.

Disc Maintenance

Windows 8 and Windows RT include two features to optimise the organisation of files and folders on your hard drive or SSD. These tools are **Disk Clean-up** and **Disk Defragmenter**, found in **Administration Tools** under **System and Security** in the **Control Panel**, opened as described on page 99.

Disk Clean-up

Over time your computer stores a lot of temporary and redundant files which can be safely deleted. Also, "deleted" files in the **Recycle Bin** aren't actually removed until the **Recycle Bin** is emptied. Too many redundant files cluttering up a hard disc may cause a computer to run slowly. **Disk Clean-up** shown below calculates how much space can be saved and allows you to delete redundant files and empty the **Recycle Bin**.

Disk Defragmenter

Files can become fragmented and scattered around a hard disc, or SSD, slowing down the process of finding and opening a file. **Disk Defragmenter** analyses and, if necessary, rearranges files to make the computer run more efficiently. **Disk Defragmenter** should be run regularly and can be scheduled for a specific time each week. You can also carry out a manual defragmentation.

Drive	Media type	Last run	Current status
(C:)	Hard disk drive	08/04/2013 10:23	OK (0% fragmented)

System Restore

This feature is available in Windows 8 and Windows 8 Pro, but not in Windows RT. When you install a piece of software or hardware, the computer may stop working properly. **System Restore** returns the computer's settings to an earlier time. **Restore Points** are "snapshots" of important settings taken automatically at regular intervals. Open the **Control Panel** as discussed on page 99 and select **System and Security**, **System**, **System Protection** and from the **System Protection** tab select **System Restore**. Select a Restore Point as shown below then select **Next** and follow the instructions on the screen.

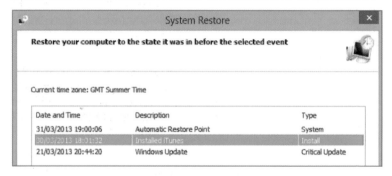

Windows Update

This feature downloads to your computer the latest updates to Microsoft Windows. Open **System and Security** in the **Control Panel** as discussed on page 99, then select **Windows Update,** and **Turn automatic updating on or off**. If necessary, automatic updates can be turned on (if not already on), using the drop-down menu opened by tapping or clicking the small arrow on the right below.

Index

Items should be returned on or before the last date shown below. Items not already requested by other borrowers may be renewed in person, in writing or by telephone. To renew, please quote the number on the barcode label. To renew online a PIN is required. This can be requested at your local library.
Renew online @ **www.dublincitypubliclibraries.ie**
Fines charged for overdue items will include postage incurred in recovery. Damage to or loss of items will be charged to the borrower.

Leabharlanna Poiblí Chathair Bhaile Átha Cliath
Dublin City Public Libraries

Baile Átha Cliath
Dublin City

Central Library, Henry Street
An Lárleabharlann, Sráid Annraoi
Tel: 8734333

Date Due	Date Due	Date Due

GERARD SIGGINS was born in Dublin and has lived almost all his life in the shadow of Lansdowne Road; he's been attending rugby matches there since he was small enough for his dad to lift him over the turnstiles. He is a sports journalist and worked for the *Sunday Tribune* for many years. His other books about rugby player Eoin Madden, *Rugby Spirit*, *Rugby Warrior* and *Rugby Rebel*, are also published by The O'Brien Press.

RUGBY FLYER

GERARD SIGGINS

THE O'BRIEN PRESS
DUBLIN

First published 2016 by
The O'Brien Press Ltd,
12 Terenure Road East, Rathgar,
Dublin 6, Ireland
D06 HD27
Tel: +353 1 4923333; Fax: +353 1 4922777
E-mail: books@obrien.ie.
Website: www.obrien.ie

ISBN: 978-1-84717-819-0

8 7 6 5 4 3 2 1
18 17 16

Printed and bound by CPI Group (UK) Ltd, Croydon, CR0 4YY
The paper in this book is produced using pulp from managed forests.

DEDICATION

To Nancy Young and the late John Young

ACKNOWLEDGEMENTS

Thanks to all my family, who allow me the time and space for Eoin's adventures. Thanks also to everyone at The O'Brien Press for their help and encouragement, especially to Helen and Emma for going the extra mile. Thanks to my pals and colleagues who help in many ways, especially Paul Howard, Alison Martin, Maureen Gillespie, Fergus Cassidy, Joe Coyle, Fionnuala McCarthy, Eoin Brannigan, John Greene, Brian Flanagan and Jack White.
I first read about Obolensky in a piece by the great *Guardian* writer Frank Keating, who enthused me about many other sportsmen and women too.

CHAPTER 1

Eoin's hands shook as he picked up the letter. It wasn't just that there was a distinctive blue 'Leinster Rugby' logo on the envelope, or even that his mum and dad had both come out to the hallway to see what the postman had brought and were now staring intently at him. Eoin had a fair idea of what the letter would say, but he was still completely torn on how he would respond to it.

'Oh well, at least it's not my school report,' he grinned as he tore at the white envelope. Inside was a booklet, and a one-sheet letter with just two typed sentences:

Dear Eoin,
Leinster Rugby would like you to attend a Youth
Academy Induction Course at our headquarters in
UCD Belfield on the weekend of July 20-21. Please
confirm your attendance to the address below by 1

July, including your clothing and equipment sizes.

Eoin flicked through the glossy booklet, which was full of photos of Jamie Heaslip, Johnny Sexton and all the other great players who had played for Leinster in recent seasons.

'They want me to go up to Dublin for a weekend,' he shrugged as he handed the letter to his mum.

'Don't look so delighted,' she laughed. 'You look as if someone has stolen your boots!'

'Ah, it's a great honour, I suppose. It's just that...'

'It's just that you're a Munster man and you won't be able to face Dylan if you play for that shower up in Dublin,' laughed his dad.

'Yeah, I suppose that's it,' said Eoin. 'And it'll be hard to break the habit of hoping Leinster lose every time they play!'

Eoin's mum smiled and patted him on the back. 'Congratulations, Eoin, that's such wonderful news. Do you want me to reply? I'm sure you don't know your shirt sizes and all that.'

'Yeah, thanks, Mam,' replied Eoin. 'I arranged to meet Dylan down the club in a little while and I suppose I'll have to break the bad news to him.'

Eoin smiled to himself as he jogged the short distance

to the Ormondstown Gaels GAA club. The letter hadn't brought bad news, of course – it was a fantastic opportunity to develop his rugby with Leinster, and could even lead to a career playing the game. But Eoin was Munster born and Munster bred, and since he started playing rugby all he had ever dreamed of was wearing the famous red shirt of the province – ahead even of the green jersey of Ireland.

A Leinster development officer had approached him a few months before as he celebrated winning the Junior Cup with his Dublin boarding school, Castlerock College. He had been taken aback by it at first, but his school coach was delighted and encouraged him to pursue the opportunity.

He felt his feet bounce a little more off the tarmac as he jogged through the gates of the club.

'Hiya, Barney!' he called out to the long-serving groundsman, who was busy painting the white lines on the playing field with a home-made contraption adapted from a broken wheelbarrow.

'Ah, is it Eoin?' he called back. 'Is it the round ball or the egg today?'

Eoin laughed. 'It will be a bit of both,' he replied. 'I'll be working on the place-kicking this morning.'

The Ormondstown Gaels pitch was where Eoin

worked on his game, and on his dreams. He had always wanted to be good at sport, but it was only when he turned his hand to rugby that he found a game that suited his temperament and his skills. Although his grandfather had once been a big rugby star, Eoin hadn't got the chance to try out the game until he went to boarding school in Dublin three years before.

Eoin had also discovered he could see and talk to ghosts, so with a little help from a long-dead friend, Brian, he sharpened his skills and soon became the best player in his year at Castlerock. The worst thing – in fact the only bad thing – about the summer holidays was that he hadn't been able to talk to Brian, who hung around the old rugby stadium on Lansdowne Road. Although Brian had made a few appearances around Castlerock, a visit to Ormondstown seemed to be beyond him.

Eoin ducked into Barney's shed and collected the rugby and Gaelic footballs that the groundsman allowed him to store there. As he emerged from the shed he heard a roar as Barney chased a familiar figure across the field.

'Hey, Eoin, tell him to leave me alone!' laughed Dylan as the old man waved his fist.

'Steady lads, steady,' intervened Eoin, 'What's going on here?'

Barney pointed to the beautifully painted touch-line which now had an ugly kink in it.

Eoin stared down at Dylan's feet, where a large white stripe now ran across his left boot.

'I just wanted to see what it would look like,' said Dylan, sheepishly.

Barney growled. 'If you ever do that again, I'll… I'll…' before he gave up trying to imagine what punishment he would have in store for Dylan. Barney wouldn't hurt a fly.

'I'm sorry,' chirped Dylan. 'I'll give you a hand with the nets later.'

'Ah, you're grand,' laughed Barney. 'But I know now who to suggest when they're next looking for a lines-man!'

CHAPTER 2

Eoin and Dylan dropped into Cleary's shop after training to buy a bottle of water. They sat outside on a bench, watching the world go by as they slaked their thirst.

'So, what's your plan for the summer, Eoin?' asked Dylan. 'You getting a job? I hear they're looking for lads to pick fruit in the farm over beyond the glass factory. The guys from the GAA club are all doing it and the crack is great. And there's a few euro in it too.'

'Nah, Dad wants me to do a few chores around the farm, and I won't have enough time to get a proper job,' replied Eoin.

'Why not? Are you going on a holiday or something?'

'No… well, not as such…'

Now suspicious, Dylan stared at Eoin.

'I have to go up to Dublin for a few days, maybe more,' Eoin admitted. 'It's for rugby.'

'Is this a school thing?' asked Dylan.

'No,' replied Eoin, realising he would have to front up to it. 'It's a Leinster thing.'

'Leinnnnnnster?' howled Dylan. 'What have you got to do with *them*?'

'Well nothing, really,' said Eoin. 'Nothing yet, anyway.'

'Yet?' quizzed Dylan, who was starting to enjoy that Eoin was so uncomfortable with his interrogation.

'Well, I never got around to telling you this… but this Leinster coaching guy came up to me at the Aviva after the final. He wrote to me today asking me to go up for this weekend camp in UCD.'

'But we're Munster through and through!' said Dylan, faking a look of horror.

'I know, I know, it's just that they asked me and I don't want to say no.'

'Well, I suppose you'll probably get good coaching and all that – it won't hurt at all, I suppose. But *Leinnns-ssster*?'

The pair stood up. 'I'm going to call by to see how Dixie is,' said Eoin. 'Do you want to come?'

'Yeah, I haven't seen Dixie for ages,' said Dylan. 'I love going to visit him. He's always great for the old stories.'

Eoin's grandfather, Dixie Madden, was a rugby legend, a former star for Castlerock College – and for Leinster.

But just before he was set to play for Ireland a tragic accident took his wife and he never played rugby again. He had fallen out of love with the sport until his grandson began playing for his old school.

Dixie was cutting the hedge when the boys called to the gate. He was delighted to see them, but not so impressed with Dylan's new spiky haircut.

'Come over here and I'll take the shears to that hair,' he laughed as he invited the boys in for a glass of lemonade.

They all sat around Dixie's kitchen table as the old man opened the bottle and poured out three glasses.

'So, what's new with you, lads?' asked Dixie, before grinning as he turned to Eoin. 'Your mum rang me with your news – congratulations.'

'Thanks, Grandad… do you think I should take it?'

Dixie stared at his grandson, silently, for several seconds.

'Well… I suppose it would be hard for you to switch allegiance to Leinster, but it's too early for that just yet. It's a great opportunity to learn more about rugby, and your own game, and I think you would get a lot out of it. At your age the team you play for is from your own choice, or your parents', and they become the team you love the most and have that passion for. It is a black-and-white issue for you now, but as you get older you start to realise that there are shades of grey in everything and who you play for is one of them.

'I played for Leinster myself, but my greatest friends in rugby were from Limerick and Cork. There are plenty of Leinster lads playing with Munster, and Connacht, and vice versa, and some of the greatest Irish players have even gone to play in France or England.'

'So that's a "yes", is it?' asked Dylan.

'Yes, it is I suppose,' said Dixie. 'It's your decision, Eoin, of course, but I think this is such a great chance for you. And, don't forget, playing for Leinster is a family tradition!'

'Thanks, Grandad. I think I will take it. It won't stop me playing for Munster later on, will it?'

'No, no, no, that's not a problem at all.'

'OK, well do you want any messages done?'

'No, I'm fine for everything, thanks. But hang on there a minute and let me tell you a story.'

Dylan grinned at Eoin and poured himself another drink. Dixie's stories were always interesting, but they did go on for ages.

'You know that big old house just before the corner?' he asked, pointing out the window. 'The one with the weeping willow trees in the garden?'

The boys nodded; the building he was talking about was well-known around the town as 'The Haunted House'.

'When I first came to Ormondstown I got to know the old man who lived there and we became great friends. He was from Russia and called himself Mr Lubov, although that wasn't his real name. He had left Russia after the Revolution in 1917 and had lots of adventures around the world before he came to live in Tipperary. I used to call up to see him every day or two and loved hearing his stories. or going for a spin with him in his sports car. We used to play chess together quite a lot, too. He was very good at it.'

'I'd love to have met him,' said Eoin. 'He sounds really cool. Why did I never hear about him before now?'

'Ah, poor old Lubov was gone before you were born,' smiled Dixie. 'It's such a long time ago.'

He resumed his story. 'Anyway, one day he got very sick and he knew he hadn't long left in the world. He called me up to the house – I remember thinking that the weeping willows were bent even lower, as if they knew he wasn't well – and gave me what he called a farewell present. He said it was a great family treasure that had once been owned by the Tsar, who was the ruler of Russia. He told me that it had been smuggled out of Russia by one of Lubov's sisters, but it had been broken on the journey.

'It's a funny thing – it looks like half a rugby ball. Since it is sort of coloured blue and yellow I thought you might like it – as a new Leinster man.'

Dixie produced a small metal dome, which was just as he described except that it was also studded with jewels.

'I never bothered getting it valued, but I suspect those things that look like jewels are made of glass. Anyway, I was clearing out some old junk and was about to put that in a charity bag when your mother rang with the Leinster news, so I thought it sort of fitted that you have it. I'm not really sure how the Tsar of Russia knew about rugby but he must have been a fan.'

CHAPTER 3

After Eoin and Dylan said goodbye to Dixie they strolled slowly back to the town.

'I suppose Dixie is right,' said Dylan. 'Leinster is better than nothing.'

'Hang on there,' laughed Eoin. 'Better than nothing? Like it or not, this is one of the best clubs in Europe! It's fantastic that they even know my name.'

Dylan shrugged. 'Well I'd NEVER play for them.'

'Wait a minute, Dylan,' laughed Eoin. 'Aren't you from Leinster originally yourself?' he asked, remembering that his pal had actually been born in County Louth.

Dylan went red. 'Oh… I forgot that. Well… I suppose I learned my rugby in Limerick so I can't turn my back on that.'

Eoin smiled and held his hands out wide. 'Well I learned mine in Dublin!'

They reached Eoin's home and parted, agreeing to

meet again after tea. Eoin needed to think, so he slipped upstairs to his bedroom. Kicking off his shoes he lay down on his bed and stared at the ceiling. He tossed around what Dixie had said and decided that he would throw his lot in with Leinster. But he was tired from the training session and soon dozed off.

Eoin was always a bit of a daydreamer, and he was soon picturing himself diving over the try-line wearing the famous blue shirt of Leinster and being shouldered off the field by his team-mates. As he walked off the field carrying the golden European trophy he spotted his old friend, Brian Hanrahan, who called him over.

Brian was a ghost, a rugby player who had died as a result of injuries he received in Lansdowne Road almost a hundred years before. He had become a great friend to Eoin, teaching him lots about rugby and guiding him in the adventures he had got up to since he moved to boarding school in Dublin.

'Well done, Eoin – that was a cracking try,' he said. 'So you've decided to play for Leinster now?'

'Yes, I think so,' replied Eoin. 'I wasn't sure at all, but Grandad said it was a great opportunity and I would miss out if I didn't take it.'

'I think he's right,' replied Brian. 'I had the same

dilemma myself, you know. I was born in Munster but went to school and then worked and played for a club in Leinster. My brother Charlie lived in Cork and played for Munster and Ireland. Shortly before I died I was picked to play in a Junior Interpro for Leinster AGAINST Munster. I wasn't sure what to do at first, but there were a few of my Lansdowne pals on the team and Charlie advised me to play. I was all set, but, well you know what happened just a week before…'

Brian had died when a scrum collapsed and had spent the years since in the Lansdowne Road stadium where the accident happened.

Eoin nodded, but he was distracted by a loud banging. He looked around the stadium and couldn't work out where it was coming from.

'Eoin!' came a shout.

Eoin shook his head and realised he had been dreaming and was now back lying on his bed in Ormondstown. The call was coming from outside the front door and he recognised the voice, which sounded a little angry.

'EOIN!!' called out Dylan, even louder this time.

He banged the door again twice as Eoin went downstairs.

'Alright, alright, I'm coming,' he called before opening the door. 'Sorry about that, I was having a nap. Now what's the emergency?'

'Do you think this is funny?' he snapped, waving an envelope in Eoin's face.

'What… what are you talking about?' replied Eoin, bewildered.

'This… this hoax letter you sent!' Dylan growled, thrusting it towards his friend.

Eoin stared at the envelope and turned it over in his hands. It was a standard white envelope, but his eye couldn't help but be drawn to the bottom corner, in which there was a crest with three crowns and a stag's head, and the words 'Munster Rugby'.

The letter was addressed to Dylan, so Eoin asked, 'Can I read it?'

Dylan nodded.

Dear Dylan,

I have great pleasure in telling you that you have been selected for a Munster Rugby youth academy training camp. It will take place at the University of Limerick on the weekend of July 20-21. Please reply to this by email immediately, letting us know if you will be able to attend, and also notifying us of your shirt size.

'So did you write it? I don't think it's very funny,' snarled Dylan.

'Scout's honour,' said Eoin. 'I swear I didn't do it. It's fantastic news!'

Dylan stopped, not sure whether to smile or not. He had been so convinced it was a mean trick that he had never considered that it might be true.

'Let's check it out,' said Eoin. 'Come in here and we'll ring the Munster branch.'

They dialled the number on the letter and a nice lady answered the call. Dylan explained who he was and how he wasn't sure if the letter he had received was a hoax.

The receptionist asked him to wait and returned a minute later, laughing, to say that the letter was genuine and that he was to send a reply today.

Eoin grinned and patted him on the head. 'And you from County Louth – I wonder do they know that at all?'

CHAPTER 4

The friends threw themselves into rugby practice with renewed energy, going through drills they had learned in school from early morning until it was too dark to see anymore. Eoin wore out the instep on his right boot with the number of kicks at goal he took.

One afternoon during a rare break in training they lay on the grass, staring up at the clouds drifting past.

'It's gas, isn't it, that we're going to be doing the same thing but for different teams on opposite sides of the country at the same time?' said Dylan. 'I wonder is this leading to some sort of interpro Under 15 competition. I've never heard of such a thing.'

'Nah, the Munster lads wouldn't be let near Dublin in case they got frightened by all the traffic,' laughed Eoin.

'Have your laugh, Eoin,' grinned Dylan, 'but at least I'll be able to wear my red Munster shirt with pride around Ormondstown after the weekend. You'll have to put yours in the back of the wardrobe for ever more. Don't even think of wearing that blue one around the town!'

Eoin's face fell. Dylan was right. He started to think how much easier it would have been if Munster had called him up. He loved the red jersey that his grandfather had bought him which, although it was getting a little tight, he wore more often than any other item of clothing he owned.

He didn't have much time to worry about what he would be wearing that autumn, though, as they were interrupted by a familiar voice.

'Hey, lads, you don't look like you're training that hard. I wonder would Leinster give me a trial too.'

Dylan and Eoin clambered to their feet to greet their best friend from Castlerock College.

'Alan!' they shouted together. 'What are you doing here?'

Eoin's mum appeared at their friend's shoulder.

'Alan's mum rang me last week and said he was a bit bored with the summer and suggested we take it in turns to host you all for a few days' sleepovers. I thought I'd keep it a surprise!' she said.

'Ah, that's brilliant, Mam,' said Eoin.

'So what have you been up to, Alan?' asked Dylan.

'Not much. It's a bit boring up in Dublin. All my mates are in Irish college or away on holidays. I was playing tennis with myself up against a wall for about three days when Mam came up with this idea.'

'I'll leave you to it,' said Eoin's mother, 'dinner will be around seven o'clock so no visits to the chipper!'

'Thanks, Mrs Madden,' said Alan, 'I'll keep them all straight and working hard at the rugby.'

The trio laughed – Alan was an enthusiastic player but wasn't very good at all. While Eoin and Dylan had leapt forward through the age groups and were now stars of the Castlerock Junior Cup team, he was still struggling to hold his place on the 14Cs.

They sat around the field chatting for a while, before Eoin and Dylan resumed their session. Alan was happy to help out running after balls and collecting them from the ditches as Eoin took his pot-shots at goal. It was good to be around the guys again.

With meal-time approaching, Alan kept checking his watch and Eoin got the message.

'That's enough for today,' he announced, tucking the ball under his arm.

As they walked back to town they bumped into Mrs Madden, who had a kitbag in her hand.

'I just dropped down to your mum, Dylan, and she

said its fine for you to stay over for the next few days. Here's your pyjamas and a change of clothes for tomorrow.'

'Ah, thanks a lot, Mrs Madden, this will be like going on holidays!'

The three devoured their dinner and started making plans for the next few days. Rugby training couldn't be slackened off, but they had to make time for Alan too. The young Dubliner insisted he was just happy to be in the same town as his buddies.

As Alan lounged on the spare bed in Eoin's room – with Dylan on the blow-up mattress on the floor – he spotted the ornament that Dixie had presented to his grandson.

'What's that thing?' he asked.

'It's some sort of broken rugby ball,' said Eoin. 'An old Russian lad gave it to Dixie years ago and he just gave it to me. I think he was making a joke about it being blue and me playing for Leinster. I think it's more green than blue.'

Eoin told Alan about the old house beside where his grandfather lived and the rumours that it was haunted.

'A real haunted house? We have to go there – NOW!' said Alan, who was a great fan of scary stories and horror movies.

Eoin looked at Dylan and nodded. 'Well… I suppose it would do no harm. It won't be dark for ages so we'll be safe enough,' he said.

The trio scurried out of the house and trotted up towards Dixie's house. The old man's car wasn't in the drive so they kept going, stopping when they reached the gates of the nearest big house.

Eoin had no fear of ghosts. He knew that visitors from the spirit world didn't wear white sheets and go 'woooo-wooooo' like those in films. He had encountered four ghosts around Castlerock since he started in the school and all had been just ordinary men, although some had done extraordinary things.

But even though he didn't feel scared of what might be inside, the way the old house appeared made Eoin and his pals slow down. Although it was a bright, warm, summer's evening, as soon as they stepped through the broken-down iron gates it seemed to grow a little darker, and a little colder.

CHAPTER 5

The Lubov house was built with dark stone and the windows were covered with shutters that had once been white. The front door had been broken off its hinges and hung at an angle, so that the whole structure looked like a face that was slightly twisted and screaming in agony.

Dylan and Eoin exchanged glances, and Eoin could see that his friend was nervous.

'Are you sure you want to go in, Dyl?' he asked.

'Yeah, sure what's the worst thing that could happen?' said Dylan.

'Well, I suppose we could caught in the crossfire between Frankenstein and the Mummy,' laughed Alan, 'And get eaten alive by zombies as we try to escape.'

Dylan went another shade whiter, regretting all the scary films he had watched with his sister.

Eoin led the trio up the driveway, which was overgrown by brambles, and past a dusty red sports car whose four tyres were flat and had begun to rot.

'What a waste,' said Dylan, 'That was a serious car in its day.'

They stopped at the front door and peered into the hallway.

'The floorboards might be unsafe…' said Eoin.

He pressed his foot to the floor and found it sturdy. He clambered through the gap where the door hung and called back to his pals.

'It's grand,' he said, 'The floorboards are all in place and they seem fine. We'll need to open the shutters to get some light in, though.'

Eoin crossed the hallway into the main room and threw back the shutters in a cloud of dust and scrambling spiders.

Alan and Dylan followed him slowly, peering over their shoulders into every dark corner.

The house had obviously been cleaned out of anything valuable, but some rickety pieces of furniture remained. There were large white spaces on the wall where paintings had once hung.

'This must have been an amazing place when it was lived in,' said Alan. 'He must have been a very rich old man.'

Eoin told him the rest of the story, explaining that the little rugby ball had once been owned by the ruler of Russia. 'Mr Lubov must have been very well connected. He certainly had some amazing stories. Grandad really enjoyed the chats they had together.'

'I wonder is there any more treasure about the place,' said Dylan.

'I'd say it's long gone,' said Alan. 'It looks like anything half-decent was taken away or robbed.'

They wandered into the last of the downstairs rooms, where a piano had collapsed in on itself after a chandelier had fallen on top.

Eoin opened a shutter to get a better look at the room. He noticed that something thin and flat was lying on the mantelpiece and walked over to pick it up.

'What's that, Eoin?' asked Dylan.

'It looks like a photo frame,' he replied. 'It's covered in dust though.'

Eoin crossed back over to the window and wiped his sleeve across the glass that covered the picture. He stared at the photograph which was brown and stained with age, but the most surprising thing was that it was of a man dressed in a white jersey and shorts running with a rugby ball clutched to his chest under his huge right hand. His flicked-back hair rippled in the wind as he ran, and he looked as if he was just about to touch down for a try as the opposition chased him in vain.

'Is that an English shirt?' asked Dylan as his friends peered over his shoulder at the picture.

'I think you're right, Dyl,' replied Eoin. 'I think I can see a rose on the chest there.'

'I wonder what that's doing here,' asked Alan. 'I thought your man was Russian.'

'Yeah, and no one ever heard of Russia playing rugby, did they?' said Dylan. 'Sure the snow would make it impossible.'

'Ah now, it's not all snow in Russia, I believe,' laughed Eoin.

'And Ireland played them in the World Cup in 2011,' chipped in Alan. 'We won 62-12 and Keith Earls got two tries.'

Eoin and Dylan stared at their pal. 'For a fellow that can't play rugby, you know an awful lot about it,' Dylan quipped.

As they moved to leave the room, Eoin stopped in his tracks and held up his index finger, pointing at the ceiling.

'Something's moving around upstairs,' he whispered.

'Probably rats, or a cat,' said Dylan, acting braver than he felt.

'Sure we've seen everything we want to see, no point delaying any longer,' said Alan, now very keen to leave the spooky mansion.

Eoin was the bravest, however, and walked to the foot of the tall, wide staircase that led to the upper floor of the Lubov home.

It was getting darker outside, and there were fewer windows allowing light into the giant hallway. But Eoin was sure he could see some movement at the top of the stairs. He took one step upwards as a figure came into view. There on the wide landing stood a man in all-white rugby gear, with a bright red rose sewn into the chest.

Eoin called out, 'Who are you?'

The man stopped and stared down the stairs at Eoin. Silently, he turned and slowly walked away.

Eoin considered following him, but as Dylan and Alan had both backed away quickly and were now clambering noisily through the front door, he decided against it. He looked back as he made his own exit and saw the figure raise a right hand in farewell. Eoin did the same then jogged after his pals, catching up as they reached the road outside.

'Who was that?' gasped Alan.

'Was it another ghost?' asked Dylan.

'I'm not sure,' replied Eoin, 'probably. But one thing I am sure of is this – your man on the staircase is the player in that old photo.'

CHAPTER 6

The boys ran home as quickly as they could and slipped into the front room, where they sat silently.

'Is everything OK?' asked Mrs Madden as she popped her head around the door.

'All fine,' said Eoin. 'We were just out for a run up by Grandad's,' he added, omitting some important details.

'I'll drop you in a drink and a snack, then,' she announced before departing for the kitchen.

'That was all a bit weird,' said Dylan. 'I wonder if it was a ghost – Alan and I were able to see them when we were with you before, too.'

'I don't know,' admitted Eoin. 'I must ask Grandad does he know any more about Mr Lubov – and that rugby player too…'

He stopped talking as his mum entered with a glass of orange squash and a granola bar for each of the boys.

'I hope today wasn't too boring for you, Alan,' she said.

'These two are rugby mad and they spend all their time at it. Hopefully you'll find something else to put the colour back in your cheeks. You *do* look a little pale…'

'I'm fine, Mrs M, thanks. There's plenty to do around Ormondstown, it seems.'

'Really?' she replied. 'Well that's good. I'll leave you to it.'

'Do you think she suspected anything?' asked Dylan after Mrs Madden had closed the door.

'Nah, she hadn't a clue. And we didn't do too much wrong anyway besides trespassing in an old house that nobody owns,' said Alan.

'Well, unless you count this as stealing,' gulped Eoin, as he took the brown, fading photograph out of his back pocket.

'Aha,' started Dylan, with a big grin on his face. 'I'm not sure what else you can call it, Mr Goody Two-Shoes!'

Eoin went red. 'Ah, that's unfair, I'm no Goody Two-Shoes!'

'Well you certainly aren't now,' quipped Alan, 'But seriously, what are you going to do with it? You can't leave it back there.'

'But I can't ask Dixie about it either, can I? I suppose I could say I borrowed it?'

'From who?' asked Dylan, with a grin.

Eoin was embarrassed and slipped the photo into his pocket once more.

'Alright, I'm off to bed,' he snapped. 'See you in the morning.'

The next day was too wet for the boys to practise rugby so they lounged around the house watching DVDs of old matches that Dixie had given Eoin for Christmas. Eoin had a good eye for spotting moves and had already learned some interesting things about tactics and how the game had changed. Alan was just as keen, but Dylan bored easily and wanted to be outdoors.

'Anyone fancy a return trip to the haunted house? We could bring torches this time and maybe a weapon or two.'

'What would we need a weapon for?' asked Alan. 'Sure if it was a ghost we wouldn't be able to hurt him, and if it was a human then we'd be better off running as fast as we could. Anyway, he didn't seem too interested in talking to us last night.'

'He never got a chance to talk because you pair were gone quicker than a snowflake on a pizza,' laughed Eoin.

Alan blushed. 'I'd like to go back. Sure what harm

could we do?'

Eoin paused the DVD. 'I don't know, I think we should keep out of there for the moment. We don't want to risk doing ourselves an injury ahead of the Leinster and Munster things.'

Dylan nodded slowly. 'Yeah, I suppose you're right. You'd look pretty stupid ringing up the Leinster branch saying you broke an ankle exploring a haunted house. They wouldn't be ringing you back in a hurry.'

Eoin switched the rugby back on. 'Look at this break by O'Driscoll, Dyl, he leaves the French fella sitting on the ground. That'll be you in a red shirt in a couple of years, wiping grass stains off your shorts.'

Dylan threw a cushion across the room, catching Alan on the back of the head.

Alan turned and fired his half-eaten chocolate bar at Dylan, and the three soon collapsed into a friendly scrum as they wrestled across the bean bags that covered the floor.

CHAPTER 7

The days flew by while Alan was around, and the trio got up to plenty of fun without risking life and limb. Eoin's trip to the Leinster academy meant Alan's holiday was nearly over.

They could tell Dylan was getting nervous about his own rugby camp as he had been getting more and more cranky as the days drew nearer.

'Hey, Eoin, I'll tell the Savage brothers you were asking how the knitting lessons were going,' he snarled one morning as they walked back to Eoin's house from training. 'And I'm sure Curry Ryan will be glad to hear you've joined the dark side.'

Eoin wasn't worried about what his old Ormondstown national school mates thought of his switch, but he was getting fed up of Dylan's constant baiting of him and his new province. He was happy he had made the right decision to take up Leinster's offer, and anyway,

Munster hadn't bothered to ask him either.

'Listen, Dylan,' he growled back. 'I'm delighted you got the Munster call-up. They obviously think you're a far better player than me. And if that's what their academy thinks, then it is obviously the best academy to be in,' he smiled. 'So best of luck with that.'

Dylan was even more incensed. 'You think this is funny? This is some excuse to be sarcastic? This is Munster ye're talking about. It's no joke! I *know* you're a better player than me, but I'm going to take my chances and turn myself into a top star.'

Eoin wasn't sure whether he should smile or keep a serious face, but in the end, as Alan made a face behind Dylan, he just spluttered out a laugh. Dylan leapt at him, fists flying, and connected one with his eyebrow before Eoin pushed him away and Alan held him back. Eoin put his hand up to his face and felt the sore spot where Dylan had made contact. He checked his fingertips and was angry to see a few drops of smeared blood.

'What did you do that for, you muppet?' roared Eoin.

Dylan had calmed down and now looked at Eoin with a horrified expression.

'Oh no, I didn't mean to cut you,' he moaned.

Eoin jogged ahead home and seethed as his mother mopped up the cut and applied a plaster.

'It was just horseplay,' he lied. 'I hope there isn't a scar, or the Leinster coaches might think I'm some sort of trouble maker.'

'Sure cuts and bruises are like medals to rugby players,' said his grandfather, who had just come into the kitchen. 'Though I'm not sure how you could have got that when all you were practising today was your goal-kicking,' he added, with a grin.

'Hi, Grandad,' said Eoin, blushing. 'We're off to Dublin tomorrow. Were you really watching us practise?'

'I was. Barney made me a nice cup of tea and we hid in his shed watching you through the cracks between the planks. You took forty-four kicks at goal and put thirty-eight of them over. And you hit the crossbar once, which counts as a miss.'

'Ah, but the GAA posts are narrower,' Eoin protested.

'True, but the crossbar is lower too,' Dixie replied, smiling at his grandson. 'That's a very good kicking record, and I liked the way you varied your kicking position and distance. You've worked very hard to get that good.'

Alan arrived at the kitchen door. 'Hi, Dixie, nice to see you,' he said. 'We were going to ask you about the Russian man and his house.'

Eoin bowed his head, still embarrassed about taking away the old photo.

'Gosh, I'm not sure I remember much. It was such a long time ago and no one has been near the house for years.'

'Did he ever talk to you about rugby?' Eoin asked.

'I don't think so,' said Dixie, 'although I didn't like to talk about it myself in those days either. I just don't believe the subject ever came up...' Dixie paused, scratching his head. 'Actually, I think he mentioned it once – way, way back when I got to know him first. He told me his family name, which was about eight unpronounceable names with lots of hyphens and dozens of syllables. He asked me did I recognise one of the names, as it was well known in rugby circles, but I couldn't always understand his thick accent and the name meant nothing to me. Is this something to do with that blue rugby ball trophy I gave you?'

Eoin looked away. 'Yes, I suppose so,' he said. 'I was wondering did he have any interest in the game.'

Dixie looked at Eoin, puzzled. 'Well, no, like I said, we never once discussed it.'

The old man stood up and walked to the door. 'I was just dropping in to say goodbye and good luck. I'm off to visit the garden centre near Limerick tomorrow so I won't be around. I'll talk to you when you get back.'

41

CHAPTER 8

His holiday over, Alan returned to Dublin the next day courtesy of Mr Madden, who offered to bring him home while he was leaving Eoin to UCD. Having Alan in the car took Eoin's mind off the weekend ahead and stopped him getting too nervous. They dropped his pal home first, and Eoin promised he'd phone him on Sunday night.

The car was silent as Mr Madden steered it into the university grounds to the place where the players had been asked to meet.

'Here we are,' said his dad as they reached the Leinster Rugby building.

HMr Madden ruffled Eoin's hair and checked he had enough credit in his phone to ring his mum that night. 'Go show them that classic Castlerock style – but don't forget the Munster passion,' he grinned.

From the boot Eoin lugged his kitbag, which was

adorned with the crest of his school. As he waved good-bye to his dad he spotted another boy arriving, this one carrying a bag which showed he played for St Osgur's, who had been one of the main rivals of Castlerock in recent years. Eoin nodded at the boy, who recognised him, and said hello.

They walked into the building, where they met a couple of coaches with clipboards and saw a long line of huge blue kitbags with the white and yellow logo of the recent European champions embroidered upon them.

'Eoin Madden and Killian Nicholson, your names are on your bags in alphabetical order so you two are along there,' the first coach said, pointing.

'How did you know who I am?' asked Killian.

'We know who *everyone* is here,' the coach replied. 'And we know everything about you too. I know you got an A in History in your summer exams, Mr Madden, and that you failed French, Mr Nicholson. And I also know you haven't got your school report yet so I've ruined your day. Sorry. Collect your bag there and move out into the car park. There is a bus waiting and we'll be leaving as soon as the last of you lot arrive.'

The boys walked over to the line of kitbags and picked up those with their own names embroidered just under the Leinster crest.

'Cool,' said Eoin, admiring the bag.

'What on earth is in it?' asked Killian, as he tried to lift it up.

The boys looked inside and were delighted to see a huge range of shirts, t-shirts, polos, shorts, socks, drink bottles and other items. Eoin fished around and pulled out two pairs of boots, which were just his size.

The coach called out their names again and jerked his thumb in the direction of the door, so they hauled the bags onto their shoulders and left quickly.

'That's an amazing amount of kit,' chuckled Killian. 'They've even given me a scrum cap and I play on the wing!'

'Here, I'm going to stick my own school kitbag inside,' said Eoin. 'It looks so tiny compared to this monster.'

Killian did the same, but when they stood up a tall blond-haired boy in a black tracksuit proclaiming he was from Dodder Woods was laughing at them.

'Embarrassed what school you're from, eh? You must be the saps from Castlerock and St Osgur's then,' he sneered.

Eoin stared at the boy, who looked like he enjoyed using the fact that he was taller than almost everyone else in his year. Dodder Woods had a reputation for looking down on other schools, but he seemed even more obnoxious than that.

They walked past him without a word, tucked their bags into the stowing area of the bus and climbed aboard.

'Eoin Madden!' came a roar as he climbed up the steps into the coach.

Eoin was confused, and he searched the sea of faces for a familiar one. All he could think was how he wouldn't need to be introduced to his team-mates – everyone knew his name now.

'Here!' came a second call as he spotted Rory's red hair and familiar cheeky grin.

He shuffled down the aisle, avoiding the gaze of the other players, most of whom knew his name already from his heroic performance in the Junior Cup Final, which was shown on one of the satellite TV channels.

Rory was seated next to another member of the Castlerock team, Charlie Johnston, and Eoin slipped into the seat behind and gestured at Killian to follow.

Eoin introduced them all and they spent the next few minutes discussing what they had been up to so far that summer.

'It's great to have a few guys from the school along,' said Charlie. 'I was terrified to tell anyone or contact you in case I was the only one.'

Killian turned to look out the window.

'Are you the only Osgur's player?' asked Eoin.

'It looks like it,' said Killian. 'Our best player broke his leg playing soccer last week.'

'Want to hang out with the Rock boys?' asked Rory. 'We're not fussy.'

Eoin laughed. 'Of course we're fussy, and Killian is more than welcome. I wonder where we're going to on the bus.'

'I hope we're staying in some big, swanky hotel with a pool and room service,' said Charlie.

'I bet we're staying in tents in a field up the mountains,' moaned Rory.

Neither boy was right, as they discovered not long after the bus pulled out of the university sports ground. It was a short, ten-minute drive to their destination and the academy head coach, Ted, winked at Eoin as they pulled through the gates and up the driveway. There in front of them was a large grey building with a stone inscription over the door which read '*Victoria Concordia Crescit*' – Latin for 'victory comes from harmony.'

Home for the weekend would be Castlerock College.

CHAPTER 9

Charlie laughed and Rory groaned as they got off the bus. A second bus was also parked in the driveway and more boys were getting off and collecting their gear.

'I didn't think we'd be back so soon,' chuckled Eoin as they went to collect the bags and make their way to the main hall where the coaches were waiting.

Ted, was at the top of the hall waiting for the boys to settle down.

'Alright everybody, welcome to the Leinster Academy, and I am delighted that every single one of you we invited was able to come, except poor Ben from St Osgur's, who we hope recovers very soon.'

Ted went through a few ground rules for the weekend, and reminded them what a great honour it was to play for Leinster. He explained how and why they had been selected, and that they were now what he called 'in

47

the system' with Leinster.

'You will still continue to play with your school or club, but your rugby will be monitored by Leinster Rugby from now until you leave school in four years' time. The very best of you at that stage, those who we believe have a future in the professional game, will be offered a chance to continue playing with this great club.

'There are ninety-nine of you here this evening, the cream of schoolboy rugby in the province. Each summer until you leave school we will invite most of you back for training and assessment. We will teach you drills and exercises for you to take back to your school or club. And once a year we will select a team from the best of you to take part in an international tournament.'

He pointed at a line of men and women in blue track-suits standing alongside him. 'On Sunday afternoon these coaches here will sit down and select the thirty-three or so boys we will be bringing to Twickenham at the end of August, where they will play in a prestigious week-long European event.'

The boys *ooh*-ed and *aah*-ed at this news, and Charlie whispered aloud, 'I definitely want to be in that team!'

'That means one in every three of you will be going to London, so that's pretty good incentive to work hard and show us what you are capable of tomorrow,' continued

Ted. 'This evening I want you to relax, go for a short run inside the grounds if you like, but get to bed early.

'Tomorrow you will be served breakfast at 7.30am and, fully dressed for the academy session, you will be taken by coach back to Belfield at 8.30am sharp. Anyone late for either of those appointments can pack their bag and head home – there's a bus stop just outside the gates.'

Ted dismissed the boys, who started forming little groups, almost all confined to the schools they attended during the year. The coach went back to the top of the hall and called them to order once again.

'I apologise, I forgot to mention that you will be staying in dormitories in the next building. You have each been allocated a room and will not be sharing with anyone from your school or club. It is important this weekend that you meet new people and make friends from other schools. This isn't about being rivals for Rostipp or St Xavier's – it's about becoming teammates for Leinster.'

After a buffet meal the boys wandered out of the hall and Eoin pointed out a few of the landmarks of Castlerock to Killian.

'Let's go to find out where we're sleeping,' suggested Rory.

'Fire ahead,' said Eoin. 'I just want to go for a walk. I've a phone call to make.'

Eoin jogged down to the quiet corner of the school grounds where a small stream flowed and where he often went to get away from it all. He sat on the large rock which had the rather obvious nickname of 'The Rock', and clicked on his mother's telephone number. He explained to her how the day had gone, and how funny it was that the sleeping quarters were in Castlerock. He promised to do all those things that his mum always made him promise when he was away from home, like brush his teeth, eat his vegetables, take regular showers and wear his mouth guard while playing rugby.

'You'll be glad to know I have a brand new mouth guard, Mam. It's blue with a Leinster logo on it – as is almost everything I've seen this weekend besides the tomatoes we had for tea.'

They made their farewells and Eoin sat back on The Rock for a moment.

'I hear you rustling around in there, come on out and say hello,' he laughed.

A man dressed in rugby gear with a black, red and yellow hooped shirt pushed his way through the bushes.

'Howya, Brian,' said Eoin. 'Bit of an early return to school for me this summer, eh?'

'I was wondering was it you – what's happened?'

Eoin explained about his selection and why he was back at Castlerock.

'And would you believe I had a dream about you too?' he told Brian.

Brian grinned. 'Was it about whether you should take up the Leinster offer or hold out for a better one with Munster?'

'Yeah…' replied Eoin, puzzled.

'That was no dream,' Brian laughed. 'One afternoon I found myself back on the pitch at Lansdowne Road getting asked this question and next thing I was standing beside your bed in Tipp. I gave my answer, but I could see you were half asleep so I didn't wake you up, and I left immediately.'

Eoin blushed.

'Really? I must have been talking in my sleep again. I took your advice anyway, as you can see, and no regrets so far. What's new with you?'

'Nothing much,' said Brian. 'It's all been quiet since the drama with Kevin and Eugene. They cleaned out that room, I see.'

The previous term Eoin had helped to solve a mystery

involving a hidden room, an abandoned arms cache and a tragic hero, which dated back almost a century at Castlerock.

'Yeah, I wonder if they have sealed up the trapdoor and the secret passage too?'

CHAPTER 10

oin wandered back to the dormitory building and met Killian coming down the steps.

'We're in together,' he grinned, 'but I never heard of the other guys – do you know Conor O'Sullivan and Marcus McCord?'

'Oh, no!' said Eoin. 'McCord is that big blond lad we met coming in earlier. I remember hearing about him. He's from Dodder Woods School and is well known as a bit of a loudmouth.'

'Oh. Well, it's only for two nights and we'll keep out of his way,' said Killian. 'Do you fancy going for a run?'

Eoin agreed, and after dropping his bag up to the dorm and locking the door the pair set off on a tour of Castlerock.

'Is it good crack being in boarding school?' asked Killian as they circled the rugby field.

'It has its advantages, I suppose,' replied Eoin, 'but you

do miss your home comforts and the food is sometimes pretty horrible. I'd never had to share a room before, although I was lucky that I got on well with the rest of them most of the time.'

'Our school is a bit boring really,' said Killian. 'The lads and teachers are grand, but unless you play rugby you just go home at half past three. It's in the middle of the city and nearly everyone has to get a bus or a train home. I'd love the crack of a boarding school.'

Eoin smiled. 'Well, there's many a night I wish I could get a quick bus home. But you're right about the crack. There's a few great characters here like Charlie that make it easier.'

'What do you think of this trip to London?' Killian asked. 'I don't think I've much chance looking at the rest of the left wingers here. They'll definitely go for Shay from St Xavier's, or maybe the lad from Clontarf.'

'I'd say you'd have as good a chance as anyone. They're going to be looking at everyone in a new light and if you put your heart into it you'll surely have as much of a chance as anyone.'

The boys rounded off their run with a warm-down and headed back upstairs to their dorm, which was on the same corridor as the room Eoin had slept in during the previous school year.

'This was Richie Duffy's old room,' Eoin remembered as he neared the door, which was wide open and the source of the loud, pulsing music that had drawn several other boys out of their rooms to see where it was coming from.

Lying on the bed nearest the door was Marcus McCord, with a music player sitting on his chest turned up to maximum volume.

'Good sounds, eh?' he roared as Eoin and Killian made their way gingerly past his bed. Eoin shrugged and turned his back on the noise.

'What's your problem?' called out McCord as he turned off the music and leapt out of bed.

'No problem, I just don't like the music,' Eoin replied.

'There's nothing wrong with the music,' barked McCord as he pulled himself up to his full height just so he could look down on Eoin.

Eoin shrugged again, not wanting to take the disagreement any further. 'Fair enough,' he said, and started to dig into his kitbag for his toothbrush.

'Just watch yourself, Madden,' growled McCord. 'You might be a big star in this kip of a school, but you're with the big boys now. You'll be mincemeat this time tomorrow if you don't keep out of my way.'

Eoin sighed and got ready for bed. He didn't need

any extra stress this weekend and McCord was already a headache.

He chatted to the third boy in the room, Conor O'Sullivan; he was a nice lad, but he kept glancing nervously at McCord.

'Don't mind him,' whispered Eoin. 'He's all mouth. I know his type.'

Later, as he lay in bed, McCord started up the music again. Eoin looked over at Killian, who had put a pillow over his ears to try to block out the din. The lights-out call came, but still the relentless beat went on. There was no point asking him to turn it down.

Eoin slept badly, and when he woke in the middle of the night the music was still blaring. He got up and walked over to McCord's bed and he was even more annoyed to see the big Dodder Woods player was fast asleep, wearing thick yellow earplugs. He pulled the cable from the music player out of the wall and jumped back into bed, desperate for sleep ahead of what would be a huge day for him.

Next morning Eoin had to force himself to get out of bed in time for breakfast. He knew he hadn't got anywhere near the full nine hours he had got used to having since school ended, but he would get a good breakfast and try to tackle the day with gusto. He prodded Killian in the ribs – his new friend was just as reluctant to get up.

'Has that music stopped yet?' he asked.

Eoin looked over to where McCord was snoring.

'Yeah, and it didn't keep *him* awake at all,' Eoin growled, pointing at the earplugs.

Eoin called up Conor and they all got ready quickly and headed downstairs.

'With a bit of luck he'll be late and they'll throw him off the program,' chuckled Killian.

The boys collected their breakfasts in the canteen and were tucking in when the door burst open and Marcus McCord stormed in, with just one minute to spare before the clock reached 7.30am.

He glowered at the trio he was sharing a room with.

'Thanks for waking me up, guys!' he snorted. 'Think you were being clever? Nice try, suckers. I had two alarms on my phone so I wouldn't be caught out.'

'But how could you hear them through the earplugs?' asked Killian.

McCord was speechless for a second, then turned his back on them and headed up to the food counter.

CHAPTER 11

The boys were quiet on the bus to Belfield, with most of them apprehensive about the day ahead. Rory tried to strike up a conversation, but Eoin ignored him, buried in his thoughts and the type of nerves that always seemed to get to him before big games for Castlerock.

As they arrived at the university sports grounds they were confronted with a sea of plastic cones as far as the eye could see, and what looked like fifty men and women in blue tracksuits carrying clipboards.

As they climbed down from the buses and gathered on the field, Ted gestured to the boys to gather around him. He welcomed them again and filled them in a bit more on what was expected of them that day, before splitting them up into groups of ten, each working with four coaches.

Eoin enjoyed the little drills and games that were

organised, but found the shuttle tests and press-ups a lot less fun. Everything the players did was measured and noted down on those clipboards.

After an hour or so, each player was grouped according to his position so Eoin went to join the out-halves. He recognised some of the players he had come up against over the past season or two, and there were a few nods of respect between them. Despite what Ted had said about everyone becoming friends and fellow Leinster men, when it came down to it this weekend was about stealing a march on the other players in your position. These were the six guys who wanted to make the No.10 shirt their own and Eoin was in their way.

A former Leinster and Ireland out-half came over to talk to them, filling them with praise for the skills that had got them to this session, but hammering home that they would have to work a lot harder to get on in the sport. He made a good point that the game was getting harder and faster and they needed to work more on their fitness than he had at their age. He told them a couple of stories from his own playing days, which didn't mean an awful lot to Eoin or the other guys, but they indulged him with a laugh when he was finished.

Ted came over and introduced the players to a few new drills and talked about developing their techniques for receiving and giving passes. He called over the scrum-halves and got the players to operate as little teams, running pass races to see who could be the quickest and most accurate.

Eoin found the new approach very interesting and made lots of mental notes for how he could bring these drills back to his sessions with Dylan, and to Castlerock too. The morning went far quicker than he expected, with a half-hour lunch break spent lying flat on his back staring at the sky, trying to rest his body.

While they refuelled with bananas, energy bars and litres of water, Eoin caught sight of Rory and Charlie holding each other up after a gruelling session in the sun.

'Keep going, guys, it's the same for everyone. Make sure you drink lots of water,' he called out. Rory tried to grin but opted to save his energy for the afternoon, while Charlie guzzled down a litre of water in one go.

By the end of the afternoon session every single one of the ninety-nine players was flat out on the grass. Ted went around between them, grinning at their exhaustion but also checking they weren't too distressed by their exertions.

'OK, that's it for today and well done to everyone. There was some serious work done today and while some of you are really coming up to the mark, everyone is still in with a strong chance of making our squad for Twickenham.

'Tomorrow morning we'll have another session measuring your performance and then we'll run three fifteen-a-side games in which everyone will get a chance to earn their place. We'll head back now to Castlerock to change and after dinner we'll all go on an outing.'

The thought of going out on the town filled Eoin with dread, as he had already made mental plans for an early night to try to catch up on the sleep that he had lost the night before. Killian sighed, too, as they climbed aboard the bus.

'I won't be able to play tomorrow unless I get a decent sleep,' he groaned. 'Is there any way we can persuade him not to put on that music…'

Eoin smiled. 'I doubt he'll listen to us, but I do have a plan.'

When they got back up to Castlerock Eoin winked at Killian and hared off up the stairs to the dorm ahead of everyone else. By the time his three room-mates had arrived he was lying on his bed with his eyes closed.

'Well how did you losers do today?' bawled McCord. 'I see Madden is already showing that he hasn't got the stamina for it.'

Marcus chuckled to himself as he went to the locker.

'This is no time for sleeping! We need to get the sounds on and the energy up for our night out—'

He stopped dead and swung the locker door open. 'Which one of you muppets stole my sounds?' he roared.

Killian couldn't help looking at Eoin who was by now sitting up staring at McCord.

'Nobody stole your sounds,' Eoin said. 'How could we? We've all been out all day and the door was locked until two minutes ago when I got here. You were following me and there's no other way out but the corridor. We're in a dead end.'

McCord checked all the lockers and wardrobes, and under the beds, turning purple with anger and frustration as he realised Eoin was right.

'I'm going to find Ted to sort this out,' he whined, storming out the door.

Eoin grinned at his room-mates. 'Ted will laugh him out of it,' he said.

'Did you have anything to do with this?' asked Conor. 'How could you have hidden it?'

Eoin winked. 'There's nothing like a bit of local knowledge,' he said.

CHAPTER 12

As Eoin predicted, Ted didn't want to know about the mystery of Marcus McCord's missing music machine. The coach was more interested in getting the ninety-nine young rugby stars fed and into the buses for their outing.

'We're going to a bowling alley,' he announced.

'But I'm useless at cricket,' moaned Rory.

'Not that type of bowling,' Ted laughed. 'Ten-pin bowling. It's a good way to relax and get to know your teammates. We'll have a little competition with a trophy and prizes for the winners.'

The mention of the word 'competition' was enough to stoke up the majority of the boys.

At the bowling alley they changed their shoes and Ted organised them into teams. Eoin had never played the game before but quickly got the hang of it. Killian was quite an expert and coached his other team-mates skilfully while scoring highly himself.

As the competition drew towards a close, Eoin and Killian's team were in second place. Ted announced they would have to play a final game against the leaders, who included Marcus McCord.

The tall loudmouth laughed when he saw who he was up against in the final, and high-fived his team before the game began.

He was so confident that he bought a hotdog to celebrate. He held it above his head like a trophy and squirted some ketchup on the sausage before tossing the sachet on the ground. He was still guzzling the hotdog while he bowled his first ball.

By the time the last round was coming to an end, Killian's team were ahead by three pins, but McCord had one more turn. As he moved to take his shot, Eoin noticed that the sachet of ketchup had stuck to the sole of his shoe. Eoin could see what was going to happen next – and even considered calling him back – but he knew that it would be McCord's own fault.

The loudmouth stepped into the lane to fire down the ball, but as he put his weight on his left foot – and the sticky sauce – it flew from under him, and he skidded head first down the alley towards the pins, wailing as he went. Mercifully he stopped before he recorded a strike with his head, but he had to let go of the ball and it ran harmlessly down the side gully.

McCord found his feet and stormed back up to where the players – even his own team – were laughing at him. 'Who put that there?' he howled, blaming his woes on everyone but himself. 'Was it you, Madden?'

Eoin shrugged and smiled. 'I think there was only one person eating hotdogs all evening…'

McCord turned and left the alley, leaving Ted open-mouthed at his behaviour.

'Well, I hope he is a better loser on the rugby pitch,' said the coach, before presenting Killian with a trophy that looked suspiciously like the replica European Champions Cup that sat in the Leinster Rugby offices.

'You can't keep that,' he laughed. 'But your team can keep these,' he added, before handing them each a carrier bag filled with even more Leinster goodies such as baseball caps, DVDs and a season ticket for all the province's home games.

'Cool,' said Andrew Jacks, who played for Springdale Secondary and was one of the best of the scrum-halves at the training camp.

Killian looked as if he was already starting to regret winning the trophy. 'Your man will be unbearable now,' he said.

'Not as unbearable as he would have been if his team had won the trophy though,' chuckled Eoin.

Killian was right though, and the double setback of losing his music player and the bowling prize had put Marcus in a particularly foul mood. He stomped around the dormitory, looking in every corner and under every sheet where he had searched five times before.

'If I find that one of you has stolen it, you'll be so sorry,' he thundered.

His three room-mates kept their thoughts to themselves and, quite exhausted, slipped into their beds and were asleep in seconds.

Eoin was woken up around 7am by a muffled noise t like the sound made by a tiger if an elephant was standing on its tail.

'That's the music player,' hissed Killian under his breath. 'Where is it coming from?'

Eoin grinned. 'It's under the floor,' he whispered. 'There's a secret passage that starts in this room. I hid the noise-maker down there. It must have been set to go off to wake him up at this time every day to that racket.'

Eoin hopped out of bed and went to the back of the room where he flipped up a trapdoor that was partly hidden by a curtain. 'Sssshh,' he gestured at Killian, 'you stay there and let me know if he wakes up.'

Eoin descended the steps into the room below, picked up the squawking device and hit its snooze button. He carried it back upstairs and carefully placed it under McCord's bed before returning to close the trapdoor and slipping back under his own duvet.

Two minutes later the music started again and McCord sat up with a start.

'What's that, what's that…' he called out.

'There's your sound system,' yawned Eoin. 'You mustn't have looked under your own bed.'

McCord hopped out of bed and picked up the player, looking confused. 'But… but…' he said, trying to start an argument with himself. 'I'm sure I checked under there.'

The other boys got out of bed and dressed silently, before heading down to breakfast. It was only when they left the room and were well down the corridor that they dared to laugh.

CHAPTER 13

The final morning of the training camp was less intensive, but the men and women with the clipboards were still buzzing around making notes. Ted and his coaching team went to each of the groups, which were split up again by positions, showing them a series of drills they could do on their own to sharpen their skills.

At the end of the sessions Ted gathered the boys all together and explained that each of the exercises he had shown them would be detailed in the log book they would be given at the end of the day. In the book they were to record the amount of exercise they did, and the games they played. Also to be recorded were any injuries and illnesses, and any extended breaks from training. He told them that becoming a professional rugby player required great effort and commitment on top of the skills that they already possessed, and the academy would need to monitor how much work each player was putting in.

After a break for lunch the teams for the three trial games were posted on a board. Eoin was out-half on the team called the Wolfhounds.

'That's a cool name,' said Rory, 'a lot better than my team… the Hedgehogs!'

Eoin laughed as Charlie explained that each of the teams was called after one of the limited range of Irish mammals available. 'There's the Squirrels, the Foxes, the Badgers and the Elks – and that last crowd are extinct.'

Charlie looked a bit glum when he realised he would be lining up behind Marcus McCord in the Foxes' pack, but not as glum as Killian, who was upset that he hadn't been selected on any of the six teams.

'I've no chance of getting to Twickenham now,' he sighed.

'Don't give up just yet,' said Eoin. 'They said everyone will get at least half a game so you'll get called up some-where. Keep warm and supple and be ready for the call.'

Ted called them all to attention, and announced that Squirrels would be playing Badgers, Elks would take on Hedgehogs, and Foxes would play the Wolfhounds.

Eoin grinned nervously and patted Charlie on the back. 'Go easy on me Chaz. I promise I won't make you look too bad when you miss your tackles.'

The groups broke up and Eoin jogged over to where his new team-mates were gathered. One of the Academy coaches had taken over and was explaining how he wanted the team to play. The coaches had kept together the famous triplets Seán, Tom and Ultan Nolan who made up the front row of the Wicklow College Junior Cup team, and Eoin knew a few of his new teammates to see from previous games. Andrew Jacks was scrum-half and the two had a chat to sort out how the most crucial partnership on the team would work.

Eoin wasn't too worried about McCord – the Dodder Woods second row wasn't quick enough to be a problem for him, but he knew he would have to keep an eye on him. The first few minutes of the game were nervous and scrappy as players struggled to get to know their team-mates. Eoin was delighted he had such a good scrum-half and Andrew ensured that every ball that he sent back was quick and straight into Eoin's hands.

The Wolfhounds led 10-3 as half-time approached, and had the put-in on a line-out close to half way. The ball took a bad bounce off the ground and came awkwardly to the scrum-half, who stumbled before flipping the ball up to Eoin. The Foxes' second row came barrelling through the line-out and crashed into Andrew just after he released the ball, sending him flying to the ground and finishing up on top of the smaller boy.

Andrew roared in agony, and the referee blew the whistle instantly. He checked how the young scrum-half was and signalled for the physio to come on, then immediately turned to Marcus and waved a yellow card in his face.

'If this was a schools' cup match I'd give you a red,' he started. 'That was a very reckless move.'

Andrew was lifted to his feet, but the way he held his arm meant everyone knew he had suffered a break. That was the end of his trial and an ambulance soon came to take him to hospital.

Ted came over to see what the fuss was. He tried to console Andrew, then he glowered at McCord before talking to the Wolfhounds' coach who realised there were no more specialist scrum-halves among the reserves. 'We only have one spare back,' Ted told him. 'He plays on the left wing for St Osgur's, but I'm sure he can fill in. It will be worth checking out how he does under pressure.'

Killian was summoned and the situation explained to him. Eoin grinned and reassured him that although he had never played No.9 before, he would be there to make him look good.

CHAPTER 14

Marcus was steaming on the sideline as he had to sit out the first ten minutes of the second half, but the Wolfhounds were unable to use the advantage to extend their lead. Killian was struggling badly in an unfamiliar position and had knocked-on the ball a couple of times in promising situations.

Eoin had a word with him. 'Don't rush things, Kil. Take your time with the ball, let it lie inside the scrum or ruck till you decide what you're going to do. The forwards can hold them up for a few seconds if you need more time. When you're ready to pass, just aim the ball at me and follow through on the throw.'

Killian was better after that, and was able to set up Eoin for a pinpoint kick into the corner with a few minutes left. Because of the hold-up with the ambulance the other two games were already over and all the other players had gathered around the pitch to watch the closing stages of the Wolfhounds versus the Foxes.

Marcus McCord won the line-out for the Foxes but dropped the ball, which broke loose at the back of the line. Killian set off like a hare and scooped up the ball at full speed as he broke through a troop of Foxes. It was as if he forgot that he was a scrum-half and had gone back to being a speedy winger. He brilliantly sidestepped the Foxes' full back and sprinted over the line before diving between the posts.

'Fantastic break, what a try,' called out Ted from behind the goal where he had been stationed. 'Well done, Nicholson.'

Killian was chuffed, and Eoin gave him a clap across the shoulders before taking the ball from him for the conversion. He smacked the ball over the bar just before the referee gave a long blast on his whistle to give the Wolfhounds a 20-6 win.

'Great try, Kil,' he grinned as he rejoined his delighted teammates. 'That was an amazing sidestep.'

The other teams had come onto the pitch and all were now seated on the grass as the coaches distributed water bottles and fruit.

'Thanks, lads, they were three good, competitive games with some excellent individual performances,' announced Ted. 'I'm going to head off with the coaches to select the squad for Twickenham. After your showers, can everyone please go into the hall here and collect your log books. There's food and drink too, and hopefully we'll be in with the names before you get too bored.'

Eoin showered and got dressed. His dad was due to collect him at 5pm and he was keen to find out how Dylan had got on in Limerick. He joined the queue for the buffet and swapped a bit of banter with Charlie about the game.

'Do you think I did enough to get the trip?' asked the Castlerock and Foxes No.8.

'You played really well,' said Eoin, 'and I'm sure they'll remember the stormer you had in the schools' final.'

'Well, I suppose we'll find out soon enough,' Charlie sighed.

The boys tucked into the food as if they hadn't eaten for a week. While the earlier meals had been healthy and nutritious, the coach had allowed them a little more junk food to mark the end of the weekend.

Charlie had no fewer than six cocktail sausages sticking out of his mouth when he spotted Ted had come back into the room – and almost choked as he tried to swallow them all at once.

'Oh no, I'm sure to miss out,' he grumbled between chewing the last of the meaty snacks.

There were lots of very nervous-looking boys around the hall. Nobody could be sure they would win a call-up.

Ted started by telling them that he had heard from the hospital that Andrew was comfortable and on the mend, but sadly he wouldn't be coming to London. Then he began reading a list of names with two or three players for each position, and there were a few low-key cheers and sounds of people being clapped on the back.

The coach got to the No.10s and Eoin was delighted to hear his name called out, but there was no luck for Rory at scrum-half. Rory shrugged and admitted that he hadn't really thought he had a chance. There was a surprise when Killian's name was called out as a utility back, covering for various positions – 'he did a very admirable job filling in today,' said Ted. Charlie, too, was called up as one of two No.8s and they were all relieved to note that Marcus McCord had been left out.

'The tournament in London takes place in two weeks,' announced Ted, 'and we will be in touch with the boys lucky enough to be selected. I don't want the rest of you to get disheartened and I want you all to start on your log books tomorrow. We'll be in touch with you before the new season starts and then throughout the year. If anyone has any questions there is a page of contact numbers at the back of the book.'

The boys started to scatter. A few exchanged emails or Twitter accounts before their parents arrived to take them home. McCord seemed a bit sheepish at the way the weekend had turned out for him, but his pride wouldn't allow him to admit he had only himself to blame.

'If I ever find out who stole my sounds they'll be sorry,' he growled as Eoin, Conor and Killian discussed the ways they would be getting home. 'If your pathetic schools get into the cup next year I'll be ruining your season.'

Eoin laughed and wished him all the best. 'We'll send you a postcard from London if we solve that mystery for you.'

The Dodder Woods bully had no answer and stormed off to grump at someone else.

Eoin made his farewells and promised to keep in touch with his old and new friends before hopping into the back seat of his dad's car. His mum had come along too, and she immediately demanded a full blow-by-blow account of the weekend.

Eoin started to explain about the trip to Twickenham, but as he lay back on the seat he found himself drifting away. By the time the car got on to the motorway he was fast asleep.

CHAPTER 15

Back home in Ormondstown Eoin filled his family in on all the weekend action, and how he would be heading off to London shortly. He rang Alan to tell him too and listed off all the kit he had been given. His mum was very impressed by the amount he had accumulated, but Eoin warned her that it wouldn't be part of his summer clothing collection.

'You think I'd wear that around the town? They'd lynch me!' he laughed. 'No, leave that there in the bag and I'll be happy with my old Munster top.'

'Speaking of Munster, I wonder how Dylan got on,' said his dad.

'Oh no, he went out of my head completely,' said Eoin. 'I'd better head down to see him now.'

Just as Eoin got to the front door there was a banging on the other side of it. He opened it to see Dylan wearing a brand new Munster jersey and a grin as wide as the River Shannon.

'Howya, Eoin, how did you get on? I had a great time,' blurted out his friend. 'We're entered in a competition too, and we're off to England in a couple of weeks.'

'Fantastic,' said Eoin. 'Me too! Where is this competition that you guys are in?'

Dylan laughed at him, 'Sure where else would it be except Twickenham?'

'I don't believe it, Leinster are going there too – and I'm in the squad.'

The pair headed out the door and spent the next hour swopping stories about their weekend. The structure in Limerick was similar to that which Eoin had experienced in Dublin, and they realised that the whole set-up must have been organised by the IRFU.

'I suppose they were probably doing the same in Connacht and Ulster too,' said Dylan.

'I wonder will they have teams in England too?'

They got their answer three days later when they both got letters from their provinces giving details of the trip and where and when to meet up for it. The teams were entered into a European competition for Under-15 players and all four Irish provinces would be taking part.

'We'll be playing nearly every day,' said Eoin. 'That's

why they are bringing such a large squad.'

'Munster have to play Harlequins, Glasgow and Toulon – that's a brutal draw,' said Dylan.

'Sure how can you tell what the Under-15s are like in any club?' asked Eoin. 'Just because the adult side is strong doesn't mean the kids will be.'

Dylan nodded. 'I suppose you're right. Who did the Leinsters get?'

'Racing 92, Bath and Cardiff. I haven't a clue what they'll be like.'

'If we get to the semi-final we could play you,' said Dylan. 'That would be deadly!'

'Well, let's not get ahead of ourselves there,' said Eoin. 'Our team have never even played together before. I think there's a plan to get a game in before we travel.'

'We better step up the training programme then,' said Dylan. 'But I can't show you any of the secret moves they gave us.'

'Listen, Dyl, secret moves or not, I've enough in my own head from this weekend to keep me in headaches for a month. I'll say nothing.'

The boys kicked a football around for a while but took an early lunch.

'Fancy heading up to that haunted house?' asked Dylan.

'I suppose so. Let's bring a torch this time and make sure you don't scarper at the first sign of anything spooky.'

A few minutes later the boys were at the gates of the old Lubov mansion. They took their time exploring the outside of the house, checking around the back where the doors and windows were all boarded over and the pathways overgrown. Eoin had brought the photograph with him, intending to return it to where it had lain on the mantelpiece.

They clambered through the loose planks in the front door, and although it was bright inside, Dylan still switched on the torch to explore the dark corners of the rooms.

'We've been around the ground floor already,' he muttered, 'Let's take a look upstairs. You go first.'

The boys climbed the wide staircase, which had once been lined with paintings. Now the carpet crunched underfoot with broken pieces of plaster and dead insects.

As they reached the landing where Eoin had seen the ghostly figure some weeks before, they stopped and looked around. There was no sign of anyone this time. They checked all the rooms and were stunned by how beautiful they still looked after years of neglect and decay. There was little evidence of the lives of the previous owners, except in the very last room they checked, which looked like it had once been a child's bedroom.

The remains of the wallpaper showed scenes from classic fairy tales such as *Peter and the Wolf*, and Eoin studied the pictures carefully. Scrawled on the wall in a tiny, thin script was a confusing word. Part of it looked English but there were other strange letters he had never seen before.

Алексе́й

'That must be Russian,' said Dylan. 'My Auntie sent me a postcard from Moscow last year and I recognise some of the letters.'

'Wow,' said Eoin. 'There must have been a Russian kid living here long ago. I wonder what happened to him.'

The boys shuffled around for a while, but there was very little to see inside the mansion and there was no sign of the mysterious ghost making a reappearance. Eoin copied the letters down on the back of the photo and then realised he couldn't now leave it behind.

'Sure it would just rot here anyway,' he said to himself as they climbed back out into the sunlight and began the slow jog home.

CHAPTER 16

he next two weeks flew by as the boys worked on their skills ahead of their first rugby tour. Barney opened the gates for them early in the morning and they were often at the Gaels ground when the sun started to set.

Eoin even devised a cruel game to sharpen his goal-kicking technique.

Using string and tent pegs he measured out and marked out four lines at 20, 25, 30 and 35 metres from the goal-line. He then borrowed Barney's whitewash to paint five blobs at equal distances along each line right across the field, from touchline to touchline.

When he was finished he had twenty spots and a daunting target – kick the ball over the bar from each of the spots in the nearest line, then the second line and so on. But whenever he missed one, he had to start again. It was a difficult exercise, especially from out wide, and it sometimes took over a hundred kicks before he converted twenty in a row.

As a result, almost every night Eoin went straight to bed, completely drained by his efforts. He and Dylan were serious about preparing for Twickenham and given Schillaci's chip shop a miss as they ate sensibly and got plenty of sleep.

While Dylan had been cranky in the run-up to the first Munster academy session, this time he was more comfortable after making friends with his team-mates. Munster Rugby was all about togetherness and passion for your team, and he was really looking forward to joining up with them again.

Eoin was always nervous before big games, and this tour was no different – worse, probably, as Leinster could have five big games, although he didn't expect that anyone would be asked to play in them all. He, too, felt reassured that Charlie would be there, Killian too, and that Dylan would be around the place.

Even though he hadn't worn any of the Leinster kit, his mum insisted on washing and ironing it all carefully in the week before he left. She completed the checklist of match and training gear and equipment in Eoin's log book and packed it all carefully in his huge kitbag. She also organised the ordinary clothes he would need for a week away and laid them all in a suitcase open on the spare bed in his room.

'Now, Eoin, I need you to decide what else you want to bring with you. I suppose you'll want the rugby book Dixie bought you last week?'

Eoin nodded and promised his mum that he would sort it out later. It was only 8pm and the sun was still streaming in his bedroom window but he was so tired that he had to sleep.

He woke very early next day, and decided to go for a run. He headed out in the direction of his grandad's house, but when he realised after ten minutes that he still hadn't seen a single person or car he checked the time. To his surprise he found that it was just before six o'clock and far too early to call in to see Dixie.

He continued on out past his grandfather's home and glanced through the old gates at the Lubov mansion. He came to a sudden halt and stared at the old house. Was that someone in the window? It was hard to tell as the low sun caused a glare which made it hard to see through the glass. He cupped his hand over his eyes to shield the rays, and again caught a glimpse of movement at one of the upstairs windows. It was someone dressed in white.

Eoin had a dilemma. He was naturally curious, and

really wanted to know what was going on at the old house, but he also knew that he had an important journey ahead in just a few hours, and he would be foolish to put that and the opportunity it gave him at risk. He wasn't afraid of any potential danger in the Lubov house, but he didn't want to take the chance.

He lifted his right hand and waved, and the figure at the window waved back. He looked closer and was sure he saw a blaze of red on the figure's chest. Fighting his instinct to rush to the house and solve the mystery, he turned his back and jogged back towards home.

CHAPTER 17

Up in his room Eoin looked at his suitcase and wondered what else he should bring. He tossed in the biography of Johnny Sexton, but suspected he wouldn't get much time to read on the trip. He gathered together his toothbrush and a few bits he would need. Almost as an afterthought he picked up the tiny half rugby ball his grandad had given him. 'You might bring me luck,' he said, staring at the odd little item about the size of a lemon before tucking it inside a sock and returning it to his kitbag.

He closed up his bags and lugged them down the stairs to where his mum and dad were waiting. His father would bring him to Dublin, but his mum had an appointment in Ormondstown, which meant she couldn't come too. She worried about him every time he left home for school or a trip, and told him he needed to catch up on his sleep in the car.

Eoin's dad let him doze until they neared Dublin, and called him again as they neared Belfield.

'C'mon, son, you'll be out playing rugby in half an hour, you'd better get yourself bright-eyed and bushy-tailed.'

Eoin took a swig from a bottle of water and rubbed his eyes. 'Thanks, Dad, I needed that sleep. Sorry I was such boring company on the way up. I promise I'll be full of chat on the way home next week.'

His dad laughed and told him he forgave him. He slipped him a few five-pound notes and wished him luck.

'I'd say the results will be on the website somewhere,' Eoin said, as he lifted his bags out and slammed the door. 'I hope I get a game now,' he grinned as his dad waved goodbye.

The Leinster offices were thronged with dozens of other boys bubbling with excitement, but all were silenced as soon as Ted arrived and raised his hand in the air.

'Great, I think that's everyone,' he said. 'It's now half past eleven but your flight is not till six o'clock so I propose we have a little practice match to get you used to playing together. We'll have another training day before the tournament starts, but we have already decided the best approach is to divide you into two teams and reserves. The way the competition works is you will play three sixty-minute games in four days, which is a completely unreasonable workload, I believe. We are going to alternate the teams and see how that goes. The group games and semi-finals are two days apart so we might take another look at the policy if we qualify.

'Whether you win this tournament or not is irrelevant to me,' continued Ted. 'I will, of course, be delighted for you if you do, but the most important thing for me is that you learn from playing with new people, and against people who play in a different way and even speak a different language. It will be exciting to be in such an atmosphere, but I'm sure you don't need me to explain how you will be expected to behave.'

The players changed into their match gear and jogged out onto the training pitch. Ted's assistants consulted their clipboards before pointing each player to the left or right where they collected an orange or yellow bib.

Eoin wore orange, as did Charlie. They introduced themselves to those fellow players they didn't know, before Ted came across to talk to them.

'OK guys, the plan is for this team to play in the second game in London, and then in the second half of the third game. It may sound a bit stupid, but we want to give as many people as possible a chance to play. Like I said earlier, winning isn't the most important thing.'

Eoin blinked as Ted revealed his thinking. It was a strange way to approach the tournament – surely an international trophy was worth winning?

The teams lined up and began a practice game, which was refereed by Ted. It was a very stop-start affair as he frequently held up the action to explain what would have been a better move, or to call the forwards coach onto the field to iron out an issue in the scrum.

But within half an hour both sides had started to gel well and had put some nice moves together. Eoin was working well with his scrum-half, a St Xavier's player called Páidí Reeves who was very quick around the back of the scrum. Killian came on as a replacement at full-back for the second half and showed great pace when he got the ball.

Ted whistled for full-time and called the players together.

'Right, men, that was a very useful exercise which has cheered me up quite a bit. We have a good bit of work to do, but you are a talented bunch and I can see where we are going with you now. With a bit of luck we could have a very enjoyable week in London. Now get your showers in and I want you all out here in twenty minutes dressed in your Leinster tracksuits for the journey. It's important when we travel together that we look like a united team.'

CHAPTER 18

As the plane descended to land in London, Eoin peered out the window at the vast city below. He had visited one of his mother's aunts here once when he was much younger, but they had travelled by ferry and car so he had never seen it from the air. He marvelled at the sights he knew so well from books and films, such as Tower Bridge and the loop of the Thames as it passed the Millennium Dome. The plane dipped low and crossed the docklands water as it jetted in to land. The airline was one of Leinster's sponsors so the whole squad got a little bit of extra attention – the pilot even announced to the other passengers that they were on board and wished them luck in Twickenham.

'It's a bit like being a celebrity,' said Killian, who had sat alongside Eoin and Charlie on the flight. 'Maybe there'll be champagne going home if we win!'

'Champagne wouldn't be much use to us, would it?'

asked Charlie. 'I'd prefer another ten bags of those spicy peanuts.'

Parked outside the airport there was one enormous coach to carry Ted and the Leinster players, while Ted's assistant Tony and the other coaches went off to collect their hire car. The coach poked its way through the busy streets past sky-scrapers and strangely shaped buildings that were taller than anything Eoin had seen before. Traffic seemed to go faster than it did in Dublin and the people looked even more hassled.

After well over an hour on the road the coach eventually pulled into the grounds of a very posh-looking school. The white marble pillars were far grander than Castlerock, and Eoin looked with envy at the shiny new swimming pool and sports pavilion they passed on their way up the drive.

Leinster were allocated two of the big dormitories and the boys were split into the teams on which they had been named back in Dublin. When settled, they walked over to the canteen and joined the queue for dinner. Eoin looked around the huge hall and caught a strange mixture of accents as the boys chatted. The bright pink tracksuits ensured that Stade Français stood out, but there were other groups that were vying for attention too with loud roars and laughter. A couple of the Scottish lads were wearing kilts and the Italians were trying to take photos of them on their phones.

'Half the sides are here and half in another school up the road,' said the cook as she doled out a bowl of steaming pasta. 'I hope you enjoy your stay at our school.'

Munster must be up the road, thought Eoin, I'd have heard Dylan before now. He, Killian and Charlie looked for a bench together and sat down across from a bunch of players from Ulster.

'Hiya guys, howya doin'?' asked one. 'We're in a different group to you boys, aren't we? We might get you in the final though – that would be some crack!'

He introduced himself as Paddy O'Hare from Enniskillen and he was sitting with his pal Sam Rainey from Belfast.

'When's your first game?' asked Killian.

'We're here since yesterday so our first game is in the morning against some Italian crowd,' replied Sam. 'You'll be doing your training in the school here; the facilities are amazing. The matches are down in a small ground near Twickenham Stadium, called the Stoop.'

'Drop down if you can, we're starting at half eleven,' said Paddy. 'They'll probably bring you on a tour of Twickers after training so you might catch the second half.'

The Ulster boys got up to go and Eoin wished them well in their game. They devoured their meal – Charlie went up for seconds – before taking a stroll around the school grounds. They sat down on a bench outside the cricket pavilion.

'What do you think of Ted's idea that we shouldn't be too worried about winning?' asked Killian.

'I can see why he's doing it,' Eoin replied. 'We hardly know each other and can't be expected to perform like a team in such a short time – but I still think it's a rubbish way to go into a tournament. We have the best guys in Leinster here, they don't need to have the pressure taken off them – they need it on!'

'Yeah, and you want them all to do their best at all times,' said Killian. 'Ted is just giving anyone who doesn't want to put the work in a chance to cop out.'

Eoin agreed, and they continued to pick holes in the coach's approach to the competition.

'That's very interesting,' came a voice from behind them, as Ted stepped out of the shadows under the pavilion awning where he had been getting some quiet time to listen to some music. 'I'm looking forward to you guys proving me wrong. Good night, Mr Madden, Mr Nicholson and Mr Johnston,' he added before strolling away.

'Oh, no! Me and my big mouth,' said Killian.

'You weren't too bad,' grinned Eoin, nervously. 'I just called the head coach of the Leinster Academy "rubbish".'

CHAPTER 19

Ted didn't seem to hold Eoin's insult against him next morning when the two Leinster sides faced off against each other on the practice pitch. He dropped a few words of praise when Eoin did anything good and grinned with delight when he kicked a conversion from the touchline.

'That's a very well-sharpened skill, Eoin,' he said. 'You obviously practise your goal-kicking very hard.'

Eoin nodded. 'Yeah, we have a GAA pitch near my home so I practise there.

'Ah,' said Ted. 'The narrower posts are obviously a good way of improving your accuracy. Keep working on that, it's a hugely important part of the game.'

When training was over the boys were walked the few hundred metres to the stadium where so many epic games of rugby had been staged, including the dramatic World Cup final they had all watched in 2015. There was a tour guide to greet them and give them a quick run through the history of the ground.

She showed them around the stadium, bringing them into some areas that the public never usually got to see. She also brought them into the main dressing rooms. 'This is where you'll be sitting if you get to the final of this competition,' she smiled. 'We always hold the final here, just to give youngsters a taste of what it is like to play in an international stadium. For some players it is the best day of their lives.'

At the back of the group Eoin smiled at Charlie. They had already played three times in the best stadium in the world – the Aviva Stadium back in Dublin.

Next stop was the museum, where the guide let them run loose for half an hour.

'Alan would love this,' said Charlie, staring at the cases packed with caps, shirts and programmes from days gone by, as Eoin went off to see if he could find an exhibit that mentioned his pal Dave Gallaher, who he had met in a previous adventure.

The boys met up again at an area where they could test their skills in passing, scrummaging and kicking. Eoin aced the kicking test, to the delight of his teammates, while Killian scored highly on the speed exercises.

As Eoin wandered towards the exit he spotted some-thing in one of the cases that made the back of his neck tingle. There was a black and white video running showing an old England player scoring an amazing try against New Zealand, but what caught Eoin's eye was the very last frame when the player turned towards the camera. He had seen that face before.

He waited for the little film to start again, but the guide called out for the Leinster squad to join her at the entrance immediately; Eoin delayed as long as he could, but there was still no clue as to who the try-scorer was by the time he was the last boy in the room and the subject of irritated waving by the guide.

'Sorry, Miss,' said Eoin, 'it was really interesting…'

'You will have plenty of time to come back here during the week, I'm sure,' she replied. 'Just show your tournament badge and admission will be free.'

The guide showed the boys down towards the pitch but they were told they couldn't even step on it today. 'When you are here to play in the final I'll let you on,' she smiled. 'Now, to finish, I'm going to take you up to a restaurant where we have some lunch for you, and you can watch a DVD of the World Cup final. Follow me, and if you get lost follow the signs for Obolensky's.'

'That's a weird name for a restaurant,' said Páidí, as

they trailed along behind the lady.

'He was a famous old England player,' she explained. 'All the other restaurants are called after England captains like Carling and Wakefield, but Obolensky wasn't a captain, just a very special player.'

'It's a funny name,' said Killian. 'Was he from England?'

'No,' replied the coach. 'He lived here for most of his life, but his family came from Eastern Europe during the First World War. There's lots about him in the museum if you want to come back and learn more.'

They arrived at the restaurant and marvelled at the array of snacks and tasty bites that had been laid out for their consumption. Eoin nibbled at a few, but wasn't particularly hungry. He gazed out the enormous windows down onto the pitch below and wondered would he ever get the chance to play there.

'I've had enough,' he told his pals. 'I'm going to head down to the car park to get some air. See you when you're ready.'

He wandered out of the restaurant and down the corridor from which they had come. He must have missed a turn however, as he was soon lost. Turning the next corner, he came to a dead end just as a man was coming out of one of the doorways.

'Are you all right, Sonny Jim?' he asked.

Eoin stopped dead and stared at the man. It was a bit odd that he was wearing an England shirt and shorts, but Eoin was transfixed by what he was seeing above the neckline. It was the same face he had seen on the landing in the Lubov house in Ormondstown, and in the photograph he had found there.

'You... you're... Well, who exactly *are* you?' he spluttered.

The man grinned mysteriously. 'Oh, I'm just an old rugby player who hangs around here. My name is Alexei, but you can call me Alex. Alex Obolensky.'

CHAPTER 20

Eoin stared closely at the young man. 'You're a ghost, aren't you?' he asked.

Alexei stared back. 'That's an extraordinary question. Why do you ask it?'

'Because I've seen you before. In an old house in Ireland. You waved at me. Twice.'

Alex's mouth fell open. 'What, at Uncle Nick's house? Who are you? What were you doing there? What are you doing *here*? Did you follow me? Were you looking for the treasure too?'

'Hang on, hang on,' said Eoin. 'I most certainly didn't follow you. I'm here to play rugby for the Leinster Academy Under-15 team. We are in a tournament down in the Stoop Ground and came up here for a tour of the stadium. I just got lost and that's why I bumped into you.'

Alex eyed him suspiciously. 'And how can you see

me? I've been around here for many years and almost nobody has disturbed me. I came across a journalist in the press box late one night – he must have been slow finishing in his work – and he recognised me. He wrote a story called 'Obolensky's Ghost Haunts Twickenham' which caused me no end of trouble. I didn't get a minute's peace for months after that, but nobody else has ever noticed me.'

'I seem to have a knack,' sighed Eoin. 'I've met four ghosts in Dublin over the last couple of years. And what's this about treasure?'

Obolensky stopped and looked over Eoin's shoulder ,from where he could hear voices. Eoin popped his head around the corner to see two groundsmen discussing their work.

'Hey, what are you doing here, son? This isn't a public area,' one of them called.

'Sorry, I just got lost. Which way is the car park?' asked Eoin.

The men showed him the way out, but when Eoin turned to look at where Alex had been standing, he was no longer to be seen.

He arrived down in the car park a little rattled by his encounter with Alex. He stared up at the modern stadium and tried to imagine what it was like when the ghost had played there. He decided to revisit the museum when he got a chance.

Killian, Charlie and Páidí arrived down soon afterwards, with Charlie's bulging pockets hinting that he had organised an unofficial doggy bag for himself. They asked one of the coaches' permission to go to watch the Ulster game and after crossing a footbridge they strolled down through rows of houses to the ground.

They arrived in time to see Sam kicking the ball over the crossbar and were impressed to see that he had just increased Ulster's lead over the Italian side to a whopping 33 points.

'These guys don't look as bad as the scoreline makes them out to be,' said Killian. 'Ulster must be a pretty good side.'

The Stoop was a compact stadium, with plenty of room for maybe 15,000 people more than the handful that were watching the game today. Eoin studied the goalposts and where they were situated. He wondered how the wind might affect his goal-kicking, and whether the grandstands were high enough to shield his kicks. He watched closely while the players were taking shots at goal.

But he found it hard to concentrate on the game, and his mind kept returning to the encounter with Alex. It was a strange coincidence and very puzzling – and why had Alex accused him of wanting 'treasure'? He really wanted to talk to Alan and Dylan about this, but one was back home in Dublin and the other was somewhere else in this huge city.

The final whistle was sounded with Ulster's victory margin over 50 points. He waved to Sam and Paddy as they came off and followed Killian down the steps as they made for the exit.

'Hey, Madden, are you not staying for the big game?' came a roar from just outside the players' tunnel. Eoin grinned down at Dylan, wearing his red shirt, and gave him a wave back. 'I suppose I'll have to, now you spotted me trying to sneak out,' he called. His other friends were just as happy to stay and watch Eoin's pal make his debut for his beloved province.

The Leinster players stretched themselves out on the nice seats in the committee box and enjoyed tossing friendly insults at the Munster team. Eoin kept quiet while this went on, still uncomfortable with the idea that Munster were the enemy.

Dylan's team were taking on Glasgow and it was a hard, close game. Roger Savage, who had been at school with Eoin in Ormondstown, was sent off for fighting with the Scottish club's second row but Munster were still two points ahead when the final whistle came.

Eoin made his way down to the advertising hoardings that surrounded the ground and called Dylan over. 'Well played, bud, it's great to get started with a win,' he told his friend.

'Yeah, it was a tough game, though,' said Dylan, showing Eoin the bruises which were starting to come up on his rib cage. 'Where are you guys staying?'

Eoin explained about the posh school and then looked around behind him to check no one was in earshot.

'Listen, Dyl, it happened again – I've seen a ghost. The same lad we saw in the haunted house back home. He's here, up in the main stadium!'

Dylan was stunned, and also checked behind him for eavesdroppers.

'What are you going to do? Can we go back and see him again?'

'I don't know. I have a team meeting later and Leinster's first match is in the morning. Let's leave it till tomorrow afternoon. We can take a look around that museum and see if we can find out more about this Alexei Obolensky.'

CHAPTER 21

The Leinster team had a good run out the next day against Bath, winning 19-10. There were players and coaches from all the Irish provinces at the Stoop and they were delighted that all four now had started the tournament with a victory.

Eoin and his pals had sat out the game, and most of the other teams were adopting a similar policy. 'I suppose they'll pick the best players from the two Leinster teams if we get to the semi-final,' said Charlie.

'You're probably right,' said Eoin. 'They can't really do it any other way. I doubt if I'll be picked after calling Ted "rubbish" though.'

The coach took Eoin's team for a run around the Stoop and a chat about tactics. As they were leaving he tossed a ball to Eoin. 'You'll need some serious practice here to get the lines right. Nicholson, Reeves, can you stay and collect the balls for him?'

Killian and Páidí didn't mind helping out, and Eoin fired over dozens of kicks before the teams for the next game started their warm-ups and he had to get out of the way. He was happy that Ted had suggested the session, as there was a definite tug on the ball from one corner of the ground and he needed to adjust his kicking line.

The boys strolled back up to the main Twickenham Stadium, where they met Dylan. The others wanted to go back to the school so made their farewells, but Eoin and Dylan went for a sandwich in one of the cafés around the ground.

They chatted about the places where they were staying, and who they had met. Dylan had got very friendly with the Connacht boys, who were the most popular in the school they were billeted. Then their conversation moved back to the ghost Eoin had met.

'Tell me about this Hopalongski fella,' Dylan asked.

'Obolensky,' said Eoin, slowly. 'He's a Russian lad, I think, which was why he was down in Tipperary. He said the house belonged to his Uncle Nick.'

Dylan nodded at Eoin, still stunned by what he was hearing.

'He must be some sort of rugby legend though because the restaurant we were in yesterday is called

Obolensky's,' Eoin went on. 'I didn't get a chance to ask him about that, though.'

'I suppose we could find out more in the museum,' suggested Dylan.

'Yeah, I reckoned that. We'll head there after this,' said Eoin. 'He asked me something about a treasure as well. He seemed a bit annoyed because he thought that I was looking for it too, but I hadn't a clue what he was on about. If it was in the Lubov mansion it was probably stolen years ago – or very well hidden.'

The boys finished their lunch and walked around to the World Rugby Museum. They flashed their tournament player badges and were delighted to be waved through free of charge. Eoin walked straight to the display he had been looking at the day before.

'That's him,' he told Dylan as he pointed to the video screen showing Alex scoring a try. They watched as he collected the ball ten metres inside his own half and cut between two All Blacks. Alex then ran wide onto the right hand touch-line to avoid the covering players, but he was so quick that he was able to cut back inside again and sprint to score close to the posts. It was a sensational try, and Eoin could see why they were still talking about it eighty years later.

A second try by the Russian winger was just as thrilling, as he cut diagonally across the field to score a second time against the powerful New Zealanders. The score flashed up as 'England 13, New Zealand 0', and the screen then revealed it was the first time the home team had ever beaten the All Blacks, and the last time they would do so at the ground for nearly fifty years.

They read the captions on the display which showed an England cap and photos of the player.

'He was a prince,' gushed Dylan. 'Wow, he must have some serious treasure.'

Eoin read further. 'Well, he was a *Russian* prince, and that didn't mean very much in the 1930s. Do you ever listen in History class?'

'What do you mean?' asked Dylan.

'Well, the ruler of Russia, the Tsar, was thrown off the throne in 1917 and he was later killed with his whole family. There haven't been any princes, or royals of any sort, in Russia since then.'

'So what was Alex doing playing rugby for England then?'

'I don't know, but a lot of people fled Russia when the revolutionaries took over. Alex was only a year old then, so I presume his family took him to England.'

Dylan read on. 'He was killed during the Second World War,' it says here. 'He was a pilot in the Royal

Air Force.'

'What an amazing life he had,' mused Eoin, 'and he was just twenty-four when he passed away.'

'So where are we going to find him?' asked Dylan.

'I'm sure he'll turn up when you expect him least,' came a voice from behind them.

The boys turned to see, grinning down at them, the ghost of Prince Alexander Sergeyevich Obolensky.

CHAPTER 22

Eoin checked left and right to make sure no one else was around in that part of the museum.

'Don't worry, you two are the only ones who can see me, it seems,' said Alex.

'I'm not worried about people seeing you,' said Eoin, 'I'm worried about people thinking I'm talking to empty air. Can we go somewhere else, like the grandstand?'

Eoin and Dylan followed the ghost as he walked out of the museum and made his way into the lower deck of the stand. They sat down on the plastic seats far away from any watching eyes and the staff going about their business.

Alex sat and smiled at them. 'Listen, I'm sorry that I was a bit snappy with you yesterday. I was a little bit rattled that you had seen me in Tipperary.'

'Me too,' admitted Eoin. 'It seemed very weird to see

you yesterday in a completely different country. What were you doing in Ireland anyway?'

'Well, I was visiting my Uncle Nick's house for the first time in many, many years. I was very sad to see what a bad state it was in. He didn't have any family left, I think, so there was nobody to take it over and move in. I had some great holidays in Ireland. I remember joining a club to play a game called "gaelic", which was a bit like rugby. I had great fun there. I used to play with a lad called Barney whose father was the groundsman.'

Eoin looked at Dylan and did some sums in his head. 'The groundsman in that club is still called Barney – it must be his father or grandfather that you knew.'

'Hmmm, that's interesting,' said Alex. 'Our family suffered enormous upheaval and tragedy in the last century at the cutting edge of history, while some people continued doing the same simple things through many generations. They were the lucky ones.'

He looked sad again, but went on with his story.

'Uncle Nick left Russia after the revolution – Nick wasn't his real name and he wasn't really my uncle, either. But he needed to find a new identity and my mum's uncle, Nikolai Lubov, had been killed in the war. The new "Uncle Nick" moved to Ireland to get out of the way and my family stayed in London. We visited him most summers until I was about ten.'

'Did you write your name on the wall in the bedroom?' asked Dylan.

Alex smiled. 'I suppose I must have. Did you see it there?'

Dylan nodded.

'Ah, they were such wonderful days.'

'How did you get into rugby?' asked Eoin.

Alex explained about how he enjoyed sport back at school in England and as a speedy runner he was always put on the right wing. He became quite good at rugby and while he was a student at Oxford University he was picked to play for England.

'I was still a teenager, can you believe that?' he asked. 'And some people grumbled that I shouldn't be picked as I wasn't English. But I could hardly play for Russia by then, could I? I got a British passport a few weeks later so that silenced all that.'

'We saw the films of your tries,' said Eoin. 'They were really amazing.'

'Yes, I was quite the star for a few weeks,' he laughed. 'But I never scored another try for England. I was dropped the next season and never got the chance to get back in the team.'

'And then the war came,' said Eoin. 'Did you join up immediately?'

'I did,' nodded Alex. 'I was a proud Englishman by then. I joined the RAF because I had done some flying, and it was the most exciting and glamorous branch of the armed services. Planes then were very different to the big white machines I see flying over here – they were so fragile. It was terrifying to be flying in what was basically a crate made from light wood and cloth.

'I hoped to be sent to France to fight the Germans, but I never saw any action. I was killed in a terrible accident when we were still on a training course.'

Eoin nodded respectfully, before asking Alex when he had come back as a ghost.

'It was a good while later, after the war. I suppose the game against the All Blacks was the highpoint of what I did in my short life, so Twickenham was where I returned,' went on Alex. 'The ground has changed a lot over the years, but I still get a thrill walking onto the turf where I scored those tries. And then they built that museum and put the newsreel in it, and people started talking about me again. I do feel at home here.'

'But why did you go back to Tipp then?' asked Dylan.

'Ah, well that, my friend, is a story for another day. A day when your coach is not about to call you away to a training session. I'll see you during the week,' he said before quickly disappearing.

'Madden!' called Ted from the side of the pitch, 'come on, we've a meeting down the Stoop in ten minutes – and I don't want to see you mixing with the enemy either,' he added, pointing at Dylan's red shirt.

CHAPTER 23

Eoin trotted alongside Ted through the streets of suburban London. 'Nice place this,' said Ted.

'Yeah,' agreed Eoin. 'It must be great to have a stadium like that so near your house.'

'Well, I'd say there's ups and downs to it,' laughed Ted. 'I'd say traffic is a nightmare on match days for example – you could be stuck in your home for hours.'

The coach slowed his pace to a brisk walk. 'So you disagree with my approach to this competition?' he said.

Eoin blushed, but decided to be upfront with the coach.

'Well, I suppose I do,' he replied. 'I don't think it's possible for competitive young lads like most of us to play less hard just because you say it's not important to win. And the lads who are just along for the ride will see it as a chance to take it easy.'

'Fair point,' said Ted. 'But maybe that was part of the

plan. Maybe I wanted to see who would take me at my word and who would continue to push themselves as hard as they could to win the trophy. Then I'd know who was worth persevering with – this is a long-term project, remember.'

They arrived at the Stoop. 'You are the first young lad I've ever heard articulate what it is like to have that competitive spirit in rugby,' went on Ted. 'I'm impressed, and I forgive you for thinking my plan was "rubbish". I think it's rubbish myself to be honest – but you're not to say that to your teammates,' he winked at Eoin.

Eoin's team were waiting for him when he arrived with Ted. The coach asked them did they know anything about Racing 92, and a few knew they wore sky-blue hooped shirts, and a few others that Johnny Sexton used to play for them.

Ted admitted he didn't know much more about their Under-15 team, but that he expected them to play a fast game with plenty of flair in the backs. He talked about how Leinster might counter this, and suggested that keeping possession was going to be important.

The team went through several drills for the next hour or so before Ted called training to a halt and told them to be in the car park in twenty minutes. That was a signal to the boys that there was a team outing and, sure enough, the bus was there to take them to a nearby cinema where they watched the latest blockbuster.

Or rather, where *some* of them watched the latest blockbuster. When the hero had finally saved the day and the house lights came back on, Eoin was just one of more than a dozen members of the Leinster squad who were fast asleep.

He slept some more on the way back to their quarters, and soon hit the pillow again when he found his bed.

All this sleep helped recharge his batteries and calm his brain, which had been overloaded by the meetings with Alex. So Eoin felt very refreshed and relaxed when he awoke early next morning. He was the first up in his dormitory and quietly slipped on his trainers to go out for a jog.

It was already warm out, and Eoin knew it would be a hot day from the way the dew was rising as steam in the morning sun. He decided not to take a long run, saving his energy for what could be a sapping day. The game was down to be played at noon, and he expected it to be scorching by then.

He sat down on the bench outside the cricket pavilion again, and thought of home. He wondered had Dixie ever had the chance to play rugby in Twickenham, or even London. Of course he would certainly have done if his life hadn't been changed by that terrible accident.

He thought of Alex too, and how his biggest moment as a sportsman had occurred in his teens, and how war robbed him of the chance to recapture that moment.

Eoin reflected how lucky he was to live in a time of relative peace, and how he had opportunities to travel to play sport that hadn't been available to previous generations. He stood up and stretched his arms wide.

'We're in it to win it, Ted,' he said to himself. 'No doubts at all.'

CHAPTER 24

Eoin got his way, too. His teammates had no doubts either and everyone put all they had into winning the game. Despite the hard pitch and the hot sun favouring the French boys, Leinster overwhelmed them in the scrums and line-outs, and Eoin's goal-kicking was perfect.

'Seven kicks out of seven – that's nearly 100 per cent, isn't it?' asked Charlie as he walked off the field with his arm draped over Eoin's shoulder.

'It *is* 100 per cent, you sap,' laughed Eoin.

'That was a brilliant win, wasn't it?' smiled Charlie. 'Everything just clicked.'

Ted said the same thing when he talked to them back in the changing room. Leinster had run in four tries and hadn't conceded even one, and were now top of their group table with two wins.

'Just to be clear,' Ted added, 'the other guys will be

playing the first half against Cardiff tomorrow, and this group will replace them at half-time. Cardiff will probably do the same thing, so look at it as two separate half-hour games – and if we win on aggregate we'll be in the semis.'

But it didn't appear quite that simple twenty-four hours later. The other Leinster side had been well beaten in their mini-game, and Eoin's group had a ten-point deficit to haul back.

'Sorry, lads,' shrugged John Young, out-half on the first-half team, in the dressing room at half-time. 'I must have left my kicking boots at home.'

Eoin nodded sympathetically to John. He liked the Newtown player, even though they would be competing for the same place in the team if they got to the semi-finals.

'Good luck, Maddser,' he replied, 'you're the 100 per cent man.'

Eoin smiled, but knew it wasn't just the missed kicks that had cost Leinster – the Welsh pack was well on top too.

Ted and the forwards coach were giving some last

-minute advice to the Leinster pack so Eoin slipped into the shower room for some peace. Standing in the corner was Alex.

'Your team are up against it, I see. Those Welsh lads are tough nuts to crack. But their back line is inclined to press too far forward at the set pieces – you could find a bit of room in behind them with a well-placed chip,' he suggested.

'Thanks for the tip,' replied Eoin. 'But what has you down here in the Stoop?'

'Ah, I'll explain it later, but I'm on the hunt for some old Russian treasure and I felt a strong tug towards the ground here. But it's probably nothing… I hear your coach calling you all together – good luck today,' he added, as Eoin dashed out of the showers.

Ted was giving a few suggestions to the team, trying to keep it simple. As the players streamed outside, he tapped Eoin on the shoulder and guided him out of the line.

'Listen, Eoin,' he hissed. 'We can win this, I'm convinced of it. Don't try and win it in the next ten minutes – if you don't rush things we will get the points on the board all in good time.'

But the half started badly for Leinster when one of their props conceded a penalty at the first scrum and the

Cardiff No.10 slotted over the kick. Eoin had a word with Páidí while the kick was being taken, sharing the plan Alex had suggested.

At the next scrum Leinster won the ball and the little scrum-half controlled it while Eoin signalled his intentions to Killian and the centres. Páidí made a move to pass inside and his dummy fooled the Welsh covering players; he quickly switched direction and sped the ball out to Eoin. The out-half had already picked his spot and chipped the ball over the Cardiff back line, who were left struggling to change direction. Eoin chased hard and reached the ball before the Welsh full-back, but went down under his tackle. As he fell he was delighted to see the Leinster backs had followed through at speed and he was able to toss the ball into Killian's hands.

The St Osgur's boy did the rest, and Eoin picked himself up to kick the conversion to make the score 13-7.

Cardiff were rattled by the try, and their coach's screaming at them rattled them even more. Eoin was enjoying himself by now, and he dropped a goal the next time Leinster got within sight of the posts. The Welsh boys hit back with a penalty, and with five minutes left there was still a six-point margin to make up for Leinster.

Eoin noticed the Cardiff full-back was arguing with

the players nearest him, and when he launched a huge garryowen towards the goalposts the distracted No.15 dropped the ball, giving Leinster a great position for a scrum. The second-half Welsh pack wasn't as strong as the first-half team and Leinster started driving forwards. Charlie controlled the ball between his feet and kept urging his pack on. At the last second Páidí slipped in and seized the ball, and snaked backwards before darting down to slam the ball onto the try-line.

The Leinster forwards erupted in delight. They knew that their hard work had paid off with a five-pointer, and under the posts too. Eoin ensured the work wasn't wasted as he fired the conversion over.

The Welsh team flailed around trying to recapture the lead, but Eoin's backs were well-organised and disciplined enough to ensure they never broke through and the final whistle brought even more delight for the team in blue.

CHAPTER 25

ed was full of praise for the second-half performance and said his team would think carefully about who they would select for the semi-final in two days' time. He ordered all thirty-three players to take it easy for the rest of the day, with recovery important for the task ahead. The squad met up later at the school swimming pool and spirits were still very high.

'Still 100 per cent, eh, Eoin?' laughed Charlie as he jumped into the pool, splashing the out-half.

'Easy, Charlie,' answered Eoin, 'a big oaf like you could cause a tsunami like that.'

The two squads were mixing together more now that they had both ensured Leinster were in the semi-final. Eoin sat on the edge of the pool with John Young, his rival for the No.10 shirt.

'No matter who gets picked we won't fall out,' John laughed. 'And I have no doubt that it's going to be you.

Your kicking has been incredible.'

'Well, kicking isn't everything,' replied Eoin. 'And there are very few players in the team with your turn of pace and power running with the ball.'

'Maybe, but this next game will be a real grudge match…'

'Why?' asked Eoin, 'Who are we playing?'

'Didn't you hear?' asked John. 'Ted just came in with the result from group C. There was a bit of a shock in the last game. We'll be playing Munster.'

Eoin was stunned. Not at the result, because he knew his native province were always capable of pulling out a winning performance, but that his greatest fear coming to London had now come to pass.

'Oh no, that'll be a tough one,' he winced.

His mind raced as he imagined what it would be like to play against Dylan, and Curry Ryan, and the Savage brothers. He could handle the banter, and even the extra attention he was sure he would get from their tacklers, but he knew he would find it hard to regard that red shirt as an enemy.

After dinner he went straight to the dorm and fished the biography out of his bag. He wanted a bit of escapism, so he lay down on his bed to read and drifted off to sleep with his head full of glorious Ireland and

Leinster victories of the past.

Next morning the boys were taken on an excursion into the centre of London. Ted told them he wanted them to forget about rugby until they had a run-around in the Stoop at four o'clock. He ordered them to enjoy the trip and everyone obeyed as they took in the Tower of London and St Paul's Cathedral before finishing with a trip in the London Eye, a giant wheel that soared slowly above the city and gave the best views short of strapping yourself to a seagull.

The boys picked out all the sights, and were thrilled to see Wembley and the Olympic Stadium and the Oval cricket ground. It was a little misty when they reached the top so they couldn't see Twickenham, but as Charlie said, 'We've seen enough of that already.'

The trip was a great success in taking the boys' minds off rugby, but mention of Twickenham brought it all back to them, and the talk all the way back in the bus was of who would be selected for the semi-final against Munster.

Ted put them out of their misery at the meeting in the Stoop. He stressed that everyone had played an important part in getting the team through the group, and that everyone would still be in the shake-up if they went any further in the competition.

'But only fifteen boys can start the semi-final against Munster, and they are…' he said, reading down the list attached to a clipboard.

Eoin twitched as his name was read out, and smiled when he heard that Páidí would be alongside him. Charlie too, was in the fifteen, but Killian was on the bench.

'I'm delighted to have got this far,' smiled Killian. 'I wasn't even in one of the four teams back at training camp, remember.'

The selectors had taken heed of the greatly improved second-half performance against Cardiff and had called up eleven members of that team. The disappointed players trailed out of the changing room, some nodding congratulations to those who had been picked.

Eoin and his three pals threw themselves into the training session. It didn't last as long as usual, but Ted and his coaching team worked them hard, bringing in a few moves that they thought would be important.

As they trooped out of the ground, the team who would be their opponents next day were arriving, and the two groups walked past each other in the car park. Eoin spotted Dylan and lifted his hand in salute.

'Howya, Dyl,' he called.

Dylan turned his head away and blanked Eoin, but just as he passed him to go into the stadium he turned again to face him, and hissed one word, 'Traitor'.

CHAPTER 26

Eoin was angry at his friend. Dylan knew more than anyone how he had agonised over accepting the Leinster offer – and there never had been a Munster offer to turn down anyway. Accusing him of being a traitor was stupid, and wrong. He seethed as he remembered the many hours he had spent with Dylan helping him improve his game, of the many nights they had spent discussing rugby on sleepovers, of the lifts his father had given him to Dubl—

'Stop!' Eoin shouted at himself as he jogged around the cricket field back at the school. A family of pigeons took flight at the noise, and two Stade Français players chuckled as they pointed at the angry Irishman.

Eoin waved a hand dismissively and jogged on. He decided he wasn't going to let Dylan's sneaky remark get to him – he needed to focus on the semi-final and the way he was going he wouldn't get a moment's sleep.

But maybe Dylan had done it deliberately to put him off his game? No! He couldn't go down that road and he didn't believe his friend could be so devious. Dylan was a hot-head when he knew him first, but had calmed down a lot. One of his team-mates had probably been goading him into some banter which went way over the top. He'd apologise tomorrow, Eoin knew he would.

But there was no sign of an apology when the teams lined up next day at the Adrian Stoop Memorial Ground. Eoin went along the line, shaking hands quickly with each member of the opposition and exchanging nods with a few of the players he knew. But although Dylan put out his hand to shake it was withdrawn quickly and he never attempted to make eye contact with Eoin.

Eoin shrugged his shoulders and strolled over to Charlie.

'What's Dylan got into his head?' he asked. 'He's being a total muppet.'

'Just answer him with your boot,' said the No.8. 'And I don't mean by kicking him – by getting more points on the board than he and his team of turnip-munchers score.'

Eoin grinned, but tapped Charlie on the shoulder. 'Listen, Chaz, I'm a turnip-muncher too, remember!'

Charlie laughed, 'You know I didn't mean it like that. Sure you're half-civilised since you came to school in Dublin.'

The banter with Charlie meant Eoin was in a better mood when kick-off time came.

The game started in a very cagey fashion, with each team trying to work out the other's strategy and neither willing to take chances. It took more than ten minutes before the ball even reached one of the twenty-two metre lines, and it was only a silly mistake by Páidí that gave Munster the lead through a penalty.

It was almost half-time when Leinster were awarded a penalty, but it was wide out on the left and more than thirty-five metres from goal. Dylan glowered at the team-mate who had committed the offence.

'What did you do that for?' he thundered.

'Arra, will you stop,' the Munster centre replied. 'Sure he's no chance of kicking it from there.'

'Wait and see,' snapped Dylan. 'I've seen him kick harder ones.'

Dylan was right of course. Eoin put the ball on the imaginary whitewash spot just like he did back in Ormondstown. He looked up at the posts and adjusted his sights before running up and easing the ball precisely halfway between the uprights.

A 3-3 half-time score meant most of the neutral spectators had almost fallen asleep, but Ted was delighted with the way Leinster were controlling possession. 'They've been attacking like tigers and will be exhausted by the last ten minutes. Keep picking off the points, Eoin, and we might be able to get some runs in by the end.'

Word of Eoin's goal-kicking skill had spread and several of the other teams' coaches had come along to marvel at the young Irishman. They saw him slot over another penalty from thirty metres out before the decisive moment of the match occurred with seven or eight minutes left.

From just outside the Munster twenty-two, Eoin hoisted a cross-field kick in the air, high above the low-slung grandstands of the Stoop. The Leinster wing, Harry, hared towards the ball, but also charging in its direction was Dylan. Both boys kept their eye on the ball as they leapt to catch it.

Crunch.

Harry beat Dylan to the ball, and his momentum carried him over the smaller boy and the two metres more he needed to cross the line and touch down. The referee signalled that a try had been scored, but also indicated that the Munster medics needed to attend to their ailing winger.

Eoin collected the ball from Harry and walked across to see how his friend was getting on. The doctors were checking Dylan's vision and asking him to stand up, which he was able to do.

The referee signalled Eoin to take the conversion and he was able to concentrate enough to send the ball sailing between the posts. But as he jogged back to his position he noticed that two coaches were standing either side of Dylan as he draped his arms across their shoulders. He watched as they encouraged him to move towards the bench, but the youngster suddenly went limp and fell to the ground.

Eoin dashed across to the touchline as the medics called for a stretcher bearer.

'Are you all right, Dyl?' he asked, but his friend was silent with his head bowed. A Leinster coach held Eoin back as the doctors attended to Dylan and signalled that the ambulance should be brought onto the field.

Eoin was distraught, and rushed back across to Ted. 'Please take me off,' he pleaded with the coach. 'I have to go to hospital with Dylan, he's my best friend. We're winning by ten points and there's only a couple of minutes left. I have to go.'

Ted chewed his lip and looked at the options on the Leinster bench. 'Of course,' he replied. 'Go. We'll work it out. Just go.'

CHAPTER 27

Eoin was terrified as the ambulance sped through the busy city. He wasn't afraid for himself, although he couldn't remember ever being in a vehicle that travelled quite so fast on such narrow streets.

They soon arrived at a large red-brick hospital and Eoin was able to give the person at the desk all Dylan's details as the doctors and nurses took him away for treatment.

'Will he be all right?' he asked everyone that came near him, and they all smiled down at him and nodded.

After about half an hour a doctor came out to see Eoin and the Munster officials who had also travelled to the hospital. He looked down at Eoin with a puzzled expression.

'But you are wearing a blue shirt – the patient is on the red team.'

'We're still friends,' replied Eoin, 'we just play for

different teams.'

The doctor smiled. 'Well your friend is going to be fine. He took a bad blow, but we've done all the tests and he's OK, except for a big bruise coming up on his cheek and a black eye.'

The doctor explained to the coaches that Dylan would be kept in for a day or two and needed to be monitored and checked by them until he was ready to go home.

'Can I see him before we go?' asked Eoin.

'Of course,' replied the doctor and showed him into the room where Dylan lay hooked up to several monitors.

Dylan was a bit embarrassed to see Eoin, and his eyes began to fill with tears.

'Ah, Eoin, I'm so sorry. I was being a bit thick with you. You know I didn't mean it.'

Eoin smiled and said of course he forgave him.

'But how did the game finish?' asked Dylan. Eoin shrugged, but one of the Munster coaches held up his phone.

'They're playing extra-time, it's 13-13.'

Eoin went white, and sat down. 'Oh, no. They'll go mad because I left early. I have to get back there.'

'Sure it will be over before you get to the ground,'

said one of the Munster adults. 'And the ref probably wouldn't let you back on anyway. Hang on here and we'll let Dylan know how it ends up and then we'll get a taxi back.'

The boys sat and chatted, but their minds were elsewhere. The phone belonging to Aidan, the coach, buzzed. Everyone stared as he swiped open the message.

'Darn it, it's 16–13 Leinster. Two minutes left.'

Eoin counted down the seconds from 120, but it seemed like he was counting down from a thousand.

The phone buzzed again, and he could tell from Aidan's face that the final result wasn't good news for Munster. He smiled, but didn't say or do anything triumphant – just in case the Munster men decided to leave him behind in the hospital.

He said goodbye to Dylan and promised to call the hospital next morning to see if he needed anything. He collected the phone numbers from the reception desk and hopped into the back of the taxi which took them back to the Stoop.

Eoin scurried into the dressing room where his team were still singing. They sent up a huge cheer when they saw he had arrived, and he was bombarded with questions about where he had gone and how was the Munster lad.

Ted slapped him on the shoulder and grinned.

'Don't you EVER do that again, Madden. We cut it very fine in the end.'

Eoin smiled and apologised, but the coach waved it away.

'Look, all turned out well in the end. How's your pal?'

'He'll be alright,' Eoin replied. 'A few big bruises but he's a tough little pup – I hope Harry was OK?'

Ted laughed. 'Yeah, he will have a sore head in the morning, but no harm done. See you back at the school. We're going to have a small party but an early night. The final is at half past two and we have to be ready to stand up to the Ulster men.'

Eoin smiled. 'Excellent, they're a nice bunch. But we'll have to keep away from them in the dining hall now.'

★ ★ ★

But there was no question of keeping away from the Ulster boys. When they got back to the school there was a welcoming banner across the doorway reading 'Congratulations'.

'We know that nobody has won anything yet,' said the headmaster, 'but we just want to thank you all for being such wonderful guests and to congratulate you on your efforts on the field. We have teams here from Wales, Scotland, England, Italy and France, but it was the two teams from Ireland that got to the final. We have made great friends with you all and we will follow all you careers closely in the future. And maybe one day those Irish boys will be on a team over in the stadium there that gets a good thumping by England!'

The boys laughed and the coaches thanked the school, and then Ted and the Ulster coach invited everyone to a party in the dining hall.

'I know the competition isn't over yet,' Ted announced. 'But we all leave too soon after the final and this is the last opportunity to get everyone together. Still, I don't want to see any of my team drinking fizzy cola the night before the final!'

CHAPTER 28

The boys were all in good form at the party, even those from the teams that were no longer in the competition. Eoin chatted with two Italian lads from Milan who told him about how their life's dream was to play at Thomond Park for Munster. Some Welsh and English players chuckled at this, but Eoin realised that Giorgio and Luigi understood just what it was that made a side such as Munster envied throughout Europe. He wondered would he get the chance to wear that famous red shirt.

For the moment blue was his colour, however, and when he bumped into Sam and Paddy they discussed the games they had played that day. Eoin realised he didn't know what had happened after he made his sudden exit and asked John Young to fill him in.

'Ted sent me on but to be honest I was so shocked the way it happened that I lost my concentration,' he explained. 'The first thing I did was fire out a loose pass and that fella they call "Curry" intercepted and ran all the way in to score. We panicked a bit after that and gave away a couple of bad penalties. They hit the post with one but put over the second to force us into extra time.

'The lads were dead on their feet but lucky enough I was fresh and once I settled down we took control again. We had one of those rucks where we kept recycling and we must have gone through twenty phases when they gave away a penalty. I'm no Eoin Madden but it was in my range and we took the points.'

The party wound down after a couple of hours. The Leinster players were on their best behaviour – even Charlie didn't pig out on the snacks for fear the coaches would spot him and leave him out for the final.

Eoin slipped away to find a few minutes on his own. He checked Ted wasn't hiding in the shadows at the cricket pavilion and sat down on the bench. He watched a couple of swallows swooping and diving across the ground and marvelled at how they never collided at such speeds. He was so caught up in their antics that he didn't notice Alex sitting down beside him.

'I see your team won today, young man. And I also see that your young friend from Tipperary was taken to the hospital. I presume he was not seriously hurt?'

Eoin nodded and explained what had happened.

'Ah, rugby can be a bruising game at times,' said Alex. 'I always found that the faster I ran the less I got hit, so I decided to become the fastest runner in all of rugby, a true flyer. I think it really annoyed those New Zealanders that I could run so fast away from them,' he chuckled.

They chatted some more about rugby before Eoin asked Alex how his treasure hunt was going.

'Ach, I am so frustrated. I have a feeling that the prize is close at hand, but it also seems so far away.'

'Why do you want to find this treasure?' asked Eoin.

'A good question, because treasure is of no use to me anymore, and all my friends and family have also passed on. But this is a rare and special treasure and it has been frustrating me for many years. However I will need to tell you the story of it first. Do you have some spare time?'

Eoin nodded and checked again that no one was around.

'Where do I start?' mused Alex. 'I suppose I must start with the revolution that ruined the lives of so many of my people. My father was a soldier and my mother was related to the Tsar, which is why I was once called a Prince. At first we thought we might be able to stay in Russia, but once they killed the Tsar and his family, everyone in Russia who had any connection to the old rulers fled far and wide – to Paris, New York, Berlin, London.

'The Obolenskys came to London but one day, when I was about four or five, a gentleman came calling at our door. My father was very disturbed at his arrival but he calmed down and made him very welcome. He stayed with us for some months until he moved away – to Ireland.

'That, as I'm sure you have guessed, was the man I called Uncle Nick. That wasn't the name he had when he first came and I explained to you before how we gave him his new one. His real name was Alexander, and his family name was Romanov. He was a cousin of the Tsar, and he came to call on us because he was afraid the new rulers of Russia were trying to kill him. They had discovered that he was now the only man in the world who could inherit the title of Tsar, and they were afraid that the Russians in exile would rally around him and take back our Motherland.

'But Uncle Nick wasn't interested. He was barely out of his teens and had no interest in becoming the figure-head in any war. He just wanted a quiet life with nice walks in the countryside and some friendly games of chess. He had a nice house in Ireland with some lovely paintings, but very little money. Some of the Tsar's friends used to send him cheques, but I don't think he ever cashed them.'

Eoin was spellbound by the story, and amazed at the fact that the heir to the throne of Russia was his grandfather's next-door neighbour.

'Anyway, on my last visit to Ireland, Uncle Nick told me the story of his hair-raising escape from Russia, and how he and his sister had been injured jumping from a train. His sister had been carrying a great treasure in her coat, but the fall had broken it in two. She was quite badly hurt so he brought her to a hospital in France and arranged to meet her later in London. They took one piece of the treasure each and resolved to meet up to make it whole again.

'However Nick had gone to Ireland by the time Olga arrived and they never did meet up. Olga's injuries were worse than she thought and she passed away soon after reaching London,' added Alex.

'But why didn't Nick have the piece sent to him in Tipperary?' asked Eoin.

'I think he wanted to forget about everything to do with Russia,' replied Alex. 'He rarely talked about the old country to me, and he never mentioned that he had the other piece. Olga had left hers with my father and he gave it to me one day not long before I died. It didn't mean very much to me, and I too didn't have very long left…'

'And just what is the treasure?' asked Eoin.

'It is one of the Imperial Easter Eggs made by the court jeweller, Peter Carl Fabergé. The Tsar had one made almost every year of his reign. They were exquisite designs and are highly prized by collectors.

'Last year I picked up a newspaper thrown away by a rugby spectator in the stadium which told all about the collection and the handful that had been lost. It described one of the missing ones, the Empire Nephrite egg, and I knew that was the one I had part of. I found my half in a box in the attic of my old home in London, but I have been searching for the other half ever since.'

'How valuable is it?' asked Eoin.

'Well,' replied Alex, 'according to the newspaper it could be worth around twenty million pounds.'

CHAPTER 29

E oin gulped and wished Alex luck in his quest, and offered to help him look when they got back to Tipperary.

'Perhaps,' said Alex. 'That would be great. I don't want the egg, or the money, but I do want to reunite this beautiful work of art, just as my father's friend and his sister had planned to do so very long ago. Good luck in your own hunt for treasure tomorrow. I will be watching from the room in the grandstand that bears my name.'

Eoin raised his hand in salute as Alex walked away, disappearing as he reached the gate of the pavilion. With the sun starting to set, Eoin headed back to the dorm, kicked his trainers off and lay on top of his bed. He hadn't planned to sleep, but was so drained by the action and excitement of the day that he was out cold in seconds. He woke again, still wearing his shirt, shorts and socks from the day before, when the sun appeared at the

147

windows at dawn.

'Yuk,' he said, as he changed out of his match kit and grabbed a shower before anyone else woke up. He skipped down the staircase in a great mood and set off on a run around the school grounds. He was particularly delighted that he had got a full night's sleep as he had often failed to do so before a big game.

After a ten-minute jog he practised a few short burst runs, then headed in for breakfast. On their way out of the dining hall were Sam and Paddy who seemed a bit nervous about the game ahead, but they all parted on friendly terms.

Eoin joined Charlie, Killian and Seán Nolan at one bench. Charlie had kept his sausage intake to his personal minimum – three – in view of the big match, but had upped his egg count to four for extra protein. The others ribbed the big No.8 about his enormous appetite, but they were glad of his power at the back of the scrum for Leinster.

'Right, boys, we're going to have a run around on the school grounds today, as the sacred turf is being cut just in time for the final,' said Ted. 'It won't be anything too strenuous, but I want all thirty-three members of the party togged out ready for action at half past ten. We'll go through a few things and I'll name the team. But we need to be back in this room here for twelve o'clock as we have some very special guests coming to see the game.'

The players looked at each other and began speculating who the guests might be. 'Joe Schmidt?' 'Johnny Sexton?' 'Justin Bieber?' were just three of the names Eoin overheard as the volume in the hall rose.

He ducked outside and asked the school secretary could he make a local call, and got through immediately to the hospital. 'Your friend had a comfortable night,' reported the nurse, 'and he said to wish you well in the final.' That cheered up Eoin even more. He was glad Dylan was on the mend, and that they had made up their stupid row.

He went back upstairs and packed all his bags, keeping everything he would need for the final in his Leinster kitbag and piling the rest – mostly ready for the laundry – into the holdall. He carried them both downstairs and left them inside the main door of the school where one of the Leinster coaches was ticking them off on a list.

Charlie dropped his bags off too, and Eoin could see he was really nervous.

'It's alright for you, Eoin,' said the big No.8. 'You've played in Lansdowne Road and you'll probably grow up to play rugby all over the world. World Cup finals, the lot. But I'm not nearly as good as you and I keep thinking they're going to drop me. I'll probably give up rugby once the Leaving Cert is over. I can't imagine playing for anyone else besides Castlerock. This is probably the only chance I'll get to play in a stadium this enormous, even if it is nearly empty. I'm terrified I'll make a mess of it.'

Eoin put his hand on Charlie's shoulder. 'Listen, Charlie, don't put yourself down, and certainly don't do it on this day of all days. You've played a huge part in getting us here and if you want to play for Leinster in future I'm certain that the only person who'll stand in your way is yourself. You haven't made a single mistake this week so there's no need to be scared of anything. Get out there and play just as you usually play and we'll win this game.'

Charlie brightened and clasped Eoin around the back of his neck. 'Thanks, mate, that's such a nice thing to say.'

'But it's true!' said Eoin.

Charlie nodded and puffed out his chest. 'Let's roll!' he called and charged off down to the training pitch with Eoin trotting on behind, laughing heartily.

CHAPTER 30

Ted made a couple of changes to the team that had won the semi-final, and Seán was delighted that he would now have both his brothers at his side in an all-Nolan front row. Killian, too, would be in the starting fifteen. Eoin was going to be captain, and John Young shook his hand after the team had been announced.

'The best man for the job, no doubt,' he smiled. 'But if you want to dash off to the cinema at half-time I'll be ready to take over.'

Eoin laughed and thanked John. He was so used to nasty little scraps for his position back in school that it was nice to be up against a good sportsman. The training session was short and sweet, and Eoin spent most of it practising his kicks from the touchline, with John and a couple of his friends helping collect the balls.

When it was over and they strolled into the canteen building, they found the doors closed and Ted standing in front of them with his arms folded. He waited until everyone had arrived and then announced that he wanted them to enter the room slowly and carefully, before he threw the doors open wide.

The players walked into the room to the sound of cheers and clapping from a crowd of more than a hundred people. The boys were puzzled but soon one or two heard their names being called and recognised who had done so. 'Mum!' 'Dad!' 'Gran!' 'Brud!' were the calls as they all realised their parents and families had gathered in the canteen.

'You're all very welcome to Twickenham!' shouted Ted above the racket. He waved his arms and the crowd was silenced.

'First of all, many thanks to our airline partners for bringing you all here today as our guests. We are very grateful to you for lending us your sons, and you can be very proud of how they have played and conducted themselves this week. I'm sure your support will be crucial in the game this afternoon. Now I'm afraid you only have forty-five minutes to spend together because we have to start the preparations for the big game shortly. So enjoy yourselves, and everyone enjoy the game.'

Eoin had spotted his parents and picked his way around several hugs and handshakes to reach them. He took several seconds to find his way around a particularly enormous group hug involving the Nolan triplets and their family.

'Congratulations, Eoin, we've been following the tournament on the website,' said his mum. 'You're a big star back home. It was even on the sports news on the radio this morning.'

'We've been up since early morning – we had to drive to Dublin for a seven o'clock flight, imagine,' laughed his dad. 'And we had to pick up an extra passenger too…'

Dixie stepped out from behind the stage curtain where he had been hiding.

'Boo!' he chuckled. 'You know they couldn't keep me away from a game like this. Would you believe the Leinster official said there were only two guests allowed per player? But I brought along my Leinster cap from 1967, and the pilot was so impressed when I showed it to him that he put me in first class. He even let me sit up the front with him for a few minutes.'

Eoin smiled at his grandfather, from whom he had got his knack for getting into adventures. 'Ah, that's brilliant, I'm so glad you could come. We never lose when you come to watch. I'd say you'll have your pick of the seats today.'

He chatted with his family about what had gone on

during the week, and explained about Dylan's injury and the trip to the emergency room. His mum made note of the directions to the hospital and said they would visit him before the game.

Eoin turned to Dixie. 'You should try to check out the museum at the stadium, Grandad, it's really excellent. There's photos and videos of some of those old players you're always talking about.'

'Oh, really? Then I must do that. I won't go to the hospital – I try to avoid them unless I'm the patient these days,' he chuckled.

When time was up, Eoin said his goodbyes and accepted all their good luck wishes. He always enjoyed having his family watching his big games – and this was going to be the biggest he had ever played.

CHAPTER 31

Ted sat on a table in the middle of the changing room and said nothing at all. He just smiled as he looked around the room at his match-day squad.

'Are you all right, Ted?' asked Charlie, eventually.

'I am, Charlie,' the coach laughed. 'I can safely say that in the eight or nine years since I gave up playing I have never felt so happy. I've been coaching lads your age, or around it, for five years, and I've never worked with a more talented bunch – in fact I can safety say we've never even *played against* a more talented group of players.

'I think the future of Leinster rugby is safe if even twenty per cent of this team makes it through to the academy, and I'm certain it will be a much higher per-centage. And I wouldn't be telling you that if I thought that any of you would be impressed by what I've just said. There's no danger of swelling your heads!'

The team laughed, and Charlie patted himself on the head.

'But… today we have a job to do, and no one remembers the great schoolboy teams who *didn't* win trophies. Do you remember what I told you right back at the start of the week?'

'Yeah,' said Ultan. 'You said, "Whether you win this tournament or not is irrelevant to me."'

Ultan delivered the line in Ted's deep voice, which got him a laugh from the boys and a wagging finger from the coach.

'Yes, I said that, I admit it,' said Ted. 'But I also gave you a list of things I *did* want you to go home from Twickenham with, such as learning about rugby and different cultures, and making friends and team-mates. You already have them in the bag, so go out there today and bring home the thing I said was irrelevant. Bring home that trophy.'

And he got up and walked out of the room.

Eoin stared at the boys, and decided to take the lead. 'OK, you heard the coach, let's go,' and he headed for the tunnel that led onto the famous turf.

The Ulster boys were already in their warm-up when Eoin reached the pitch. He nodded to Sam, but this wasn't the time to exchange words with the opposition. Eoin looked around the ground and was a bit taken aback by how tall the stands looked compared to Aviva Stadium. Then he remembered that they could fit 30,000 *more* people into Twickenham.

Not that there was any need for that sort of capacity today. A few of the other teams had come along to watch the final, and were identifiable by their brightly coloured tracksuits. The Connacht boys were already singing songs, and had prepared banners for each of their fellow Irish teams. Just around the halfway line Eoin spotted the Leinster parents, all dressed in blue and waving the scarves they had been given on the flight over. He couldn't see his mum and dad yet, but Dixie gave him a thumbs-up as he passed.

Eoin tossed the coin with Paddy O'Hare, who was captaining Ulster, and opted to kick off. He liked to get an early feel of the ball. His kick fell right into the hands of Charlie Johnston, who fed the ball straight to Páidí. Eoin raced to catch up with the action, and signalled to his scrum-half to pass it to one of the forwards, who put his head down and charged at the Ulster boys. Eoin wanted to test out the opposition early and see how ready they were for action. The second row turned and passed to his partner, who did the same. Leinster were inside the Ulster twenty-two and looking unstoppable.

The defence panicked and conceded a penalty, which Eoin smashed high over the bar into the second deck of the enormous stands. Less than two minutes were gone and it was 3–0 to Leinster.

But Ulster fought back, and the rest of the half wasn't nearly as straightforward for Leinster. Their scrum was struggling as Ulster's powerful forwards began to take control and just before half-time they overwhelmed the Leinster defence with a series of drives ending with a try near the posts and a 7–3 lead.

Ted was still smiling at half-time, and didn't seem at all concerned at the scoreline. He stood at the table in the dressing room, took three eggs out of his pocket and started to juggle. The eggs were painted yellow, blue and white, the Leinster colours, and he was quite slick in the way he tossed them in the air and caught them. After half a minute he stopped and began to speak.

'Did you see that?' he asked. 'That's the handling I saw from you guys earlier in this competition. You were fantastic. Remember the first try against Bath, and when we demolished Racing, and Killian's try against Cardiff? You juggled the egg like it was red-hot and you moved it at speed. Now let's see that again. Any questions?' Nobody spoke up, and Ted moved away to talk to the front-row.

Eoin stared at Ted's back, puzzled by something he had said. He had called the rugby ball 'the egg', which was bugging him for some reason. He walked over to the table and picked up the eggs. He examined the blue one, rolling it in his hand, before he had a sudden flash.

'Oh no, oh no, oh no,' he said to himself, turning quickly to find his kitbag. He tore it open and rummaged about inside. It took a minute but he found what he was looking for tucked inside one of his spare boots. He pulled out the crumpled blue sock and stood up.

'Sorry, Ted,' he called across the room. 'I have to go somewhere urgently. But I promise I'll be back for the second half – this time.'

Before Ted could object Eoin was gone, charging along the corridor and taking the stairs two at a time. He didn't even stop for breath as he climbed all the way up to the third level of the East Stand. He barrelled down another corridor until he came to a door with the name of the restaurant painted upon it. The restaurant named after a man who had scored just two tries in his international career.

He pushed the door and entered an empty room, the bars shuttered and tables stacked along the wall. 'Alex,' he called, 'are you here?'

Out from behind a pillar stepped Alex, with a puzzled

look on his face.

'Aren't you supposed to be playing down there?' he asked. 'The Ulster boys have just started to come out.'

'I am, I am,' rushed Eoin. 'But I had to give you this in case it got lost again. I only realised a minute ago what it was and I was terrified to leave it in the dressing room – and I couldn't bring it out on the field.'

'But what are you talking about – that's just a smelly old sock,' said Alex, pointing at Eoin's outstretched hand.

'It's not,' said Eoin, 'Look, look what's inside.' And he peeled back the sock to reveal the missing half of Alex's priceless Fabergé Easter egg.

CHAPTER 32

'I have to go,' said Eoin. 'See you after the game.'

He turned and dashed off as fast as he could back to ground level. He hadn't even stopped to check Alex's reaction to completing his family treasure.

Eoin found the first door he could that would take him out to the pitch and vaulted an advertising hoarding just in time to see the referee signal that he was fed up waiting for Leinster's missing out-half.

'I'm here, ref, sorry,' called Eoin as he raced into position. 'Bit of an emergency.'

'Where did you go?' hissed Páidí. 'Ted was going mad on the touch-line a minute ago. He had Johnny Young ready to go on.'

Eoin said nothing and prepared to see what the Ulster kicker would do with the ball. As he awaited his kick he glanced into the grandstand and saw his mum and dad had arrived. But he was confused by the person standing between them – was he wearing a red shirt and a blue scarf?

Ulster kicked off and Eoin could see that they had got a new confidence in their step from being ahead on the scoreboard. Sam gave him a wink as they waited for the next scrum to form, but Eoin kept his eyes focused on Páidí.

Both sets of teams flagged as the second half went on. Many of the players had played four games in a week, in warmer conditions than they were used to, and their stamina was being tested. Eoin recognised this and took a swig out of a water bottle at the next break in play, close to the ten-metre line inside the Leinster half.

'I'm going to go back a few metres at this scrum,' Eoin whispered to his scrum-half. 'Can you give me the ball on the run heading out to the right. A couple of their backs look wrecked and I have a plan I want to test before their coach replaces them.'

Páidí nodded and fired the ball out to Eoin as he charged through the midfield. Ulster were taken aback by the move, and their centres were left waving as Eoin dashed between them. He veered out to the right, and charged down the wing. As the Ulster winger came out to intercept him, Eoin stepped inside and put his foot on the accelerator. His turn of pace shocked the opposition and he sprinted in to score, going to ground feet first and touching down as he slid across the grass.

Eoin was swamped by his team-mates as he tried to stand up.

'What a try!' roared Seán. 'That was unbelievable.'

'Nice score, son,' smiled the referee.

Eoin stood up and trotted back to kick the afters.

'Good man, Eoin, that try was pure Hopalongski!' came a familiar voice from the stands.

Eoin stopped and stared into the crowd. There between his parents sat Dylan, newly released from hospital with not a whit of damage done to his vocal chords. He slotted the ball home and chuckled to himself at the sight of the boy wearing a Munster shirt cheering on the team in blue.

Ulster struck back, and Paddy O'Hare kicked a penalty to tie up the scores again. Eoin looked around his team-mates and could see their faces fall when the ball went over the crossbar. They were down-hearted not just at losing the lead, but even more because it meant they might now have to play another twenty minutes extra time.

Eoin checked the clock and saw there were less than two minutes left of normal time.

The Leinster forwards were stuck around half-way,

finding it hard to make progress. Every metre was hard won, and sometimes lost. As the clock ticked down Charlie stood with the ball between his feet as Páidí decided what to do next. Suddenly an Ulster hand reached in and tried to scoop the ball back. The whistle blew.

'Penalty, blue,' said the referee.

'We'll kick it, ref,' Eoin announced immediately.

'You sure, Eoin?' asked Páidí, pointing at the ground. 'That's the half-way line.'

'I'll give it a go,' said Eoin. 'There's a strong wind behind me. We're going nowhere as it is and I want to get this game over with. The lads are dead on their feet.'

Killian walked over and patted Eoin on the back. 'Go for it, hero,' he grinned. 'If there's anyone who can do this, it's you.'

'Listen, Kil,' whispered Eoin. 'Follow the ball, will you? It's a huge distance and I'm not sure I can make it. Maybe you can frighten one of them into fumbling if you come charging in. You never know what could happen.'

Killian nodded, and went to stand on half-way. He let the other quick runners in on Eoin's suggestion.

Eoin stepped back and prepared to kick. He thought back to the hours of practice with Barney's whitewash spots. The longest of those kicks was from 35 metres, but didn't he clear the bar by miles – surely that would be enough to make up the difference to 50 metres?

His right leg swung back before he drove it forwards – whump! – the ball flew high off his boot, high towards the clouds and past Alex, watching in his restaurant on level three. It dropped, toppling over itself as wind and gravity did its work. And it fell – smack! – on top of the crossbar and bounced backwards... into the arms of Killian who was still moving at speed. The Leinster wing kept running and dived over the line despite the frantic scrambling of the Ulster defence.

The referee, just as shocked as everyone else, hesitated before thrusting his left arm in the air and pointing down at the ground where Killian was buried under several boys in white. Moments later he was buried under even more boys in blue, but he escaped to allow Eoin complete the conversion just before the referee blew his whistle for the last time.

CHAPTER 33

As soon as Eoin had fought off his own team-mates, he sought out Sam and Paddy to commiserate with them on the result. He knew the pain of defeat and suspected it would be even harder to take in the cruel way it had come for them. The pair looked a bit shocked, but a group hug sorted that out and they congratulated Eoin on his amazing, if strictly unsuccessful, kick.

'There goes your 100 per cent record,' said Charlie, 'but I bet you wouldn't have it any other way.'

'Too right, Chaz,' grinned Eoin. 'And it gives me something to work on when we get back to school. I fancy my chances of getting a few 50 metre kicks in the Aviva.'

A former England international made a short speech before presenting the cup to Eoin, who really didn't know what to say so just thanked his team, Ted and all the coaches, and the families that came along.

After he had showered and changed, he joined the families in a suite behind the dressing rooms where a reception had been laid on. He grinned at Charlie, who had no fear of being dropped now and was making a bid for the Guinness World Record for cocktail sausage consumption.

'Well, Mam, I see you picked up some dangerous bug when you were at the hospital?' Eoin said, straight-faced.

His mother looked horrified for a moment until she heard her husband laugh and Dylan shout, 'Hey, I'm not dangerous.'

'Well, irritating, maybe,' Eoin laughed, before apologising to his mother.

'How you feeling, Dyl, you gonna be OK to fly?'

'Yeah, they said there was no problem with that,' answered his pal.

'Lucky sucker,' said Eoin. 'You're flying into Shannon so you'll be home a lot quicker than us. And of course, we have a lot more in our baggage too,' he chuckled, pointing at the silver trophy.

The mention of baggage reminded Eoin he had left his second bag in the changing room, and he excused himself to go back to get it.

He opened his locker in the dressing room, and sitting

on top of his bag was a small box with his name written upon it.

'I want you to have it,' said a voice behind him. 'I don't need it, and you helped me complete it. It is right that you have my part.'

Eoin turned and looked into the sad blue eyes of Prince Alexei Obolensky.

'You're a very good rugby player,' Alex went on. 'Very good indeed. Your try today reminded me of my own here in 1936, even down to the way you touched the ball down. Did you mean it to be so?'

'Well...' replied Eoin. 'I suppose I spent a lot of time studying that move and I saw a chance to try to repeat it. I could have sworn you were at my shoulder all the while I was running.'

'Yes, I was, in a way,' said Alex. 'And I hope you get as much fun out of this sport as I once did. I must go now, my little quest is over and I must rest. But it was wonderful to meet you and I hope we can see each other again some day.'

'Wait,' said Eoin. 'I can't take the egg. It's worth twenty million pounds! That sort of money could ruin my life. Can't you find someone else to take it?'

'No,' replied Alex, firmly. 'The egg is yours now. You must decide what to do with it. Farewell.'

And Alex was gone, leaving Eoin with a small, priceless gift which he stuffed back inside a sock and hid in his kitbag.

He rejoined his family, and with them was Dixie, who had earlier been deep in discussion with an elderly Englishman about the good old days when a try was worth three points.

'I've just been talking to that man there,' he said, pointing, 'and he was talking about the remarkable similarities between your try and that of a very famous player back before the War. We dropped into the museum again to check it and he was right. And the funny thing is, the chap who scored the try was very familiar. Obolensky was his name and I have a vague memory that was the same name old Nicky Lubov mentioned to me.'

Eoin grinned. 'What a remarkable coincidence,' he said.

CHAPTER 34

All the way home to Ormondstown Eoin worried about the egg.

'You don't look like a man who won the cup,' said his dad as they were bringing the bags in from the car.

'I'm just tired, Dad, sorry,' replied Eoin, although he had slept on the plane and in the car all the way home.

He soon hit his bed too, glad of the familiar mattress after a week away, but sleep was slow in coming.

His clock said 2.15am, but he decided to get up. He rambled downstairs and into the washroom where he had left his bags. He rummaged in the pockets and took out the small box in which Alex had placed the blue-green egg.

Back in his room he examined the treasure that had so bewitched the dead rugby player. Now he knew its true value he realised the tiny jewels must be diamonds, and the decorative bands wrapped around it were solid gold. On the side of the egg was a gold medallion which showed a serious-looking man with an oval-shaped head and a bushy moustache.

Eoin switched on his computer and typed 'Tsar of Russia' into a search engine. Up came lots of pictures of men in uniform, most with bushy beards or moustaches. But he eventually narrowed it down to one who resembled the man on the egg, who he now knew was Tsar Alexander III.

He typed in 'Tsar of Russia Easter egg' and his mouth dropped open at the stunning jewels that appeared. There were dozens of the Fabergé eggs, covered in gold and precious stones and with little intricate paintings of Russian royals. Eoin checked the prices that collectors paid and saw that Alex had been right.

He lay back in bed, now more disturbed than ever by the situation in which he found himself. He dozed off, but woke with the dawn chorus.

Eoin dragged himself out of bed and decided to go for a run, his usual solution to a problem that needed serious thinking. There were very few people about as he trotted along the pavements past the homes of his friends and the shops he called into every time he was in town. Having twenty million pounds in his bank account would mean he couldn't do that again easily. He probably couldn't go for a run without being stopped by someone – or worse.

He jogged out of town towards his grandfather's house, and past it to the gates of the old Lubov mansion. He was sure there was someone standing at the doorway this time, but who could it be? They certainly weren't wearing rugby gear.

He paused, unsure whether he should venture inside, but a friendly wave from the figure encouraged him. He knew he was a fast runner and this person looked very old, so he could surely escape if there was any danger.

'Good morning, Eoin,' said the stranger.

'Eh, good morning...' replied Eoin, 'but how do you know my name?'

'I know quite a bit about you, actually,' he smiled, 'but don't worry, it's all good. My nephew Alex filled me in.'

'Are you Uncle Nick?' asked Eoin.

'Yes, that's what he called me, and your grandfather too. But as you now know, my real name is Alexander Romanov and I was once the last uncrowned Tsar of Russia.'

'Why did you come here?' asked Eoin. 'I've never seen you here before.'

'I have been gone a long time,' said Alexander. 'And I am sad to see what has happened to my old home. I wasn't very good at paperwork and I should have made better plans for what would become of it.'

'So why did you come back?'

Alexander smiled. 'I understand you know just what the gift I gave Dixie was. Alex was very grateful that you helped him to put together the mystery at last, and I am delighted that he has presented you with the complete treasure.'

Eoin looked at the ground.

'And I also understand that you are burdened by the ownership of the egg. But I am here to tell you not to be. It is too much a treasure for one man to own, or one young boy. Ireland has been good to me. Perhaps the people of your nation would enjoy it more than if it were stuck in a bank vault, or a smelly old sock.'

Eoin grinned and suddenly saw the solution. He thanked Alexander, who said goodbye and walked back into the old mansion. Eoin turned on his heels and raced home as fast as he could.

CHAPTER 35

Back in his bedroom he collected the egg and returned to his grandfather's house. It was still very early so he waited outside for a few minutes until he saw the curtains being drawn and Dixie waved him in.

He sat at the kitchen table as Dixie made tea and toast, and when the old man sat down he produced the little cardboard box from his pocket and placed it in the middle of the table.

'Do you remember that little rugby ball, Grandad?'

'Oh, that old thing? Yes, why do you ask?'

'Well I brought it to England with me as a sort of lucky charm. It obviously worked, too. Anyway, after the final I found this box in my locker, and inside was the other half of the ball, or the Easter egg as it really is.'

He opened the box and removed the treasure. Dixie was amazed how beautiful it looked when complete, and how it really did look more like an egg than a rugby ball.

'This is really very special. What have you found out about it?'

'Well, I've found that it could be worth twenty-five million euro for a start…'

Dixie dropped his toast.

'Twenty-five…' he started.

'… million,' Eoin finished the sentence for him.

'Oh, lord, and I nearly threw it in a bag for the charity shop.'

'Well, that would have been a pity – but they might have made something out of it, I suppose,' chuckled Eoin.

'What are you going to do with it?' asked Dixie.

'Well, I don't want it,' said Eoin. 'It's a stupid amount of money and it would change everything. I love living here and going to school in Dublin, and all that. If I had twenty-five million I'd need security guards and we'd probably have to move.'

Dixie smiled at his grandson. 'That's very sensible of you, but what are you going to do with the egg? You can't leave it in your room.'

'I thought I'd give it to the National Museum up in Dublin,' he said. 'They could fix it and look after it, and maybe more people would go to see the museum if this was in it. We'd all be winners then.'

Dixie nodded his approval, and Eoin thanked him for his support. He would still have a bit of explaining to do, and maybe even the Gardaí would want to talk to him, but he reckoned he would be able to tell them the story without mentioning ghosts.

Eoin closed the gate carefully and jogged back towards Ormondstown with a huge weight off his shoulders. It was time to call for Dylan – school was just around the corner again and it was time to get the banter started about London. Eoin would never let him forget about the day he wore that Leinster scarf.